I Started All This

The Life of Dr. William Worrall Mayo

A Biography

by

Judith Hartzell

Credits:
Written by Judith Hartzell
Design and Layout - Suzanne J. Curtis
Photo by Judith Hartzell
Photo Contributors-Barbara Berkman Withers,
Chemical Heritage Foundation, Philadelphia, PA, and
Olmsted County Historical Society, Rochester, MN.
Also by permission of
St. John's Catholic Church, Rochester, MN and
Department of Development and
Mayo Foundation for Medical Education and Research.
Printing: Doosan Printing, Korea
ISBN 0-9703569-1-9 Price $18.95

Copyright © 2004 by Judith Hartzell

All rights reserved. No part of this work may be reproduced or used in any form by any means - graphic, electronic, or mechanical, including photocopying, recording, taping, nor any information storage and retrieval system - without written permission from the publisher.

Published By
Arvi Books, Inc. • 12 Sawgrass Court • Greenville, SC • 29609

Preface

William Worrall Mayo, a "little" country doctor, was the man who started it all – the patriarch of the Mayo Clinic. Unfortunately, history is often not kind, and the contributions of the father were soon overshadowed by the accomplishments of his sons, Will and Charlie. Many remember the elderly Mayo as only a strange, restless, wild-eyed man. His influence on his sons, however, remained strong. As Charlie said, "One of the best things that Will and I ever did was to pick the parents we had."

Judith Hartzell tells us why this later statement was so true. From thorough research and a gifted pen, she presents a rich tale of one of America's most fascinating persons. W.W. Mayo was indeed a remarkable man. Uniquely educated and with many diverse talents, he was brought up in England during times of great social unrest, which strengthened a deep devotion to caring for and about his fellow man. We follow him across America, traveling throughout the early frontier regions of Minnesota until he eventually settles in Rochester. This explorer, tailor, farmer, newspaper editor, politician, riverboat operator, veterinarian, and daring surgeon became known as the one to see for medical care when others could not help.

As a civic and political activist, he gave much to the city of Rochester. As a pioneer physician on a life-long quest to improve his craft, he gave too; all who have been touched by Mayo Clinic owe him much. Though Dr. Mayo was devoted to the development and expansion of the medical knowledge of his sons, perhaps even more important were the values and character he lived and taught to his boys. Ms. Hartzell seeks to truly understand the man and discover his many influences on his sons and Mayo Clinic. The team concept of medicine, a clinical practice supported by education and research, the availability of the latest technology in diagnosis and therapeutics, and mutual respect and support of his staff are but a few of his lasting influences.

His penchant for treating everyone respectfully and with the best care possible is alive today at Mayo. Picturing him standing in suit and top hat by his horse and buggy, ready to see his patients, those who work at Mayo will fondly smile and say thanks. Everyone will enjoy getting to know this man a little better. It is time to give him his credit. At last, his biography is here.

Kerry D. Olsen, M.D.
Consultant, Department of Otolaryngology-Head and Neck Surgery
Professor, Mayo Clinic College of Medicine

Words are but breath,
But when great deeds were done,
A power abides
Transferred from sire to sons —
And daughters
And grandsons and granddaughters

THIS BOOK IS DEDICATED TO

Linda Balfour Aikens, Robert Bruce Aikens III, Christopher Mayo Aikens, Gregory Vermeil Aikens; Alan Damon Balfour, Alan Damon Balfour, Jr., Ava Ralphs Balfour; Dr. and Mrs. Donald Church Balfour III; James M. Balfour, Laurie Balfour Tremain, Wendy Balfour; Walter Mayo Balfour, Beverly B. Balfour, Walter E. Balfour, Andrew Church Balfour; Douglas John Balfour, Jeanne Louise Balfour; William Worrall Mayo Berkman, Elizabeth Hammond Berkman Wirth, John Mayo Berkman II, Nancy Hammond Berkman, Karen Sherman Berkman; Martha Judd Kirklin Byrne, Elizabeth Ann Byrne Dugan, Thomas Judd Byrne; David H. Cole and Judith M. Cole; Dr. and Mrs. B.F. Eckardt; Elyda S. Elwinger; Ann Mayo Hartzell Graf, Claude Graf, Christina Graham Muir; W. Howie Muir III, Dr. Constance E. Gaulter, Ian Mayo Muir, William Kerr Muir; Dr. and Mrs. John Mayo Hartzell, Donna Hartzell-Shepherd, John Stewart Hartzell; Allan and Gertrude (Trudy) Judd Hughes; Suzanne Berkman Johnson; Thomas H. Judd, Ellen B. Judd; Andrew B. Judd, Susan Judd Dely; Edward (Ned) E. Kirklin; Starr J. Kirklin, Eleanor Judd Kirklin; Eleanor Sanberg Lish and Raymond Lish; Penelope Mayo Lord, Debra Ann Adams, Sharon Lee Hatch, David Mayo Hatch, Steven Edward Lord; Ann Withers Martin and Russell Larson; Dr. Andrew Mayo, Maren Mayo, Sofia Mayo, Ahna Mayo; Carolyn J. Mayo and Dr. Charles H. Mayo II; Drs. Chester and Julie Mayo, Chester Mayo, Chloe Mayo, Charlotte Mayo, Chandler Mayo; Joseph Graham Mayo II, Jodi Catherine Mayo, Jennifer Catherine Mayo Kremen, Elizabeth Anne Mayo Kremen; Dr. and Mrs. Joseph Graham Mayo III, Kathryn Mayo, Joseph Graham Mayo IV; Muff Mayo; Sarah Kirklin Pacchetti; Mary Judd Patton; Charles Mayo (Bo) Rankin; Mr. and Mrs. Fred W. Rankin, Jr; Edith (Missey) Rankin Redden; Dr. Chris and Laura Ricketts, Caleb and Rachel Ricketts; Suzanne Withers Schrader, Michael W. Schrader, Veronica Schrader, Alex Schrader, David Schrader; Karin Rankin Sisk, Dr. Allen Sisk, Allison Sisk; Christopher Graham Trenholm, Rita Rosalyn Trenholm, Louise Mayo Trenholm, Christopher Graham Trenholm, Jr; Robert Mayo Walters, Susan T. Walters, Matthew Mayo Walters, Bradford Mayo Walters; Mr. and Mrs. Waltman Walters, Sandra Damon Nichols; Mr. and Mrs. Charles and Barbara Berkman Withers, Mr. and Mrs. Chrispen and Kelly Withers Behnke, Mr. and Mrs. Christopher and Alyssa Martin, Mr. and Mrs. Jonathan and Carrie Martin, Erin Withers, Michael John Withers, and Mr. and Mrs. John and Patricia Withers,

GENEROUS DONORS TO MAYO CLINIC, STILL LIVING THE GIVE-BACK ETHIC IN THE MAYO FAMILY.

Table of Contents

Genealogy of Louise Abigail Wright and William Worrall Mayo .... page 6-7

Chapter 1: On Giving Back .... page 9

Chapter 2: The Beginnings .... page 15

Chapter 3: Finding His Way in America .... page 23

Chapter 4: Married Life .... page 31

Chapter 5: Wilderness in His Blood .... page 37

Chapter 6: The Sioux War and the Civil War .... page 49

Chapter 7: Moving to Rochester .... page 63

Chapter 8: Beginning to Give Back at Last .... page 75

Chapter 9: The Boys' Education .... page 87

Chapter 10: Cyclone .... page 101

Chapter 11: Battle for the Hospital's Survival .... page 115

Chapter 12: Mayos' Clinic Grows .... page 127

Chapter 13: Travels and Celebrations .... page 135

Chapter 14: Last Years .... page 145

Chapter 15: The Legacy of Louise and William Worrall Mayo .... page 153

Author's Note: Thanks to many who helped me .... page 161

End-notes .... page 162

Index .... page 174

Praise for *I Started All This* and *Mrs. Charlie* .... page 177

Genealogy

William Worrall Mayo

(1819-1911)

&

Louise Abigail Wright

(1825-1915)

Horace Mayo	(1851-1852)
Gertrude Emily Mayo	(1853-1938)
Phoebe Louise Mayo	(1856-1885)
Sarah Frances Mayo	(1859-1860)
William James Mayo	(1861-1939)
Charles Horace Mayo	(1865-1939)

(W.W. Mayo's parents were Anne Bonsall and James Mayo, Sr.)

(Louise Wright's parents were Sarah Totten and Horace Wright)

Gertrude Emily Mayo

&

David Mack Berkman

(1850-1912)

Daisy Louise Berkman	(1878-1976)
Martha May Berkman	(1880-1971)
Helen Phoebe Berkman	(1883-1952)
David Mayo Berkman	(1886-1958)
John Mayo Berkman	(1898-1978)

Genealogy

William James Mayo

&

Hattie May Damon

(1864-1952)

Carrie Louise Mayo	(1887-1960)
Worrall Mayo	(1889-1889)
Helen Phoebe Mayo	(1892-1893)
William Damon Mayo	(1893-1894)
Phoebe Gertrude Mayo	(1897-1994)

Charles Horace Mayo

&

Edith Maria Graham

(1867-1943)

Margaret Mayo	(1895-1895)
Dorothy Mayo	(1897-1960)
Charles William Mayo	(1898-1968)
Edith Mayo	(1900-1982)
Joseph Graham Mayo	(1902-1936)
Louise Mayo	(1905-1993)
Rachel Mayo	(1908-1910)
Esther Mayo	(1909-1971)
Marilynn "Sally" Mayo	(1920-1984)

Chapter 1

On Giving Back

"Our father recognized certain definite social obligations. He believed that any man who had better opportunity than others, greater strength of mind, body, or character, owed something to those who had not been so provided; that is, that the important thing in life is not to accomplish for one's self alone, but for each to carry his share of collective responsibility."

— Dr. William J. Mayo

On a wintry Saturday in Rochester, Minnesota, Dr. William Worrall Mayo was hurrying to reach a patient in the country. As he peered through bundled layers of warm clothes, seated in his light open sleigh, he urged his spirited horses too fast around the corner of Fourth Street and Broadway. Suddenly, the sleigh skidded sideways across the icy street, struck the sidewalk, and tipped over, dumping the short, slim doctor out, onto the ice. Unfazed, Mayo jumped to his feet and chased his two horses a block down Broadway. With the help of some neighbors, he brought them under control. It was only an inconvenient interruption in the 53-year-old doctor's day. He led the runaway horses back to his barn and harnessed his other two horses, which like the runaways, were selected for speed. Then he continued on his way, making his country calls. In 1873, his life more than half lived, Mayo was at last fully engaged in his life's work — giving back to others from his abundant and hard-won stores of wisdom and skill. Most of his youth and middle age had been spent not doctoring as he wished, but struggling to survive. He had endured near starvation, Indian attack, and the blindness of his wife. Now these problems were behind him, and he was able to fulfill his life's purpose as he saw it.

The "give-back" ethic is an idea from the European aristocratic code of "noblesse oblige," which says those highly gifted are obliged to give to the less endowed. How Mayo acquired this idea is unknown. He was not an aristocrat, but grew up in a middle-class English family impoverished by the early death of his father. Of course, the same idea is in the Bible: "To whom much is given, from him much will be required" (Luke 12:48 NKJV). Possibly, Mayo picked it up in church.

Wherever he got it, Mayo not only believed in giving back for himself, he taught his family the same code. "Now my father had certain ideals," his son Will said. "He believed that any man who had physical strength, intellectual capacity or unusual opportunity held such endowments in trust to do with them for others in proportion to his gifts."

Left to right: Drs. Charles H., William W., and William J. Mayo, around 1900

Photo permission of Mayo Foundation for Medical Education and Research. All rights reserved.

It was upon this "give-back" ethic that Mayo Clinic was built. From what resources were the Mayo sons, Will and Charlie, to build the Clinic? From the wisdom and skills taught to them first by their father and mother.

In 1873, William Worrall Mayo was living life abundantly, primarily as a doctor. He kept office hours for town patients with almost religious exactness and wore out his four horses in trips to the rural sick. Patients from all parts of southern Minnesota sought his advice, for they respected his forthright diagnoses and treatment.

"Lang, if you get sick like this again, there won't be anything I can do for you; so don't send for me," Mayo had warned Thomas Lang while successfully treating him for pleurisy. When Lang did get sick again and died, Mayo's reputation, far from being harmed, was enhanced, for sturdy Minnesota pioneers honored his honesty.

An inquisitive Mayo was beginning to push the frontiers of medicine. His was a pioneer's mind, daring to seek out what was new and promising. Surgery was the unexplored territory which beckoned to him, especially surgery to cure women's problems. Since frontier American physicians then knew nothing of antiseptic methods, and wound infection was thought normal, any operation other than on the surfaces of the body was considered by many to be foolhardy. But Mayo was successfully managing to heal his women patients by means of internal surgeries.

One operation that women requested of him in those days involved draining large ovarian cysts. The surgery was always done in private homes, since no hospital then existed in the Rochester area. Mrs. Titus of Mantorville was close to death when Mayo arrived to drain her ovarian tumor. He used the lady's kitchen table for a surgical bed and operated with her family observing from vantage points in the doorways. Rarely had he seen a growth of this size – her girth around the cyst was 54 inches, and the newspaper report said it "had become so great as to render her perfectly helpless and endanger her life." Inserting a trocar (metal tube with a sharp point used to draw out fluid) through a one-inch incision, Mayo was able to tap and drain the cyst of nearly five gallons of fluid and restore his patient to health.

In addition to his medical work, W.W. sought every opportunity to give back to the community of Minnesota doctors by promoting some ideas of good they had never considered. For instance, in 1873 he was sponsoring Dr. Harriet Preston for membership in the Minnesota State Medical Society, because he believed her as capable as her male peers. The other doctors, wanting to preserve their all-male club, voted against her.

Unrelenting, Mayo continued to press for her admission. Reporting to the society on a new and successful surgery he had performed, he interrupted his case study and held its members' feet to the fire: "At this point I wish to make public acknowledgement to Miss Harriet Preston, M.D., a graduate of the Women's Medical College of Philadelphia, for her very able assistance to me while performing this and other operations on women." (Preston was not admitted to the medical society until 1880.)

He enjoyed fighting for good. In the arena of the State Medical Society, he tried to eliminate quacks from medicine by strengthening the collegial ties of competent physicians. At this time, Minnesota did not license its physicians, and any unscrupulous and uneducated person could advertise himself as "Doctor," as he prescribed snakeoil or whatever he chose to unsuspecting victims.

Mayo had declared, when he became third president of the society the previous year, that belonging to this group would "enable you to do silent battle against the parasites of our profession." Men belonging to the society, he said, could be instantly recognized as "a healthy outgrowth of science," whereas men who didn't belong were caught in "the brutal ignorance of the pretender."

As president, Mayo also eagerly led the medical society doctors in a fight against wrongful malpractice lawsuits. Patients deformed by accidents – their hands chopped off by mechanical reapers, for example – often sued and won because of the juries' pity at seeing the deformities. But the injury was not the doctor's fault. Mayo advised the doctors to seek protective legislation, because "the impecuniosity of one class and the avarice of another will seek to make the deformity an excuse to get an amount of money from the surgeon which they never could accumulate by honest industry."

In his hometown too, Mayo fought in frequent political speeches for what he believed. He addressed crowds initially as a Republican, then as the leader of a faction that bolted the party to back a "people's candidate," finally as a Democrat. This was all part of a struggle to protect poor farmers who suffered from price-setting monopolies in the early '70s. The plight of the poor touched Mayo's heart always; he identified with them.

His most important arena for giving back, however, was not public but private – in his family and especially among his two youngest children, Will, who was eleven in the spring of 1873, and Charlie, seven. They were his only living boys, the last of six children, Charlie born when Mayo was 46. The doctor bonded strongly with these sons and began teaching them his passion for medicine as soon as they could walk, talk, and understand.

He taught them to doctor ably and with unwavering dedication. They went along after school in the buggy when he visited country patients, who came to expect the boys at their sickbeds along with the father. After the visits, on the long buggy rides home, Mayo quizzed Will and Charlie on what they had observed. In this way, they learned what symptoms to look for in a patient and how to diagnose. Later, Will said of those days, "When we were small boys we assisted [my father] as much as we could, gradually growing into the profession much as a farmer boy learns by working with his father."

At age eleven, Will was already studying, under his father's guidance, Gray's *Anatomy* and Holden's *Anatomical Landmarks*. Charlie, only seven, had mastered the names of all the human bones. By this time, he also knew the botany required of a pharmacist. In the summers, while the boys weeded the herb garden alongside their mother, she taught them the names and medicinal properties of all her plants.

Mayo also showed his sons, by his own example, how to doctor with a servant's heart. He answered every call for help, no matter the time of night or the inconvenience, and without regard for race, sex, religion, age, or ability to pay. Many times the boys had seen him refuse to charge a poor patient anything at all.

Mayo challenged Will and Charlie to be surgeons by making them assistants at his operations, all conducted in patients' homes. Charlie was so young that he helped mostly by standing alongside his father with appropriate sutures threaded through needles, stuck in his lapel for ready use. Will heated surgical instruments in the fire for his father and assisted with the sponges.

A lesser teacher might have provoked his sons to rebel and seek other interests when he saturated them so thoroughly in medicine, but W. W. Mayo had studied under a master tutor in his youth. He knew how to teach with infinite, loving patience and how to fascinate his boys by the mystery of unanswered questions. Research was the means of enlarging knowledge and finding cures as yet unknown, and the microscope was a key tool in this research.

A dedicated microscope-user from his first days at medical school, Mayo taught both boys how to preserve pathological tissue samples on slides, and how to examine them by microscope. He owned a crude one during the boys' early childhood. By 1873 he had, in a dramatic move, bought an expensive, up-to-date model for their use. He did it, with his wife's permission, by mortgaging their home to raise the funds.

In addition to imparting his passion for patient care and for research, Mayo taught the boys that a doctor, to remain effective, must pursue self education his entire life and, for the good of the sick, must share his knowledge with others. Will and Charlie went along to meetings of the Olmsted County Medical Society, where Mayo taught them to sit quietly and learn from the discussions of his doctor friends. The boys became acquainted with all the outstanding local doctors in this way.

To continue his own education, Mayo liked to observe other surgeons. Once, when he found a procedure that looked promising for his female patients, the ovariotomy (surgical removal of a diseased ovary), he traveled to Lancaster, Pennsylvania, to see the technique performed. Back home, he discussed the procedure with Will and Charlie. How did Mayo know which doctors to visit? He diligently read medical journals and kept notes on outstanding men and methods. His boys were always to do the same.

Because Mayo pioneered new surgeries, he began to attract other doctors to observe his operations. As he worked, he taught them verbally. His work with state and local medical societies, too, was designed to encourage and teach other doctors.

In short, Mayo taught his sons three dimensions of a doctor's life: 1) to provide the best possible patient care; 2) to pursue further knowledge by research, and 3) to continually learn better techniques and to teach other doctors whenever possible. Today, W.W. Mayo's three emphases are represented as the three interlocking shields of the Mayo Clinic logo. The middle and largest shield stands for patient care. The two side shields are for medical research and education.

Finally, Dr. Mayo taught his sons to work as a team. Hadn't they always been a team – father and sons? "No man is big enough to be independent of others," he told his boys.

In the booklet "Teamwork at Mayo: An Experiment in Cooperative Individualism," Carolyn Stickney Beck, Ph.D., explains the ethos which has resulted in the Clinic becoming the largest private medical system in the world dedicated to group practice, including research and education. "At Mayo," she says, "education and research have always been essential to serving patients' needs.... This logo conveys the fundamental Mayo principle: the needs of the patient come first."

Mayo's son Dr. Will put this idea even more forcefully: "The best interest of the patient is the only interest to be considered." This statement is quintessential W. W. Mayo.

October 24 380 No. 556	Alice Daughter of	James and Anne	Hardman	Croftsbank	Laborer	Wm Keeling Curate
October 24 381 No. 557	John Son of	Thomas and Anne	Partington	Winton	Weaver	Wm Keeling Curate
October 24 382 No. 558	Mary Daughter of	George and Anne	Valentine	Worsley	Sawyer	Wm Keeling Curate
October 24 383 No. 559	William Worrall Son of	James and Anne	Mayo	Salford	Joiner	Wm Keeling Curate
October 31 384 No. 560	Hannah Daughter of	Richard and Mercy	Bradburn	Leigh Parish of Leigh	Toll Bar Keeper	Wm Keeling Curate

Chapter 2

The Beginnings

"Father was always talking about [John] Dalton.
He simply enthused him with chemistry."
—Dr. Charles H. Mayo

A week after the birth of the future Queen Victoria, William Worrall Mayo was born on May 31, 1819, in the town of Salford, England, near Manchester. He would grow up to be a physician and surgeon on the American frontier and the founder of what was originally called "Mayos' Clinic" in Rochester, Minnesota–the forerunner of today's Mayo Clinic. Though his life's goal was to give back to his community from his superior endowment of gifts, he appeared, at first, to have nothing to give back.

Because William's family was neither rich nor poor, their expectations and hopes for the boy were reasonably modest: to acquire some education in Church of England schools and to work respectably at a trade, like his father. James Mayo was a skilled carpenter who finished wood products in his own shop–things like paneling, window sashes, and doors–and then installed or "joined" them in new homes and businesses. He called himself a "joiner." In a city growing as rapidly as Salford-Manchester, which was the center of England's industrial revolution, James Mayo could always expect to be employed, but he would not have considered himself prosperous enough to be required to give back.

William's mother was Anne Bonsall Mayo, daughter of John Bonsall and Timminson Worrall Bonsall of Salford. John Bonsall maintained a large farm, where he raised crops and children: Anne was the oldest daughter in a family of thirteen children, eight of them girls. Her mother's father, James Worrall, had established the largest dye factory in Salford, making the Worralls William's most prosperous immediate relatives. Both of his maternal grandparents were still living.

His father's parents, James Mayo, Sr., and Esther Mayo, had already died, but many of their twelve children still lived in the area. At home with William were his sister Anne, four, and his brother James, two.

On October 24, the family took the baby to nearby Eccles to be baptized in St. Mary's Church, the ancient parish church for their Anglican community. This christening, almost five months after William's birth, was later than usual. Since records are scant from William's early years, nothing can be deduced from the late christening except that the baby was strong and healthy. If he had been born a frail infant,

Baptismal certificate of William Worrall Mayo from the Eccles Parish register, St. Mary's Church, England. The certificate is now in Manchester Library, England

Photo permission of Mayo Foundation for Medical Education and Research. All rights reserved.

the baptism would have taken place within days.

After William, three more children were born to Anne Mayo—Esther in 1821, Sarah in 1823, and Mary in 1825. The boys, William and James, began elementary school. No records survive to tell us which school it was.

The children learned from their parents that they had distinguished scientists as ancestors, including John Mayo, who worked out a theory of oxygen a century before Joseph Priestley. They also learned from their mother of the difficult experiences her family had endured when they were Huguenots (Calvinist Protestants) in France. From her stories, William developed a strong dislike of religious persecution.

Life moved comfortably along in the Mayo family during William's early years. But when he was only seven, he met his first and lifelong enemy—death. In September 1826, at the age of 49, his father died. Within the next four and one half years, death struck twice more, taking two sisters, Anne and Esther. From these early brushes with death, William began developing his life-long passion to heal the sick.

He was acquainted with death in his community as well as in his family. Life was brief in the Manchester area. The average lifespan of workers was only 17, less than half that of England's worker population. Even the professional class had an average lifespan of only 38 years, which was 14 years less than the national average of 52.

Part of the reason for these depressing statistics was the city's amazing growth rate. During William's youth, Manchester's textile mills, bleaching factories, and dyeing businesses attracted immigrants in huge numbers. Between 1801, the time of Britain's first census, and 1831, the city more than tripled, growing from 75,000 to nearly 240,000. Though many of its more prosperous citizens lived in pleasant neighborhoods, the influx of newcomers simply outpaced the city's ability to provide adequate housing, clean water, clean air, and sanitation.

Early 19th century Manchester mills were unhealthful workplaces too. All the mill workers, but especially the children, were prone to sickness and injury, worn down by long workdays, from 6 a.m. to 9 p.m. in some cases. Charles Dickens' pitiful descriptions of London's working children are accurate descriptions of Manchester's working children at this time too. It was not until 1847, the year after Mayo left England, that an English law limited the hours which 13 to 18-year-olds could work to 10 per day.

The mill environment was also unwholesome from air pollution. In cotton mills, fabric production created inside dust. Outside, coal-burning factories of all types polluted the air. By 1827, when William was eight, smoke from Manchester's many factories had created a semi-permanent cloud of black coal dust over the city.

James Mayo's death might have been expected—he lived 11 years longer than the average Salford professional. To the family, it was a calamity, leaving Anne with six children to raise, alone.

Possibly with the help of her father and the Worrall family, Anne managed. She moved to a smaller, more affordable house in Salford, on Regent Road at the bottom of Oldfield Road, and continued to seek formal schooling for her sons, James and William. Somehow, she paid the fees for her boys to complete their elementary education, mastering reading, writing, and math. William did not study science, however, since English schools followed a classical education curriculum; it would be another 50 years before they considered science an important subject for children.

Anne Mayo wanted her sons educated in the common pattern, so she hired a French-born tutor to teach them Latin and Greek. But she could not afford to boost them up the Anglican ladder of education, into church-run secondary schools leading to Cambridge or Oxford. Paradoxically, being barred by poverty from continuing his classical education proved a boon to William.

He sought out a brilliant, self-taught scientist to be his tutor: John Dalton, the chemist and physicist responsible for formulating the modern atomic theory of matter and devising the periodic table. He also was the first to describe color-blindness, based on his own and his brother's experiences.

When and for how long Mayo studied with Dalton is uncertain, since all the Dalton papers were destroyed by fire during the 1940 German blitz of Manchester, and Mayo himself left no history of his youth. It is, however, certain that Dalton's influence on the fatherless Mayo was profound. More than 50 years after the two worked together, Mayo's son Charlie said, "Father was always talking about Dalton. He simply enthused him with chemistry."

Most likely, Mayo studied with Dalton in his early and mid-teens. Before May 1833, when Mayo turned 14 (Dalton was then 66), he could have studied during the day in the little school of eight or ten pupils Dalton ran in his room at the Literary and Philosophical Society ("the Lit. and Phil.") on George Street, Manchester. Anne Mayo's house was about a mile away, within easy walking distance. At the age of 14 though, with the serious responsibilities of adulthood pressing upon him, Mayo apprenticed himself to a tailor. He was then occupied from early morning to evening every day learning how to make and alter clothing. Still, he could have continued studying with Dalton in the evenings. Dalton taught as many as eight students a week after tea, between 5:30 and 9 p.m. each evening, at a cost of two shillings a lesson.

A devout Quaker and member of the Society of Friends, Dalton dressed in plain gray clothes all his life. His speech was plain too, never courtly or flattering. He tried always to speak the truth as clearly and simply as he could. Consequently, some contemporary biographers, used to a more worldly look and manner, described him as awkward, gruff, morose, and overly serious.

To his students, however, Dalton presented another face. He was "robust, athletic, muscular and stooped slightly as if hasting forward, for he was a rapid walker," according to his biographer Elizabeth Patterson. One of his pupils, Samuel Giles, described him: "Dr. Dalton's manners were extremely simple.... Amongst his intimate friends ... he was exceedingly cheerful and facetious.... He was fond of society ... regular, methodical, orderly, and temperate."

Later in life, William Mayo was also known by some outsiders to be crusty and irascible, but to his sons and other intimates, he was affectionate and cheerful. Several of Dalton's other personal traits could be seen in W.W. Mayo – his habitually rapid walk, his love of good books, and his blunt, honest speech.

Some values which in the early nineteenth century were unique to the Society of Friends, through Dalton's influence became Mayo's values, such as his respect for women. Quakers educated girls along with boys at a time when Church of England schools were male only. When Mayo attended classes in Dalton's room at the Lit. and

John Dalton, Fellow of the Royal Society
Engraved by Worthington after a painting by Allen, 1823

Fisher Collection, courtesy of Chemical Heritage Foundation

Phil., for the first time he had girls as his classmates. Later, Mayo did not hesitate to choose intelligent, independent women as his first professionally trained nurse, some of his doctor associates, and his wife. As long as his daughter Gertrude was interested, she learned doctoring skills from him along with her brothers.

From Dalton's strong Quaker beliefs, Mayo learned another lesson which proved vitally important to him — to respect hard work and individual effort. Quakers differed from other Christians in their assessment of how one gains salvation. Many Calvinist Protestants (like the Huguenots in Anne Mayo's family) believed that a man could not gain redemption through his own efforts and works, but through divine election. Church of England believers (like Mayo's immediate family) valued the sacraments, especially communion, as instruments of salvation. Patterson sums up Dalton's different belief: "To the individual Quaker, the fashioning of one's own salvation and one's own life through one's own exertions was not a possibility but a certainty.... The Society [believed strongly] in individual responsibility and independence and in the dignity of labor."

Mayo's summation of his own spiritual life would have been thoroughly acceptable to a Quaker: "My own religion has been to do all the good I could to my fellow men, and as little harm as possible."

A third, very important value Mayo learned from Dalton was a keen respect for science. The Society of Friends encouraged children to learn natural science a century before other schools taught it. They believed people could perceive God's plan in nature, and so God Himself. Because they wanted to rear their children to serve others, they looked for ways to apply scientific facts to practical use.

James Joule, another one of Dalton's outstanding students, said of his tutor, "Dalton possessed a rare power for engaging the affections of his pupils for scientific truth; and it was from his instructions that I first formed the desire to increase my knowledge by original research." It was from Dalton that Mayo too first developed the interest in scientific research which he passed to his sons.

Dalton especially enjoyed observing, measuring, and weighing physical phenomena, and then trying to answer questions he put to himself about what he saw. That is, he practiced (and taught) an inductive, scientific method of thought. When he was 20, he began a meteorological journal, noting measurements of weather data every day from 1787 until and including the day before his death on July 27, 1844. In all, he made more than 200,000 entries, which is about 10 measurements for every day of 57 years. Similarly, Mayo much later developed a habit of systematically recording important data in a book called *Index Rerum*.

As a young man, Dalton made a study of human digestion, using himself for the subject. For two weeks he noted the quantity and weight of food he ate and the quantity and weight of his waste, in an effort to discover which food gave him the most satisfaction and energy. Years later, Mayo's research on urine analysis followed similar research lines.

Even Mayo's interest in becoming a doctor may have come from his tutor. In his youth Dalton had wanted to study medicine, but his uncle dissuaded him because he considered the young man more suited to teaching. He learned about medicine anyway, through self study. By 1825 (when William was six), Dalton had gained sufficient medical knowledge to found, with some friends, the Manchester School of Medicine, also called the Pine Street School. There he taught pharmaceutical chemistry, a subject Mayo later mastered. Some writers say Mayo studied under Dalton at the Pine Street School, but since Dalton taught only a few years at Pine Street during William's early boyhood, it is unlikely he took a course from him there. Perhaps Mayo studied at Pine Street at a later time, however, when Dalton gave an occasional lecture there.

All assertions about Mayo's later education in England are conjecture, based on oral reports more than 20 years after his death. He is said by various writers to have attended Owens College or some other college and to have "walked the wards" in a medical apprenticeship at the Manchester Royal Infirmary as well as in London and Glasgow. No evidence can be found for any of these activities.

Whatever higher education Mayo sought had to be fitted into his life as a tailor. After completing his apprenticeship at age 21, he operated his own shop in Manchester for making men's clothes. To have continued full time as a tailor and at the same time studied medicine in a regular program in London or Glasgow would have been next to impossible.

When Mayo was nearly 18, Dalton suffered his first stroke, which caused him to curtail teaching. However, he never quit teaching entirely, and some students continued regularly visiting him at the Lit. and Phil. Mayo became Dalton's assistant in doing chemical experiments and recording the results.

On July 27, 1844, Dalton died at the age of 77. He was given a funeral befitting a king in Manchester, where he had – towards the end of his life – become a celebrity. His body lay in state on the Saturday after his death while 40,000 persons filed past his bier to pay their respects. The funeral procession on Monday was almost a mile long, with about 100 carriages and many persons, probably William Mayo as one, following on foot. Four hundred policemen were hired to keep order.

With his eminent tutor dead, Mayo concentrated on earning a living. The following year, when he was 26, a listing in the Manchester city directory referred to him as a "tailor and draper," that is, a master tailor. His brother James, who would later call himself a "chemist," was a cloth dyer. Their younger sisters, Sarah and Mary, made and sold dresses.

About this time, an inner restlessness began to grow in Mayo. He was not satisfied with his future prospects in a country which rewarded privileged birth before it rewarded merit and hard work. The temptation to seek a better life abroad grew until on July 19, 1846, at the age of 27, William Mayo boarded the *Oxford*, an American three-masted sailing ship bound for New York City. This ship was part of the Black Ball Line of packet ships often called the "covered wagons of the Atlantic," because they carried so many immigrants west. Of the 248 passengers on the *Oxford*, almost half (119) were Irish, escaping the Great Famine in Ireland caused by the potato blights of 1845-49.

Like other people on their way to America from Manchester and Salford, Mayo would have said his goodbyes to family in his hometown and boarded a boat in the Manchester turn-around basin, traveling down a newly-dug canal to his ship in Liverpool.

Helen Clapesattle, in her book *The Doctors Mayo*, says that William's leave-taking was entirely impulsive. Other writers have followed her lead, so that a small legend has grown up about his habit of making quick decisions. Clapesattle says, "His mind made up, he went straight to the nearest seaport and boarded ship for America. He asked no permissions and said no goodbyes. Not that he was being secretive about his going, or that there was any ill feeling between him and his mother. Taking unceremonious leave was just his impetuous, independent way."

This scenario is highly unlikely. Mayo's trip to America required much preparation, which he would have done with his family's knowledge and help, since he was living with his brother, two sisters, and mother in the family house. To travel in steerage, which was all he could afford, Mayo had to carry on board ship his own bedroll and blankets, his clothes and essential papers, and, most difficult of all, the food, dishes, and cooking pots he would need for a six weeks' journey. (The duration of trips varied.) He stocked up on cheeses wrapped in paraffin, oats for porridge, twice-baked bread, fresh eggs wrapped in paper, lentils and beans, salted codfish, dried beef, salt pork, potatoes, onions, garlic, vegetable oil, salt and pepper, whiskey and rum, nuts and dried fruit—-the ordinary foodstuffs for the Atlantic traveler too poor to be fed onboard. Enterprising steerage passengers could fish for food, and when in dire need, they ate rats.

Sailing across the ocean on a three-masted packet boat in 1846 required courage and endurance. Nearly a century earlier Samuel Johnson had said of a trip like Mayo's, "Being in a ship is being in a jail, with the chance of being drowned."

In fact, the former master of the *Oxford*, John Rathbone, had drowned just five months before Mayo sailed, when he was washed overboard during a storm. Samuel B. Yeaton of New Hampshire, only 24 years old, replaced Rathbone on the summer voyage. Storms and rough water were common in the North Atlantic, and even when they did not endanger life, they made it miserable, especially for steerage passengers, who were not allowed on the afterdeck, the most stable place on board and reserved for cabin-class passengers.

Mayo slept on a wooden bunk, as did the others in steerage, about 230 persons. Stacked rows of bunks lined a place between the two decks under a ceiling less than six feet high. Ventilation was minimal. The sleeping area smelled of urine and excrement, which routinely escaped from the toilets in the forward part of the ship into the bilges, along the ship's sides. Foul air and rough water made many people seasick.

Fortunately, Mayo was hardy enough to survive the trip. By his own description, he was "small of stature, five feet four, thin of flesh, weighing 120 pounds, but wiry and active and capable of great endurance and fortitude."

The *Oxford* docked in New York City on August 22 after a voyage of 34 days, and Mayo disembarked. Who was this young man, newly arrived in America? Some might have said he was merely a master tailor. In reality, he was an unusually hard-working man of science, a lover of learning and fine books, and a man of action.

Chapter 3

Finding His Way in America

"William W. Mayo ... makes the following report of himself; upon his solemn oath, ... that it is bonafide his intention to become a citizen of the United States of America, and to renounce forever allegiance and fidelity to any foreign prince or potentate ... whatever, and particularly to Victoria Queen of Great Britain and Ireland."

From W.W. Mayo's application for U.S. citizenship, filed in the Tippecanoe [Indiana] Circuit Court on September 7, 1849

William Mayo climbed off the *Oxford* in New York City and very soon found work at Bellevue Hospital, making medicines as Dalton had taught him. Here he met his childhood enemy again. Death presented itself as a common condition in the smelly, dirty, foul wards of this place, which was not only a free hospital but also a poorhouse and mental institution. Until a short time before, it had been a prison, with nursing done by prisoners; now care of the sick was handled by anyone who could be hired with the promise of a little pay.

Doctors with the title "Resident Physician" were supposed to attend the sick; these never entered the building. Instead, they charged their medical students extra tuition fees to do the unsupervised work, as if it were a legitimate part of their training.

Infection – typhus, typhoid fever, yellow fever, and cholera – spread rapidly through the hospital on dirty sheets, patients' gowns, doctors' clothing, and medical instruments. No one understood then that sickness was caused by bacteria and viruses spread through unsterile hands, fabrics, or implements.

Mayo didn't remain long in this place – just long enough to solidify his life-long detestation of ignorance and incompetence when people's lives were at stake. In early 1847, he moved westward. He went by the water route, as most other settlers did. (The Hudson River Railway from New York to Albany was not completed until the early '50s.) Traveling up the Hudson River to Albany, Mayo took the 340-mile Erie Canal to Buffalo. He was lucky he left when he did; months later, a typhus infection swept through Bellevue Hospital, and ten of the thirteen student "doctors" died of it.

After hearing reports of prosperity out in Indiana, Mayo decided in 1848 to go there. He traveled by boat across Lakes Ontario and Erie to Toledo, Ohio, and journeyed to Lafayette, Indiana, via the Wabash Canal (completed only three years previously) and the connecting Wabash River.

Lafayette was a prosperous town and growing rapidly as a trading center for the rich farmlands surrounding it. By 1850 the population would reach 6,216 – nearly one-third of Tippecanoe County's total of 19,558. The town had nearly quadrupled from its 1840 population of only 1,700, with immigrants pouring in, many from

England, Ireland, and Germany.

Mayo quickly solved the immediate problem of earning a living by reverting to the trade he had already mastered, tailoring. With a partner, Alphonso W. Roath, he opened a men's clothing shop which they called the "Hall of Fashion." It soon prospered. After several months, the men invited E. B. Schonfeldt, an experienced tailor, to join them. They added women's clothing to their stock, promising garments which would "give additional grace and eloquence to the female form."

About this time, on September 1, 1848, Mayo received a gift from a friend, George S. Hull. *Index Rerum: or Index of Subjects* was a blank book or journal, with an introduction from the publisher, the Rev. John Todd of Northampton, Massachusetts, encouraging its use "As a Manual, To Aid the Student and The Professional Man, in Preparing Himself for Usefulness."

Apparently, Hull believed Mayo would find the book valuable. He was right. Over the next 20 years, it became a record of W. W. Mayo's intellectual life as he methodically recorded more than 1,000 subjects in it.

Even though he was prospering as a tailor in the autumn of 1848, Mayo was not satisfied, and by the next spring, at the age of 29, he had decided to sell his interest in the Hall of Fashion and become a doctor. He announced his decision April 3 in the *Wabash Atlas* newspaper. Making this career change was not difficult; he was encouraged by a new friend in Lafayette, Dr. Elizur H. Deming, 51. A man of merit and experience, Deming became Mayo's mentor during the following six years.

As with John Dalton, Mayo chose an outstanding teacher in Deming, who had graduated with honors from Williams College in Massachusetts before studying medicine. Chairman of Lafayette's Board of Health, he was the most respected doctor in the county. At Indiana Medical College in LaPorte, Indiana, which he co-owned with the other faculty members, he taught "materia medica and therapeutics." And, significantly for Mayo's future, Deming was skilled in the use of a microscope.

The summer of '49 was a good time for Deming to acquire an assistant; in early July cholera struck middle Indiana, causing near panic. It was to claim 300 victims in Tippecanoe County alone. The two men fought it with the few weapons they possessed. Their common-sense advice to frightened townspeople was — stay as healthy as possible, clean your house and barn, and use lime on cellars, privies, and stables. Later a newspaperman said that Mayo's patients that summer had recovered in "fortunate" numbers.

Not all of Mayo's patients recovered, however. He was so disturbed by one patient's death that he wrote of it in *Rerum*, breaking his pattern of taking notes on the histories of ancient Greece, Rome, England, and America.

A page of the *Rerum* book

Photo by permission of Mayo Foundation for Medical Education and Research. All rights reserved.

On Tuesday, August 27, 1849, Mayo listed under "Cholera" the case history of Emeline Bates, 11-year-old daughter of Isaac Bates, who lived one mile southeast of Lafayette. He had called on her the previous day about noon and was told she had been vomiting and suffering diarrhea for two days. "Found her extremely low," he wrote, "no pulse at the wrist, hands and arms cold, legs and feet warm, warm applications to the feet, face anxious."

He administered a powder to settle her stomach and left more of it to be given her every three hours, noting, "Vomiting and purging permanently checked."

When he called to see her again the next day, he wrote, "The powers of life appeared to be sinking." She had experienced some diarrhea and a return of her stomach irritability during the night, "which was promptly checked as before." He prescribed stomach-settling powders to be taken every hour, and in between, valerian infused from its root, combined with camphor and cinnamon tea, to be taken by spoonfuls. Her parents were instructed to apply mustard plasters.

Even so, when he returned in the evening, he "Found the patient still lower ... a very rapid flickering pulse at the wrist, with difficulty aroused from slumber, answered questions correctly but voice almost inaudible." In an effort to help her rally, he ordered "port wine, a tablespoonful every hour with three grains of quinine." The patient "Sank into death at two o'clock in the morning."

Emeline's death troubled Mayo. Like other doctors at that time, he did not know that cholera was caused by bacteria spread in contaminated water and food. Although he only knew how to treat symptoms, he was trying to figure out the root cause of the disease. In *Rerum* he made nine entries, dating from 1849 through 1867, which show dawning understanding: "Cholera/ Microscopical researches, 1864," and "Cholera/ Water as the cause of its spread, 1867."

By early September, cholera had run its course in Lafayette, and life returned to normal. Mayo then made an important decision: he would become an American citizen. On September 7, he went to the Tippecanoe Circuit Court and, paying the one dollar recording fee, signed an application to the judge. He stated that he was "an alien and a free white person" and that "it is bonafide his intention to become a citizen of the United States of America." Further, he asserted that he was born in Lancaster County, England, and Victoria, Queen of Great Britain and Ireland, was his monarch.

Next he was asked to agree
"...to renounce forever, allegiance and fidelity to any foreign prince, potentate, state, or sovereignty whatever; and particularly to Victoria Queen as aforesaid, of whom he is a subject."

William W. Mayo

To all this, he signed his name, William W. Mayo.

By temperament and faith, he had been an American for some time; the freedom and opportunity of the new country, especially in the unsettled West, appealed to him. He preferred meritocracy to aristocracy.

Mayo made one other important decision in the fall of 1849: he would attend medical school. With Deming he traveled to Indiana Medical College in LaPorte, where he paid $100 tuition plus $50 room and board for a four-month term's work. This college, like other frontier medical schools, had no admission requirements and gave its students no grades. It was a "proprietary school," owned and operated by its professors. The first medical school west of Cincinnati, founded only seven years earlier in 1842, it was already well enough known in America to attract 100 students, some from as far away as Vermont and North Carolina.

Faculty members at Indiana Medical College were chosen for their teaching ability and integrity; they acted as "preceptors" or mentors in a kind of medical apprenticeship system. Mayo learned medicine and surgery mostly from their lectures, but he also had opportunities to watch firsthand as professors demonstrated surgical procedures in an amphitheatre of the college. (LaPorte had no hospital.)

Doctors Meeker and Shipman of the college used chloroform as an anesthetic for their surgeries only if the patient agreed, and many did not, preferring whiskey to dull their senses. The doctors used no antiseptic agents, since the germ theory was not yet understood. They performed surgeries only on external parts, like removing skin growths, or, in emergencies, arms or legs. The cavities of the body were never invaded by the surgeon's knife at this time, because of the fear of infection.

In the LaPorte school Mayo learned to believe in microscopy as a means of solving medical puzzles. The college – ahead of its time – had purchased from England one microscope "at great expense" for its students. Harvard Medical School did not yet own a microscope and would not for another 20 years.

The college offered courses in pathology and physiology, as well as in anatomy and dissection. Anatomy was taught only from books and lectures, illustrated by pictures. Even though the dissection class was not mandatory and required a fee, it is likely Mayo took it, as he later demonstrated an ability to dissect. Students' fees were used to hire someone to dig up corpses, since this was the only way the school could provide cadavers for the class. This difficult and even unlawful activity, "body-snatching" as it was called, was done by night and at risk of paying a stiff fine if caught.

The medical education offered at LaPorte was slight, but it was of good quality for the American frontier school. If, as some have said, W.W. had previously studied medicine in England, he would have known that the four-month curriculum of lectures, followed the next year by another four months of the same lectures, was inferior to the curriculum medical students encountered in England. Joseph Lister, who attended medical school at University College in London about the same time W.W. attended Indiana Medical College, completed three years of work, including clinical instruction in a hospital, studying throughout the 12 months.

Obviously, the preceptor system used in the American frontier schools was only as effective as its preceptors, since they were the ones who brought student doctors along to the bedsides of sick patients to observe symptoms, diagnoses, and treatment. Mayo judged well when he chose to work with Deming. Later, when Mayo taught his own sons, it was the preceptor model he followed.

Though requirements for graduation at LaPorte were two sessions of lectures and three years of mentoring, Mayo was exempted from one year of lectures and two years of mentoring, probably because of his earlier studies in England with Dalton and his work at Bellevue Hospital. He passed both his oral exam and written thesis and received his doctor's degree on February 14, 1850. At the graduation ceremony, Mayo stood with the other graduates and promised "that you will, to the utmost of your abilities, exert your influence for promoting the welfare and respectability of the Medical Profession; that you will demean yourselves honorably in the practice thereof; that you will not put forth any nostrum or secret method of cure; and that you will not publish any matter or thing derogatory to the Institution."

It was an oath he would honor for the rest of his life.

Not all of Mayo's time in LaPorte had been spent pursuing knowledge. He also wooed the woman who would become his wife, Louise Abigail Wright. When they met in the autumn of '49, she was 23, Mayo, 30. Louise was slender and shapely. Her long brunette hair framed expressive brown eyes. She stood slightly taller than his 5 feet 4 inches.

William appreciated Louise's courage and intelligence. When she was only 18, she had journeyed alone more than 530 miles as a passenger on canal boats and covered wagons, from her hometown of Jordan, New York (near Syracuse), to a section of southwestern Michigan known as the Galien Woods. She lived there in the home of an aunt, sister of her deceased father, Horace Wright, who had been a mechanic of Scottish descent. Two uncles, Milton and Samuel A. Wright, also lived in the Galien Woods. When they moved 20 miles southwest to LaPorte, Louise went with them, and in 1849, she was living in their home.

Louise loved reading and could remember well whatever she read. Persons who met her in later years assumed she was well educated because of the range of her interests and knowledge, but she had been taught only at home. All her long life she was known as a person who enjoyed others and was quick to help anyone in need.

She found the intense medical student from England interesting. His British accent and strong sense of purpose set him apart from others. William stood proudly erect. His walk was impatient and quick. In arguments, his keen smoky-blue eyes were piercing — and he never avoided arguments. Always his speech was honest, and sometimes it was blunt. When Louise met him, William was already focusing his energies on decreasing human misery caused by disease and injury. Realizing how much he needed to learn made him restless. Idealistic, energetic, compassionate, eager to learn, these qualities in William attracted Louise, for she shared them.

They did not, however, marry immediately. After graduation, Mayo returned to Lafayette, where he was employed by Daniel L. Hart, who owned a drugstore on the west side of Lafayette's public square, a prime location. Hart agreed to pay Mayo $75 a month for acting as pharmacist, mixing up the medicines he prescribed, as well as seeing his private patients. Hart owned the store but was not a druggist. He expected Mayo to prescribe medicines which would increase his drugstore sales.

"Dr. W.W. Mayo, Physician and Surgeon" read the sign on the doctor's office door.

Three months later, a letter from England informed Mayo that his mother was gravely ill. Because of his love and great respect for her, he immediately arranged to leave his business at the drugstore and begin the arduous journey back to England, traveling by boat to New York City and by ship across the Atlantic. Sadly, he arrived in Salford too late to see his mother alive. She had been buried in the churchyard of St. Mary's Church in Eccles on May 25, while he was still in Lafayette, even before he received the letter telling of her illness.

Nevertheless, in England again, Mayo could visit his brother, James, and his sisters, Sarah and Mary. He appears to have spent the summer with them. By September 25, he was back at Hart's Drugstore.

In late January 1851, Mayo disappeared for a few days from his patients. He traveled to the Galien Woods in Michigan, and there he married Louise Abigail Wright.

Louise Wright Mayo

Photo by permission of Mayo Foundation for Medical Education and Research. All rights reserved.

Chapter 4

Married Life

"There is one thing I try to do which is not natural to me and hard—-that is not to regret anything. Let it all go, like the pieces of a broken dish [or] spilled milk. There is no use in looking at, or regretting, the accident in life or mistakes."
Louise Abigail Wright Mayo

It was a cold Sunday on February 2, 1851, when Louise Wright married William Mayo in the home of a friend, Erasmus Shedd, who lived in the Galien Woods of Michigan. Louise had planned the wedding months in advance so that her mother could come, traveling by canal boat and covered wagon. This journey from the village of Jordan, New York, was a formidable trip even in summer, as Louise well knew from her own experience.

Louise's mother, Sarah Totten Wright Ostrander, was twice widowed. After Louise's father died, Sarah married again, but Mr. Ostrander also had died by the time of Louise's wedding. Intending to settle in Michigan with her sister-in-law, Sarah brought along her son Horace (Louise's younger brother), and her two Ostrander step-sons. The wedding thus became a family reunion for Louise's kin. Because they were all in England, no one from William's family could come.

After the ceremony and refreshments, the couple left for their new home in Lafayette. Their prospects for success and comfort seemed bright now that Mayo had established himself in Lafayette as a doctor.

In the spring of 1851, when Louise discovered that she was expecting their first child, William decided to make a career move to increase the family's income. He quit his work at Hart's Drugstore in May and went into partnership with Dr. Deming. Hart had not paid Mayo the monies owed him, and so he sued Hart, alleging that Hart, "contriving and fraudulently intending craftily and subtly to deceive and defraud … hath not as yet paid the said several sum of money [of one thousand dollars] … or any part thereof … although often requested so to do." Mayo called his former partner E.B. Schonfeldt as one of many witnesses on his behalf.

Soon Hart countered with a list of monies and goods he said he had already provided Mayo. The suit dragged on through the court of common pleas for a year, until finally Mayo agreed to dismiss it and pay court costs. He had made a major mistake in judging the character of another person. From this time, he deliberately associated with the best, ablest, most trustworthy persons he could find, and he taught his children to carefully judge others. Mayo's son Will said much later, "As I look back on these men who influenced me so greatly, I realize that their influence lay not in their craftsmanship, but in their high qualities of mind."

The first of William and Louise's children was born in November 1851. They named him "Horace," after Louise's deceased father. Having delivered his first baby some months earlier, William knew the birth experience well enough to be able to assist and comfort his wife.

In the account he wrote of that earlier birth in his *Rerum* book, William provided a glimpse of a frontier doctor's life. He was called to "a shanty on this side of Wood's Mill in the hollow," at 8 a.m. He traveled on horseback and "got there at half after nine. Waters had broken at half past three.... Determined to wait as ... there was [sic] no proper labor pains. It was a miserably cold place. The female was very chilly, sick at the stomach."

He administered $1/4$ grain of morphine to relieve her pain, a small dose of ipecac as a sedative, and an iron compound. He also did what he could to warm her.

"At one o'clock strong pains came on, and at two o'clock the child was born, a female."

Louise recovered from the birthing experience, but her baby did not thrive, and six weeks later, in January, Horace died. This was the first sorrow for the couple. In the manner of frontier people at that time, Louise and William set their faces towards the future as a means of overcoming grief. Louise wrote a letter of advice 40 years later in which she explained to a young friend how one copes with personal tragedy: "There is one thing I try to do which is not natural to me and hard – that is not to regret anything. Let it all go, like the pieces of a broken dish [or] spilled milk. There is no use in looking at, or regretting, the accident in life or mistakes."

Having no baby to occupy her time, Louise wished to contribute to the family's income. It was probably William who came up with the idea which established her career as a businesswoman: she could make and sell hats. With 13 years' experience as a tailor, it was natural for William to think of making clothes as a good means of earning money.

To get started, Louise ordered supplies of satin ribbon, lace, crepe and velvet leaves, rosebuds, bunches of flowers, and bonnet frames from New York City. Soon her shop, "The New York Millinery," on Lafayette's Illinois Street (now Fourth Street) was thriving. It was located two doors north of the public square, a place well selected for serving customers. Louise and William lived near their places of employment, on the north side of Main Street. Their house was large enough so that Louise accepted boarders to supplement their income and even permitted one lady boarder to open a small school in the house.

Mayo was continuing his education by extensive reading, which he noted in *Rerum*. He was beginning to prefer medical subjects to historical ones, having already read and noted through four volumes of "Gillie's Greece" and two volumes of "Marshall's Washington." Occasionally he continued to break the prescribed pattern of *Rerum* when a medical case particularly intrigued or puzzled him, such as that of Thomas Long's baby Nathaniel, born in Lafayette on May 1, 1852.

Mayo was summoned to the house when the baby was three days old and "on examination found not the slightest appearance of Anus. Cut in 1 inch and a half with thumb lance. Found no sight of feces. Child lived 61 days, without much show of distress, took the breast ... no distention of abdomen, no vomiting.... Before death was reduced to skin and bone ... no post mortem."

The cases Mayo described in *Rerum*, as well as cases he wrote up in Louise's millinery accounts book, are the earliest examples of what became, years later, a key feature of Mayo Clinic: its intricate and extremely valuable library of patient case histories.

In addition to being partners in medical practice, Deming and Mayo decided to begin making and selling medicines. They opened the "Family Medicine Warehouse at the Sign of the Infant Hercules." The business was located in "the Purdue block," which was one large, impressive, new building stretching an entire block on Second Street built by John Purdue, the man who was later to endow Purdue University. In this "warehouse" the doctors made medicines, which they sold to other doctors and pharmacists. They maintained their office for consulting with patients in another building on Second Street. At this time, judging from his businesses, Mayo appeared to be a successful and rising doctor. He and Deming were both elected in 1853 to membership in the Indiana State Medical Society, and Deming was named president for the following year.

Also in the spring of 1853, Dr. Deming accepted a faculty position at the University of Missouri Medical Department in St. Louis (now Washington University), teaching "general pathology and clinical medicine." These were subjects of great interest to Mayo, and he entertained the idea of going to St. Louis in the fall along with Deming.

But in the meantime, on July 18, 1853, Louise gave birth to their second child, Gertrude Emily (Mayo), a healthy, beautiful girl. Both parents were delighted. Business at the "New York Millinery" shop had by now grown so much that Louise moved to a bigger shop and took in a partner. Her grandson Dr. Charles W. (William) Mayo later said: "She had a great talent for business, that woman. When a daughter was born..., Grandmother didn't lose stride – she took in a partner and the business continued to prosper."

Soon Louise was put to her first test as a wife. Deming was to begin lecturing in St. Louis on November 1, 1853, and Mayo expressed a desire to seek another medical degree at Missouri Medical Department. After giving it some thought, Louise encouraged her husband to go and leave her at home with the baby, if by so doing he could benefit his patients. It was a pattern she was to repeat often in the future. With little Trude to care for, and the hatshop to supervise, Louise stayed busy and content.

In St. Louis, Mayo studied anatomy with a competent

teacher, Dr. John T. Hodgen, who became president of the American Medical Association many years later. To support himself, Mayo tutored other students in chemistry and physics.

In the spring of 1854, the University of Missouri in St. Louis granted him a second medical degree. This one was "*ad eundem,*" a degree added to the one he already had. To qualify, Mayo had to submit written documentation that he had graduated from an accredited school of medicine and practiced medicine for at least a year preceding the application. In addition, he had to prove that he "sustains a good moral character," and to pledge in writing that he "intends to devote his time wholly to the practice of his profession." This was Mayo's promise in the spring of 1854. During most of the next nine years, he would be unable to keep it.

In May of '54, though, Mayo was practicing medicine full time. In addition to seeing his patients in the Lafayette area, he had conducted some chemical experiments and was ready to deliver a paper on which he had worked for one year, "Report on the Pathological Indications of the Urine." He and Deming traveled to Evansville, Indiana, for the fifth annual meeting of the Indiana State Medical Society, where Mayo instructed the assembled doctors in how to diagnose disease by studying the urine of sick people. The paper shows, for that time, unusual knowledge.

To prepare for this paper, Mayo had experimented on himself or another person and found that if the rectum is evacuated, and a solution of one part salt to sixty parts water introduced into it, salt will be found in the urine. Further, he found if potassium is introduced instead of salt, the urine fifteen minutes later will yield "a copious precipitate with the persalts of iron."

Mayo described in the paper a medical puzzle which Deming had solved by urine analysis. A patient unsuccessfully treated by another doctor for liver disease had come to Deming, who tested the man's urine for albumen. When "that fluid became almost solid from the large proportion present," Deming concluded that the patient suffered from kidney disease, not liver disease. A proper diagnosis brought the patient much better results.

Finally, Mayo urged his fellow doctors to begin urine analysis as a routine part of their patient care. "Its [urine's] most important pathological changes require very simple reagents for their detections, and as such are within the reach of every practitioner," he assured them. "Various poisons are eliminated by the kidneys, and their existence in the urine will furnish hints for treatment, and valuable evidence for the medical jurist." Early Bright's disease cannot be detected unless the urine is analyzed, Mayo said. Using this method, doctors can also identify diabetes, some cancer, pneumonia, puerperal fever, typhus, and inflammation of the kidney, bladder, or prostrate.

When Mayo spoke to the Indiana doctors, he was performing two functions which later were systematized into the Mayo Clinic Model of Care – research and education. The triple emphases of the future clinic were thus already in place: patient care, research, and education.

At this time, Mayo seemed to be well connected and flourishing in Lafayette, although the appearance was never quite the reality there, as many patients were unable to pay doctors adequately.

Though they were still partners, Mayo's association with Deming was now only part-time, since Deming was teaching through the winter in St. Louis. In fact, Deming was able to teach only two sessions at the Missouri school. On the way home to Lafayette in February, 1855, he became severely chilled when his unheated train got stuck in a snowbank during a blizzard. He contracted pneumonia and died on February 22 at the age of 58.

Mayo, at this point, had left Indiana for Minnesota. The calamity which shook him loose from Indiana was his own severe illness, which he thought might kill him. During their years in Lafayette, he and Louise had come down with malaria every summer.

"Hell," William had said, "is a place where people have malaria." The wet marshy lands around Lafayette were breeding grounds to millions of mosquitoes, which carried the disease. No one understood why people got malaria; they only knew to expect it to come along with the summer rains. Always before, both William and Louise had been able to shake off the sickness.

The summer of '54 was different. Mayo was irritated beyond endurance by the chills and fever, followed by extreme lassitude, which malaria put him through. Years later, when Louise was 88, she described to an interviewer her husband's surprise announcement: "One morning…, in the midst of an attack of chills and fever, he hitched up his rig and said to me, 'Good-bye, Louise. I am going to keep on driving until I get well or die.'"

She added, "That was the parting. That was Doctor Mayo."

It was the beginning of his wanderings in Minnesota Territory, a place whose wild, pristine beauty deeply satisfied him.

Note: Le Sueur is just north of Traverse des Sioux, on the east side of the river; New Ulm is between Mankato and Fort Ridgely, on the south side of the river.

Chapter 5

Wilderness in His Blood

"I was perfectly charmed with the new country, and I was anxious to see it in all its wild beauty and to tread where the foot of man had never trod before, unless it be that of the Indian."

W.W. Mayo

"Throw away your guide books; heed not the statement of travelers;…believe no man, but see for yourselves the Mississippi River above Dubuque." Pleas like this one in the *New York Times*, from newspapers throughout the northeastern United States in the summer of 1854, called forth an impetuous, enthusiastic migration of settlers towards Minnesota Territory.

The Chicago and Rock Island Railroad had organized a clever and successful advertising venture, the Grand Excursion of 1854, to celebrate completion of railroad tracks from the East Coast to the Mississippi. They invited 1,200 influential people – including ex-President Millard Filmore – to travel by railroad to Rock Island, Illinois, and from there by steamboats to St. Paul, Minnesota. The large party visited St. Anthony Falls, Minnehaha Falls, and Fort Snelling. In the evenings, they enjoyed sumptuous dining and dancing. According to the *Chicago Tribune*, the travelers were "the most brilliant ever assembled … statesmen, historians, diplomats, poets, and the best editorial talent in the country."

Fifty newspaper editors were among the group. Their published letters during the trip and editorials written upon their return home praised the Upper Mississippi River in extravagant terms: "Perhaps you have beheld such sublimity in dreams, but surely never in daylight…. Over one hundred and fifty miles of unimaginable land, genie-land, and world of visions, have we passed during the last twenty-four hours." The same *New York Times* reporter declared of St. Paul, "[It] looks like a long civilized city…. There is glorious, boundless country behind."

W.W. had already heard enticing stories in Missouri of Minnesota territory from settlers who came down the Mississippi to shop for basic supplies in St. Louis. Word of the healthful climate was everywhere: no ague, no malaria. The air was cold and clean. People with tuberculosis were cured just breathing the air. So ran the tales.

Years later, after having lived through many Minnesota winters, W.W. still believed these stories. He repeated them to others, claiming "that the West pays tribute to [Minnesota], that the South sends its debilitated to our invigorating climate, and that the East contributes of its ambitious youth to mingle their phthisically-tainted blood [tuberculosis-tainted blood] with the … streams of the Teutonic and Scandinavian which the old world has sent hither."

Why did all these people emigrate to Minnesota? W.W. explained: "We have a far more powerful source of attraction than any of these [states], and one which compels every state in the Union to contribute to our population. It is that climatic property of our atmosphere which conduces to the re-establishment and preservation of health."

This was the belief which lured W.W. northwest in the summer of 1854. If cold, clean air could prevent malaria, then Minnesota was his desired home.

By the time he reached Galena, Illinois, in early July, after a month of travel from Lafayette in his horse-drawn rig, W.W. had overcome his chills and fever. The Grand Excursion had passed that way only two weeks before, and everyone was buzzing with excitement about Minnesota Territory. He joined the eager people lining up to buy steamboat tickets to St. Paul.

The boat W.W. took was overcrowded, and it was summer cholera season on and around the Mississippi. Soon he was called to doctor the sick. He did the best he could, but often the boat stopped at night so men could carry off dead cholera victims and bury them in wooden coffins on shore or on little islands in the river.

Arriving in St. Paul, a city of about 4,000, Mayo liked what he saw. The place was not entirely without cultivation and sophistication – though a frontier town, some of its houses were white frame or brick, and its shops included a bakery, a bookstore, and a china shop that imported dinnerware from Europe. Louise could be happy here, he believed. Mayo himself thrilled to descriptions of the unsettled miles of wilderness north of St. Paul, some of it never explored, except by Indians. He heard too that in the north lay vast deposits of unmined minerals.

Returning to Lafayette in late August, Mayo persuaded Louise to move with him to St. Paul. They decided to move her hatshop as well. In a town where she would have no rivals, Louise expected her business to flourish.

On September 26, Mayo was in Chicago, buying new hat materials for Louise and supervising the packing of her Lafayette hat supplies to be shipped ahead of them. He bought such items as braid, ribbons, velvet trimming, orange blossoms, rosebuds, bunches of flowers, little ornamental birds, and silk bonnets. Louise and W.W. then traveled by train to New York to order more supplies which they optimistically expected Louise would soon need. Louise was now planning to add dresses and other ladies' items to her hat merchandise, so they bought dress goods and their most expensive item, a sewing machine for $105.

In October, the couple packed their household goods in Lafayette, plus their clothes and books, and loaded them all on a covered wagon. Among the books, W.W. carried *Rerum*. During the next nine years, he would have little need for it though, because his life as a doctor would virtually cease. Oxen pulled the wagon, carrying W.W., who was then 35; Louise, 28; and little Trude, 15 months, to Galena, where they took their belongings aboard a Minnesota-bound boat.

As soon as she could, Louise opened her new St. Paul hatshop, "The Fashionable Millinery," on Third Street (now Kellogg Boulevard). It was an immediate success.

Louise at this time was still slender and attractive, her long, dark brown hair and large brown eyes set off by the beautiful hats of her own creation which she modeled about town. Soon she added to her wardrobe dresses copied from the latest fashions in New York and Paris. After one winter in Minnesota, she began wearing, and selling, fur stoles, cuffs and muffs.

Unfortunately, Mayo found St. Paul already heavily populated with doctors, about 25 of them, or one for each 160 people. Despite the abundance of doctors, most people avoided calling on one for healing help, preferring to dose and treat themselves. Consequently, he did not even establish a medical office. In later years, Louise's granddaughter asked her why she opened her shop in St. Paul. "To put food on the table," was her answer. Another reason was her enjoyment of the work.

Louise had already proven herself capable of caring for Trude and the hatshop while her husband was out of town. So with his wife secure, and no doctoring to be done, Mayo decided to explore the territory which stretched away to the north. Twice in the autumn of '54 he walked the 260 miles round trip to Lake Superior and found the experience exhilarating.

"I was perfectly charmed with the new country," he wrote later, "and I was anxious to see it in all its wild beauty and to tread where the foot of man had never trod before, unless it be that of the Indian."

To a man who had spent his boyhood in the smoggy city of Salford-Manchester, the natural beauty of Minnesota was irresistible. He especially enjoyed traveling alone. "Once I had trod the Indian trail alone for three days without seeing the face of man or beast," he said. "Once again in a birch bark canoe I had paddled the length of the Saint Croix [River].... [I made my bed] on the bottom of the canoe, swung to sleep by the light, rippling waves, while the boat was tied to the banks waiting for the morning's light.... Thus three days passed, floating through wild scenes, viewing nature in all her wildness and grandeur of stillness.... These scenes had given me a taste for trips in solitude. To notice a small rabbit cross my tracks ... to be glared at by wolves through the day and to be regaled by their wild concert of howling during the night, had for me a real pleasure."

In January, 1855, property on the north shore of Lake Superior became available for settlement when the Chippewa Indians of Minnesota Territory signed the Treaty of LaPointe, ceding their lands to the United States. America already owned the south shore of Lake Superior, in Wisconsin. Settlers in the town of Superior, Wisconsin, had heard so many stories of rich copper ore on the Minnesota north shore that, as soon as it was legal, they rushed there to stake claims.

W.W. made a third trip to Lake Superior about this time with two new friends, Edwin Hall and Edmund Ely. In six days they walked to the north shore of Lake Superior on snowshoes. Arriving on January 20, Mayo claimed land which he believed to be rich in copper west of what is now Duluth (Minnesota). Then, the purpose of his trip accomplished, he left his friends for several weeks to go off and live with Chippewa Indians.

Returning to the Duluth area, W.W. found another man staking his claim. Since the squatter refused to budge, in Mayo's words, he "cussed the fellow and let it go." In mid-March he returned to Louise, disappointed in his search for copper riches.

On May 15, Minnesota Governor Willis A. Gorman appointed Mayo one of three county commissioners assigned the job of organizing St. Louis County (originally Superior County) government. Men living along the north shore who had met the doctor on one of his trips north had recommended him — such was their impression of his competence and honesty. Mayo also agreed to take a census in the new lake county so that proper representation in the state legislature could be established.

In late May, W.W. set off again for St. Louis County with two companions. He had already walked the land route north along Indian trails and also traveled the alternate water route. This time, he wrote, "I induced them to take a new route, a foolhardy one; it was to strike as near as possible a beeline from Saint Paul to the lake."

One of the men was a 30-year-old tailor newly arrived from Philadelphia. He was tall and stylishly dressed in a "suit of fine black cloth and a stove pipe hat and small, neat-fitting boots." W.W., more experienced, wore "a straw hat, red flannel shirt, coarse, thick pants and stockings, with Indian moccasins — and of the last, three pairs." The third man was, like Mayo, accustomed to outdoor life and appropriately dressed.

Each man carried a heavy backpack of camping gear. It included a coffee pot, frying pan, tin cup, camping knife, flour, pork, tea, coffee, and a generous supply of sugar, all wrapped in a blanket. The entire pack weighed about 50 pounds. After a short time, the tall tailor felt the weight of his provisions. As Mayo put it, "The long man's pack gets heavy, but he will not own it. His body continues to bend under its increasing weight. There are frequent hitches to give it better position, but of no use. At last to get relief from his bent position he straightens up to his full height. The effort is too great…; he is over balanced, and we look back to find him sprawling upon his back, unable to rise without being relieved of his pack. So passed the first stage of this eventful journey."

The "beeline" trip began in comedy, but it turned to disaster after the men lost their way trying to cut straight through the thick woods. One night they inadvertently set the forest on fire with sparks from their campfire while they slept near it on their blankets. The wind shifted. Sparks blown onto dry pine needles ignited and grew into flames, fanned by the rising wind. Awakening just in time, they fled upwind of the rapidly-spreading fire.

Mayo described what happened next: "The hot fire ran along the ground licking up the dried pine needles and vaulting up the tall spruce trees, making beautiful cones of flame and throwing out from the long branches overhead volleys of scintillating blaze,… fireworks far excelling the art of pyrotechnica. The great clouds of smoke rolled away dire, black, tremendous. The fire passed us, but we heard its sounds through the dreary woods and saw at times dreadful gleams of light as some tall tree became food to the devouring element.… The fire still glittered through the now gloomy woods; a deathlike silence began to pervade the scene.… My companions stood trembling with a weird and pale look."

All their food and cooking gear had burnt up in the flames. For five days the men had no food but berries they plucked from bushes as they passed. Nor did they know where they were. In desperate hunger, they killed, roasted, and ate their little dog, a spaniel. They feared it might be the last meal before they died. Then they met friendly Indians, and with deep gratitude, Mayo and his companions accepted food. The Indians guided them to an established trail which led to Lake Superior.

These experiences built more toughness into Mayo's character. In later years, people described him as "fierce" and "peppery."

He had always been described as honest. But his honesty was tested when he attempted to count Minnesota settlers in St. Louis County. The task was impossible to carry out – Mayo was not even given expense money enough to travel the 150 miles of lake shore to count the men living in claim shacks scattered along it. He wanted to admit defeat and return to St. Paul without census figures, but the men who had asked the governor to appoint him now offered to help, rather than lose him. One man said he would make a list of settlers at Fond du Lac; another counted those in Grand Portage, while a third drew up a list for Grand Marais. When the census papers from these helpers arrived, Mayo recognized names of men living in Superior, Wisconsin, on the list of Minnesota settlers. He couldn't certify the lists without compromising his honesty, so he decided to send the lists to the governor as they were, without signing for their accuracy.

His other task, to organize some kind of government in St. Louis County, was quickly accomplished. Mayo was named county commissioner; one of the three men quit, and Mayo and the remaining commissioner, Henry S. Burk, held a single meeting in which they drew the election precincts for the county and named the county seat: site of the present city of Duluth.

In the summer of '55, W.W. also accepted a private job while he was still up north. He worked for Richard B. Godfrey of Detroit, an agent for the Northwest Exploring Company. His task was to examine copper specimens in all the claims along the north shore of Lake Superior and judge their value, so the company would know which ones to develop. For one delightful month, Mayo sailed along the shoreline in a Mackinaw boat with three French-Canadians, who rowed when the wind died down and who accompanied him inland where the copper was located. He completed this work and returned to Louise in late August, after three months' absence.

Working together, W.W. and Louise made an extensive inventory at this time of her dress and hat-making goods and then took the train to New York City to buy more. W.W. bought furs, including six opposum stoles in a variety called "Victorines," because Queen Victoria liked the style. That same day, Louise also bought furs, as well as ten glass-covered fur display boxes. On this trip, Louise made her last entries in the millinery accounts notebook. She now had plenty of stock to last until spring. At that time, her thoughts would turn to other matters than hats and dresses.

On October 2, 1855, Louise ran an ad in the St. Paul *Daily Minnesotian* newspaper announcing, "Mrs. L.W. Mayo is now prepared to supply all the LADIES who may favor her with their patronage with the prevailing styles of the NEW YORK AND PARIS FASHIONS for Millinery and Dress Making. My Stock is replete with all the most exquisite can desire in Dress Hats and Trimmings.... Dress making executed in a superior manner."

During the winter, W.W. was exasperated by a political brouhaha which took time he would have preferred spending in another manner. The census counts from St. Louis County were hotly contested after an election on October 9 produced more voters than men W.W. had counted in July. (The law stated a person had to be a resident six months to qualify for voting.) Mayo became a key witness as Minnesota legislators tried to figure out which votes were valid; he testified many times at long hearings, answering the same questions over and over.

By the spring of 1856, he was tired of politics and city life and ready to uproot Louise and Trude to find another home, where he hoped to earn enough for the three of them plus another baby, for Louise was expecting in June.

According to their grandson, W.W. also wanted to be a doctor again. "He must have been missing medicine," Dr. Charles W. Mayo observed, "for he returned one day from a solitary, rugged canoe trip and told Grandmother he wanted to move somewhere that he could set up a practice. She loyally agreed and they went up the Minnesota River, pausing to visit some friends from Indiana who had settled along its banks. Grandfather ... decided he had found the location he wanted."

These friends were the Dunham family, who lived on the western side of the Minnesota River in a beautiful area about four and a half miles south of the village of LeSueur (Minnesota). It was called Cronan's Precinct, after an Irishman whose house was the voting place, and was on the edge of the "Big Woods," a hardwood forest which stretched from Iowa north into northern Minnesota and east into Wisconsin. Around LeSueur, areas of open prairie were lovely in the spring, when the Mayos first saw it.

Alice Mendenhall, who was Trude's age and later became her friend, lived here and described it later in a little book she wrote for her family, *The Story of My Childhood*. "The open prairies were covered with wild flowers and wild strawberries," she said. "The grand old forest trees still grew where God had planted them, and the Indian roamed over land he called his own."

W.W. had no cause to fear living near Indians; they had saved his life the previous year.

The prevailing reason the Mayos moved to this remote spot was that they could do so for little money – they now planned to live on W.W.'s earnings alone. Louise's uncle, Nathaniel Wright, held title to some land in Cronan's Precinct. He was not using the one-room log house built on his property and offered its use to the Mayos.

W.W. took their belongings up the Minnesota River on a flatboat in the spring, soon after they decided to relocate. Louise and Trude remained behind in St. Paul while Louise sought a buyer for her business and made dresses and hats to reduce her stock.

With typical optimism, W.W. decided at once that he would become a farmer, as well as a doctor. He joined the Nicollet County Agricultural Society and was elected a member of its board of directors, where he served three years, though he knew next to nothing about farming. His confident, intelligent, decisive manner won him friends and positions of leadership all his life.

On May 7, 1856, Louise advertised her hat-making skills for the last time in the St. Paul *Daily Minnesotian*. Weeks later, she paid $4 each for two stagecoach tickets, and she and Trude traveled the 70 miles to their new home, breaking their two-day trip with overnight lodging in a place called "House-on-the-Rocks," located near Shakopee. They were happy to rejoin W.W. after two months' separation.

He at this time began making occasional entries in the *Rerum* book again, such as one on "Acoustics" from the "Lectures by Joseph Henry" and another on "Ventilation," both from an 1856 magazine published by the Smithsonian Institution. He was returning to his former medical life, but slowly. Three things made it difficult for him to practice medicine. First, he had no access to patients from his isolated home. Second, his one-room cabin was crowded, especially after their second daughter, Phoebe Louise (Mayo), was born there on June 26. Conditions at home were not favorable to solitary study or to seeing patients. Third, pioneers depended on mothers and grandmothers to care for their sick families. They rarely called on doctors.

For Louise, the move to Cronan's Precinct began three difficult years. She had never lived on a farm. Now she found herself in what she later called a "hard country," far from any neighbor. She was lonely, though after they met other settlers, there was some social life for the family. Alice Mendenhall wrote, "Sunday was visiting day. Everybody living within 10 or 12 miles – if we liked him – was a neighbor, and visited back and forth frequently."

The work of a pioneer housewife was difficult for Louise. She had no training for it. Once, while making soap, she began bleeding profusely from her mouth and nose. Trude ran screaming to her father for help. He prescribed rest and fresh air, which, in time, restored Louise to health. The incident had occurred because she knew no better than to cook her soap indoors, not, as a competent pioneer woman would have done, over an outdoor fire. She had breathed in lye fumes, and her lungs had hemorrhaged. Because of this experience, she developed the habit of remaining outside in the fresh air as much as possible every day. In time she became a gifted botanist and astronomer.

Louise had enjoyed operating her own business, but she never liked housework. Now there was no relief from it. She had to make almost everything her family needed, including candles, clothes, carpets, and all foods like cheese, butter, jams, and cured meats.

They were sometimes hungry, especially during the winter. Much later, describing her experiences at Cronan's Precinct, Louise spoke "with unmistakable grimness." She said, "Those were very hard times – particularly hard for a physician…. It was a rough, hard country. A few folk were comfortable, but most of us had to struggle to keep body and soul together."

W.W. bought eight animals, cows and oxen, and arranged with a farmer across the river to board the animals through the cold winter in his barn. But in two years, all Mayo's animals were gone, some sold, some starved.

At first, the Dakota Indians living near the Mayo family were not a threat. Trude, much later, told her children that she and little Phoebe used to run outside the cabin each morning as soon as they woke up, to see if they could spy any Indian footprints. Often Indians would come to the cabin and beg for food and liquor, especially if bread or some other good-smelling food was baking.

But even when the Indians were friendly, they had a frightening sense of humor. One morning two big Indian men dropped in on Alice Mendenhall's family south of LeSueur after her father left to do farmwork. They helped themselves to every food they could find, even raw potatoes. Then they cleaned their guns and one of them pointed his toward the window to see through the barrel. By so doing, he set the older children screaming, because the baby lay in a trundle bed under the window. Laughing at them, he did it again, and continued until Mrs. Mendenhall ordered them out of the house.

For amusement and from curiosity, the settlers sometimes went to "scalp dances," held by the Dakotas after they had fought other Indians. Since these were at Traverse des Sioux, an Indian trading post located about six miles from Mayo's cabin, it is likely that his curiosity led him to attend them too.

Alice Mendenhall went only once. "I can yet see the flicker of the firelight and the squaws with their long hair … throwing themselves upon their faces with grief for friends killed. Their cries were louder if the dead warriors had been scalped, for that meant that they could not go to the Happy Hunting Ground.

"The warriors, in paint and breech cloths, stood close together in a big circle around the fire, jumping up and down to the noise of the tomtom, yelling, 'Yip! Yip! Yip! Yip!' and at the same time dancing around the fire. Some of them had taken scalps, which they carried fastened to long poles. The white people, in their eagerness to see, crowded us very close to the Indians, and a scalp swung out and hit Mother in the face."

One day Mayo, riding on horseback to a sick patient in the country, met three intoxicated Dakota Indian men. He forded a stream, and when he approached the bank, they emerged from the bushes and demanded his horse. One of the Indians he would see again – a fierce brave whose nose had been partly bitten off during a fight with another Indian. Afterwards called Cut Nose, he stood six feet, six inches tall. Nevertheless, the five-foot, four-inch doctor did not hesitate to order him out of the way, and he continued on his trip unimpeded.

W.W. added to his few patients' fees by accepting whatever other work came to hand. He doctored animals and served as justice of the peace for Cronan's Precinct from 1857 to 1858. So that his neighbors could conduct business in Le Sueur, he established a ferry service across the Minnesota River.

In August, 1857, a bank failure of the Ohio Life Insurance and Trust Company in New York City caused panic and bank failures in every sizeable town in America, including in Minnesota territory. Up to this point, sales of land had boomed: town lots were selling for as much as $2,000 each in larger towns. When Mayo moved to the valley, having observed the heavy influx of settlers along the Minnesota River, he had expected the area to thrive. It even looked like nearby St. Peter might become the capital of Minnesota, since it was more centrally located than St. Paul.

However, by sundown on August 24, word had reached Minnesota of the Ohio Life failure, and banks began declaring bankruptcy in Minnesota too. Businesses were ruined; people already in debt found themselves in dire poverty, and money flowed out of the territory. The population of St. Paul was cut in half, but it remained the capital city. Bright prospects for the LeSueur area dimmed.

By December, 1858, W.W. was planning to move his family from the farm to a house in LeSueur, then a village of about 200 people. Louise was six months pregnant with their third daughter, the already-crowded cabin was becoming unbearable, and a town location was better than a farm for his medical practice. He bought two large lots on Main Street from the village on December 9 for one dollar.

On January 9, 1859, Louise wrote to a friend, Mrs. Lucans, using for stationery a page of her now-unused millinery accounts book. "I have had many ups and downs since you wrote me," she said, "and still I keep about on a level."

Mrs. Lucans had been to Pittsburgh for medical treatment, and Louise was not sure if she had returned home yet. "I'll direct this to your old place, hoping it may find you well. Well'er than it leaves me. The stove smokes and my expressive eyes are red and angry. We have had very cold weather for a few days, but today it is very pleasant, but too bright, too light, for my eyes."

For some reason, Louise never mailed the letter. It remained in the millinery book, giving evidence of her depression at this low point of her life.

On March 11, 1859, she gave birth in the little house to their third daughter, Sarah Frances. Trude was now five and a half, and Phoebe two and a half. When the Minnesota River flooded its banks several weeks later, the Mayo family was stranded in their cabin home for a time, because all the nearby trails were under water. The river was too swollen and swift for W.W.'s ferry to cross it.

W.W.'s older brother James, 42, was living in America, and in the summer he came to LeSueur to help W.W. construct a new white wood house. Plans for it came from a mail-order company; in those days, house-building plans could be bought like dress patterns. During the summer and early fall of '59, the brothers worked together.

The doctor had never built a house, but that didn't discourage him. The plans seemed clear enough, and James was there to assist. They managed to construct a solid structure, which still stands, even though their

The W.W. Mayo House, LeSueur, Minnesota

Photo by Judith Hartzell

measuring was inexact, and they built the house seven inches off the square. Under the roof, the brothers ran into some problems and had to "butt join" (splice) two or three short boards to make rafters, rather than following the usual practice of using rafters made from one board. The Mayos used no insulating materials in the original structure.

On the first floor of the house were two rooms, a kitchen and a sitting room, and upstairs three small rooms, two of them bedrooms and one the doctor's office. W.W. dug a well and built an outhouse and a barn large enough for a horse, cow, and wagon on their double lot, bordering the Minnesota River. During the four years the family lived there, Mayo added a big kitchen at the back of the house and above it, a workroom/storage room. At this later building time, he placed insulation between the walls, using his discarded newspapers and periodicals. Below the kitchen, W.W. dug a cellar for storing fruits and vegetables.

The doctor's office had a large gable window which looked out on the street. By its light he could read or mix medicines. He kept his rolltop desk in this room, and, on a table, his doctor's tools, including surgical instruments and the little pocket case he carried them in, his microscope, bottles, and a mortar and pestle for mixing medicines. The door into this room was only five feet and seven inches high – plenty of room for the five-foot-four inch man people sometimes called "the little doctor."

While W.W. and James were roofing the house, a farmer, J. L. Drake, rode up and asked if W.W. would come and examine his sick horse – did the doctor treat animals?

"Sure, I'll come," W.W. answered. "I'll look at a horse or any other damn thing you've got."

The horse got well, and W.W. made a friend.

Sadly for the family, James Mayo became ill while he and the doctor were working on the house. Census records in LeSueur state that he died in November, 1859, after a sickness of 35.6 days. The family had moved into the house only a short time before.

When W.W. and Louise recovered from their grief, they began to befriend their neighbors. Louise was glad to be back in a town. She preferred a busy life in the midst of family and friends, especially if she could help people. And W.W. was encouraged, living closer to potential patients, for he had missed medicine. Perhaps the happiest was Trude, now more than six years old, because she could attend school with other village children.

Soon after moving the family to LeSueur, W.W. made a courtesy call on the only other doctor in town, Dr. Otis Ayer.

Ayer gruffly commented, "Dr. Mayo, this town is not big enough for two doctors."

Mayo answered, as if surprised, "Why, Dr. Ayer, were you thinking of leaving?"

Chapter 6

THE SIOUX WAR AND THE CIVIL WAR

"I have no purpose directly or indirectly to interfere with the institution of slavery in the States where it exists.... Physically speaking, we cannot separate.... No State, upon its own mere action, can lawfully get out of the Union."
President Abraham Lincoln, March 4, 1861

Now happily settled in his upstairs office, W.W. returned to reading and occasional noting in the *Rerum* book. Entries from this period suggest how varied were his interests: in the *Smithsonian Report* he read about cuttlefish, and in *Medical Times*, about "Homicidal cut throat cases," and "Poisons/Belladonna case."

But W.W.'s medical studies were sporadic. Again he found that patients were too few and too poor to provide a living for himself, Louise, and his three little girls. He found sicknesses common enough. True, there was no malaria. He left that behind in Indiana, but Minnesota presented pneumonia, frostbite, problems associated with malnutrition, and children's diseases like scarlet fever and diphtheria. Occasionally, epidemics of cholera or typhoid fever struck on the frontier, killing hundreds. Hunting and farming accidents were common, but unless the emergency or illness was severe, settlers treated themselves. Even when they came in desperation to the doctor, they often could not afford to pay him, except in goods.

To help provide food for the family, Louise planted a vegetable garden and tended their cow. She also began studying the properties of various herbs, and whatever was useful she grew in an herb garden in the backyard. She planted hyssop, to be prescribed as an infusion of leaves in water or alcohol for sore throats, coughs and indigestion. The whole tansy plant was used for many complaints – in a cold drink for indigestion, jaundice, and worms. Heated, it treated fever, delayed labor, and gout. As a poultice, doctors applied tansy to reduce swelling, cramps, and inflammation, and its seeds were used against worms. Yarrow for diseases of the uterus, along with comfrey, the "healing herb," for diarrhea and dysentery, and catnip for fevers, also went from Louise's garden to her husband's medicine stores.

Though his medical practice did grow a little when W.W. moved to LeSueur – for town patients as well as his former Cronan's Precinct patients consulted him – he still needed to supplement his income with outside work. He continued to doctor animals and operate his ferry between LeSueur and the west side of the Minnesota River. In late spring, 1860, he accepted a full-time job on a small steamboat, transporting people and goods up and down the river from St. Paul.

When the Minnesota River was highest from melting snow and abundant rainfall each spring, large steamboats could travel from St. Paul all the way upriver to the towns of St. Peter, Mankato, and New

Ulm. But when the waters dried up in summer and fall, the big St. Paul steamboats could travel only a little distance before sandbars blocked them. Then smaller boats, directed by local residents, took the food, farm supplies, and other provisions onboard for the up-river travel, carrying back downstream passengers, farm produce, lumber, and other goods for sale.

During the summer of 1860, W.W. enjoyed river life and extended his reputation for directness and honesty as he met people in the river towns. One acquaintance was a 21-year-old Canadian named James J. Hill, who had decided to seek his fortune in Minnesota and was working for a St. Paul wholesale grocer, handling freight transferred to steamboats. He was the sort of young man W.W. liked, with a life story similar to his own. Hill's father had died when the boy was young; he had been taught in an excellent Quaker school until he was 14 and so had mastered practical subjects like math and English. He was intelligent and had a will to work. Hill later told a newspaper reporter that the secret of his success was "Work, hard work, intelligent work, and then more work." The two men would meet again in later years.

Mayo's boat made two trips a week, sometimes towing a barge from St. Peter past New Ulm, all the way to Fort Ridgely. Since travel between the valley towns was mostly by boat, a community of sorts formed from the river commerce. As W.W. made friends up and down the river, he established a fund of potential patients.

In the winter, when no boats could travel up the frozen river, people living in LeSueur enjoyed parties and sleigh rides, and in the summer, every Fourth of July the town held a big picnic.

The baby, Sarah Frances, died in the fall of 1860, when she was 18 months old. As with little Horace, there was nothing Louise and W.W. could do but grieve this loss and then turn their faces towards the future. At this time they still had two living children from the four that had been born to them. Trude was now seven and Phoebe four.

Soon after Sarah's death, W.W. had his second experience in a lawsuit. A Mrs. Wirt of LeSueur asked for $10,000 in damages from Dr. Otis Ayer, alleging that she now had a stiff wrist, due to Dr. Ayer's treatment. While lancing an abscess, he had cut into her wrist joint, causing the synovial fluid to drain out. Mayo testified that, according to his knowledge and the best medical books, Ayer had indeed acted negligently.

Nearly everyone in town avidly followed the case. Dr. Ayer had six doctors from nearby towns witnessing on his side, and Mayo alone testified against him. (As it happens, Mayo was wrong on this issue, but he testified honestly, basing his belief on current medical theory.) The jury decided against Ayer but asked only $57 from him as penalty. This case – like the lawsuit against Daniel Hart in Lafayette nine years earlier – left W.W. dissatisfied with lawyers, judges, and juries as a means of solving problems.

Mayo likely voted for Abraham Lincoln for president on November 6, 1860, since the two men held similar views on slavery and preserving the union. Lincoln triumphed in Minnesota. Louise never had the opportunity to cast a ballot during her long life; Minnesota granted women the right to vote in 1919, four years after she died.

Lincoln had been chosen by Republicans as their candidate only on the third ballot. William Seward of New York led the first two ballots, but because he was an antislavery radical, the convention decided to throw its support behind the more moderate Lincoln, balancing the ticket with Hannibal Hamlin of Maine for vice president. The Republican platform affirmed the right of each state to control its own institutions and took no stand against slavery. However, it opposed reopening the slave trade with Africa and extending slavery into the territories.

Lincoln's moderate views did not satisfy the South. On December 20, the South Carolina legislature, with no dissenting votes, declared that "the union now subsisting between South Carolina and the other States, under the name of the 'United States of America,' is hereby dissolved."

At a dinner held by the First Baptist Church of LeSueur in December, W.W. discussed these events with friends. To raise money for painting their new building, the church people had invited generous acquaintances along the Minnesota Valley to the fund-raiser. One of these was Harry H. Young from Henderson, whom W.W. had known when both men lived in Indiana.

Now Young was editor of the *Henderson Democrat*, and he proposed that the two men together begin another paper, a weekly which they named the *LeSueur Courier*. Mayo would publish it and write articles about agriculture; Young would edit and write about politics. One month later the first issue appeared. It lasted for only 12 issues, but it gave W.W. his first experience writing his opinions for newspaper readers, an exercise he enjoyed and would repeat in coming years.

Mayo and Young differed in politics, and this was a time when political views were ardently held and expressed. Perhaps that is why the paper failed so quickly. Young was a Democrat, Mayo now a Republican, though he had been elected justice of the peace for Cronan's Precinct as a Democrat. His views in early 1861 were like Lincoln's: he did not believe in abolition of slavery at any cost; he believed in promoting understanding and gradual progress.

In a letter to the editor appearing in the *Henderson Democrat* on March 2, 1861, Mayo decided "to proclaim our own political faith. Upon mature reflection, we think it quite as well that we should have a few journals in the free States to uphold the views of the South and make known their grievances, be they real or imaginary. It shows to the South, too, that our institutions must be preferable to theirs to live under, in that we can tolerate freedom of speech and of the press."

Such a statement was designed to provoke both northerners and southerners. To be sure he was catching the attention of his readers and properly representing southern views, Mayo continued, "And with regard to slavery, we do believe that it has its rights and that its advantages have been great.... There are many things both in the moral and physical world which are difficult for finite minds to comprehend."

He further argued for the South: "There are very few religiously rabid abolitionists who allow themselves to think for a moment that if they had been brought up under slave institutions, and had slavery surrounding them from their earliest infancy, they would themselves be slavery propagandists, and as violently so as any Southern fire eater. Yea, we believe that Wendell Phillips himself, had his lot been cast in a Southern clime, would have out-Yancied Yancy." (Wendell Phillips was a prominent abolitionist from Massachusetts; William Yancey from Alabama had tried to persuade Democrats in their convention to adopt a platform plank "that slavery was right.")

Mayo did not believe slavery was right, but he felt if northerners would try to understand the southern position, their differences of opinion could be settled peacefully in another 20 or 30 years, when the South would come to accept "the right of human freedom from servile bondage." In the meantime, he argued for peace, even if it meant extending slavery in the territories, because he had faith that justice would prevail from "a higher power than even this combined generation of men that shapes our political actions, 'let us rough hew them as we will.'"

During the short months Mayo was publishing his newspaper, seven states in addition to South Carolina seceded from the union because of what they called northern aggression against their institutions. They met in Montgomery, Alabama, and by February 8 had framed a constitution and set up a government. On February 9 they chose Jefferson Davis as their president.

When Lincoln was inaugurated president on March 4, he said, "I have no purpose directly or indirectly to interfere with the institution of slavery in the States where it exists." He was firm against secession. "We cannot separate.... No State, upon its own mere action, can lawfully get out of the Union."

One month later, civil war began, precipitated by the

attack on U.S. Fort Sumter in Charleston, South Carolina, by General Pierre Beauregard of the Confederacy. All these events W.W. observed with great interest, reading whatever newspapers and magazines he could get, coming to him up the Minnesota River on packet boats.

However, on June 29, 1861, civil war was not uppermost on his mind. Life, not death, preoccupied him as he assisted Louise in their little upstairs bedroom. She gave birth to a healthy boy, their second son, the first to survive. They named the baby "William James" after his father and his uncle, who had helped build their house two years before.

In early 1862, a traveling photographer visited Le Sueur and photographed the Mayo family — baby Will, Phoebe, five; Gertrude, eight; Louise, thirty-six, and W.W., forty-two. Louise is squinting in the photo, her brown eyes hyper-sensitive to bright light. Her brunette hair is carefully coifed in long curls. Slender and fashionably dressed, she holds her son, bare-foot, wearing a baby dress. The doctor looks handsome and tough, with a full dark-brown beard and mustache. His hairline is beginning to recede. With penetrating directness, he stares at the photographer.

W.W. was still in LeSueur in the spring of '62, though he had applied to Republican Governor Alexander Ramsey months earlier, on September 22, '61, to serve as surgeon to the Minnesota volunteers who had already left for the battlefield. This surgeon appointment was a political plum, and, with such short experience as a Republican, Mayo was not the man picked. Dr. Levi Butler of Minneapolis, who had not practiced medicine in four years but was an influential Republican, won the position.

Instead, the Minnesota governor named W.W. examining surgeon in LeSueur County after President Lincoln announced on August 4, 1862, following the Union army's second defeat at Bull Run, a draft of 300,000 men. Lincoln called for a quota of men from each county to be raised by volunteers until September 3, and after that by draftees. W.W.'s task was to examine the men for fitness to serve.

But another battle was brewing, this one much closer to home. On Tuesday, August 19, a horseback rider with urgent news woke Mayo before dawn — the Dakota Sioux Indians in southwest Minnesota had declared war and were murdering settlers southwest of New Ulm, a prosperous town about 34 miles away. Before Trude and Phoebe were out of bed, W.W. had left to plan a response with all the other able-bodied men in LeSueur. They spent the morning preparing for battle, gathering guns and gunpowder and making bullets from lead. H.W. Mendenhall, Alice's father, and her Uncle Jim Swan were among the band, which became known as the "LeSueur Tigers."

Louise and William W. Mayo with their children, from left, William, 10 months; Phoebe, 5, and Gertrude, 8

Photo by permission of Mayo Foundation for Medical Education and Research. All rights reserved.

At mid-morning, the men left town and crossed the Minnesota River by ferry. Dr. Ayer traveled in a buggy with the medical supplies, but Mayo chose to walk with the other men. Twelve miles south in St. Peter more volunteers joined them, including Judge Charles E. Flandrau from Traverse des Sioux, making a force of 125.

From St. Peter they again set out on foot for New Ulm, 22 miles away. Dr. Asa Daniels of St. Peter at this time joined Dr. Ayer in the buggy; Mayo continued on foot. By 10 p.m., soaked by torrential rains on the way, they arrived at New Ulm to learn that five persons had been killed, five injured, and six houses set on fire in an Indian attack earlier that day. Refugees, some of them wounded, were beginning to crowd all available shelters. Though the carnage was minor this day, townspeople were panicky, expecting another, more effective attack.

The citizen-soldiers elected Judge Flandrau their commander. He immediately posted guards around New Ulm and established emergency hospitals for the doctors. Dr. Mayo, with Dr. William R. McMahon of Mankato, joined New Ulm's own young doctor, Carl Weschcke, who was already working in a hotel called "the Dacotah [sic] House." Across the street, Ayer and Daniels established a hospital in the basement of a store. Meanwhile, more men arrived from Mankato and elsewhere, swelling the volunteer army to nearly 300.

Wednesday and Thursday passed, with no new alarms. The doctors tended growing numbers of injured patients, as rescue parties brought in more from the countryside. The other men built barricades from wagons, farm machines, logs, and rocks around the business district of the unfenced town, an area three blocks long and two blocks wide. (The Indians' preferred method of fighting was to shoot flaming arrows at wooden houses, forcing the whites to flee into the open, where they could be picked off by arrows and bullets.)

Late Thursday, a fleeing settler told of 13 women and children hiding in a marsh 10 miles southwest of town. Next morning, 100 men, including Drs. Mayo, Ayer and Daniels, hiked to their rescue, stopping on the way to examine houses and barns and bury any dead they found. At last they reached the terrified and hungry women and children, who for three days had eaten nothing but flatbread and drunk marsh water. After caring for the refugees, the men set out walking toward Fort Ridgely to rescue more settlers, if possible. When sounds of gunfire from the fort, which they had heard all day, ceased, they held a council. Believing an attack on New Ulm imminent, they voted to return and bolster its defenses. About 1 a.m. on Saturday, Mayo arrived back at the Dakotah House.

He did not know what the Indians' warplans were and might not have known the source of their unrest. Dakota men, especially the warrior types who belonged to a group called the "Soldiers' Lodge," hated the white traders who often cheated them and government agents, who sometimes withheld food. They longed to return to the years before 1851, when they had signed away 28 million acres of hunting land to the United States in the Treaties of Traverse des Sioux and of Mendota in exchange for food and annuities of nine dollars per year per Indian, paid over 50 years. The Dakota warriors resented U.S. efforts to change their culture – to destroy the old warrior-hunter pattern and recreate them as American farmers, each settled on his own piece of land. In the summer of 1862, the farmer-Indians (about one-tenth of the whole) were harvesting plentiful crops, while their hunter brothers were hungry, unable to find enough game on their reservation.

Government agents gave preferential treatment to farmer-Indians, delivering their annuities and food on time, and sometimes building them houses. They often delivered annuities and food late to the warrior-Indians.

Agent Thomas Galbraith had refused food to the tribes in the spring, causing distress and wrath, saying that though the food had arrived, the annuity money had not, and he wanted to distribute them together. The Indians had waited through the summer on the edge of starvation, and finally on Friday, August 15, they met again with Galbraith. Chief Little Crow spoke for them, "When men are hungry, they help themselves."

Frightened, Galbraith asked the traders if they would give the Indians credit until the money arrived; he wanted to give them food. One trader, Andrew Myrick, answered, "As far as I'm concerned, if they are hungry, let them eat grass."

The Indians responded with cries of fury.

The actual incident which began the war occurred two days later, when four hungry young Indian braves went into the Big Woods to hunt. One of them, finding a hen's nest filled with eggs, took them, causing another to say, "Don't take them. They belong to a white man and we may get into trouble."

From this simple comment an argument erupted and escalated into a series of taunts between the braves as to who was the most courageous. The argument ended when they shot and killed the farmer who owned the eggs, Robinson Jones, his wife, son-in-law Howard Baker, and two other people, one a 15-year-old girl.

Returning home directly, they reported what had happened, and their tribal leader took them to Little Crow, a highly-respected Dakota chief, in the middle of the night. He advised, "War is now declared. Blood has been shed, and the [government] payment will be stopped. The whites will take a dreadful vengeance because women have been killed."

A Soldiers' Lodge meeting of about 100 warrior-hunter Indians followed. Aware that many Minnesota white men had left the state to fight in the Civil War, the Indians decided this was their chance to reclaim their hunting lands. The council declared war, with the purpose of driving all whites out of western and southern Minnesota, as far as St. Paul. They planned to capture the strategically important Fort Ridgely and New Ulm and then sweep down the Minnesota Valley. LeSueur – with Louise and the three children – lay in their projected path.

At dawn the next morning, Monday, August 18, Indians in battle paint and regalia attacked the Redwood Agency, upriver from New Ulm, killing 24 traders and government employees and causing everyone else in the agency to flee. They began their killing with Myrick the trader. Into his dead mouth, they stuffed grass.

Then Dakota warriors looted the agency's food and ammunition stores, taking away what they could carry. Bands of Indians spread out to kill settlers on farmsteads in the area and set their houses and barns on fire. More than 400 settlers were killed this first day, attacked without warning as they worked in their fields.

Tuesday, the Indians attacked New Ulm in the skirmish which had drawn W.W. and the other citizen-volunteers from Le Sueur, St. Peter and Mankato. While the doctors treated patients in New Ulm on Wednesday, Thursday, and Friday, the Indians twice attacked Fort Ridgely. Both attacks failed because of the soldiers' valiant defense, and by sundown Friday, Ridgely was saved, but 40,000 residents of a 10,000 square mile area were fleeing the Dakotas, having heard grim reports of the events at Redwood Agency and elsewhere.

Concerned that New Ulm might soon receive U.S. soldier reinforcements, the Indians decided to strike there the next day and then return to attack Fort Ridgely again.

So it was that on Saturday, August 23, Dakotas attacked New Ulm a second time, in greater numbers, better organized, and better led. Little Crow was in charge, assisted by other chiefs – Mankato, Wabasha, and Big Eagle among them – , 650 Indians engaging in all. Only 225 of the 300 citizen-soldiers stood against them. Early in the morning, Flandreau had fallen into a trap when he sent 75 men off across the Minnesota River to investigate fires set by the Indians, who soon cut the whites off from the only ferry back to town.

Only two-thirds of the 225 men had guns, and many of these were old-fashioned muzzle-loaders, whereas the Indians were better armed with good rifles and double-barreled shotguns, as well as bows and arrows. Fighting on this day was the most ferocious of the brief war and proved to be its turning point.

About 9:30 a.m., the Indians assumed positions on an upper ridge two miles above the town. Flandreau ordered his troops to stand half a mile south of town, facing them. At mid-morning, the Dakotas attacked. Flandreau wrote, "Their advance upon the sloping prairie was a very fine spectacle, and to such inexperienced soldiers as we all were, intensely exciting. When within about one mile and a half of us, the mass began to expand like a fan and increase in the velocity of its approach, and continued this movement until within about double rifle-shot, when it had covered our entire front. Then the savages uttered a terrific yell and came down upon us like the wind."

The sound of the Indians' war whoops plus the sight of them, naked except for breechcloths and headbands and smeared in warpaint, so terrified the settlers that they fled back to the barricades. The Indians could have pursued and taken them there, but they hung back, fearing a trap. Instead, Indians took over houses outside the barricades and used these for cover. Twenty brave Le Sueur Tigers, including Mendenhall, stopped during the retreat and took shelter in the wooden, four-story windmill. They were some of the best-armed citizen-soldiers and excellent marksmen. From the windmill they fired upon the Indians, stopping the advance of some.

A few of the New Ulm defenders were so unnerved by the battle, they ran to hide in cellars with hundreds of women and children refugees. Incensed, Dr. Mayo drove them out and armed them with whatever was handy. For some, it was pitchforks.

"What will we do with these?" they asked Mayo.

He swore and answered, "Run your forks through the Indians, of course!"

After the Sioux's flaming arrows set some houses on fire, a stiff wind spread the flames and caused dense clouds of smoke which choked and blinded the soldier-volunteers and gave cover to Indians. Fighting became desperate, with New Ulm defenders pushed back behind the barricaded three-by-two blocks by a powerful Dakota attack.

Within these blocks, the five doctors worked steadily. In 90 minutes of fighting, 10 whites were killed and 50 wounded and brought to the doctors, carried on doors torn from houses. The room in Dakotah House, where Mayo worked, filled up rapidly with wounded and dying men, lying on beds and mattresses that lined all four walls.

Once, while amputating a settler's leg, Mayo looked up and through a window saw two of the citizen-guards sneaking away. He streaked out the door, waving his bloody knife, and ordered the men to return and fight. They did.

Some time later, the citizen-soldiers were at the point of surrendering. Three men made impassioned appeals for them to continue fighting: Father Sunrisen (a Catholic priest), Captain Dodd (who was killed later that day), and Dr. Mayo. At stake were not only their own lives, but the lives of more than 1,000 refugees, helpless and huddled in cellars and deserted buildings.

About 3 p.m., the soldiers rallied. Flandreau led them on the offense against 60 Indians who were forming to attack. The whites charged, mimicing the Indian warcry to bolster their courage. They managed to rout the Dakotas, with help from marksmen at the barricades. This charge turned the tide of battle, which the Indians had nearly won.

As evening fell, the Dakotas retreated, and settlers burned the windmill and outlying houses, to prevent their use as Indian shelters the next day. All through the night the five doctors worked on, as flames from the burning buildings lighted the area. About 190 buildings, one-third of the town, burned during and after the Saturday battle. Of the 225 citizen-soldiers, 34 were dead and 60 wounded.

Discouraged by the stout defense of both New Ulm and Fort Ridgely, Dakotas did not attack again. They retreated upriver. In both places, they misjudged, from the intensity of the resistance, how many men were fighting. Flandreau believed the defense of Ridgely and New Ulm was critical: "Had they [the Indians] carried the Fort and New Ulm, they would undoubtedly have pushed their success through the length of the Minnesota Valley."

On Sunday, leaders in New Ulm decided to abandon the burned-out town, which had more than doubled its population with a steady influx of refugees. There were not enough provisions for such a large group. Store-owners made foodstuffs available to everyone, and on Monday, 153 wagons carrying women, children, and the wounded slowly rolled out of town towards Mankato, 30 miles downriver. Leading the caravan were Drs. McMahon and Mayo, who went ahead to make preparations. Following were more than two miles of people on foot.

Tuesday, when the caravan (which included Dr. Ayer) left Mankato and moved on to St. Peter and LeSueur, Mayo stayed behind to help McMahon tend the injured. He remained another week.

Louise was thus two weeks alone in LeSueur with the three children. With no men in town, the women, including Louise, half expected an Indian attack at any moment. On Saturday, a man from LeSueur deserted the fight at New Ulm, thinking the large number of Indian attackers would easily win. He returned home and told the women of LeSueur that all their men were dead. When they later discovered he had lied and deserted, they threatened to kill him. One woman carried a handgun with her for weeks, to shoot him if she saw him.

Louise many years later described her experiences while her husband was away. "Will was a baby in arms and safe enough, and I scared the other two children into staying indoors. When it was necessary for me to go to the barn or well, I'd put on a pair of overalls and tuck my hair under one of the doctor's old hats.... What a figure I must have cut in those overalls. I often think of it. So brave and manly, and my heart in my mouth!"

A family story says Louise organized the women of LeSueur to scare away would-be attackers. As her grandson put it, "My resourceful grandmother conceived the brilliant plan of having the women dress in men's clothing and move around the streets with sticks on their shoulders which, from a distance, would resemble rifles. As an added touch, she fastened spoons to the ends of the sticks, to twinkle in the sunlight like bayonets."

When refugees from the Sioux War began passing through LeSueur, Louise said she "would run to the gate and ask, 'Who dressed your wounds?' And when they said, 'The Little Doctor,' I knew my husband still lived."

Once, Louise took seven fleeing families into her house for the night, and three more families stayed in the barn. Trude and Phoebe gave up their beds to the visitors and slept with other little girls on the parlor floor.

"Trude and I had to work day and night to feed them," Louise said. "One day I baked a whole barrel of flour [into bread] to feed the homeless who quartered on us."

When Louise told the story to Mrs. William Brown Meloney much later, she simply stated, "The Doctor was needed there [in New Ulm] and he went."

Meloney interrupted her, "And left you and the babies all alone?"

"Why, of course," Louise answered. "He was needed at Ulm."

Meloney commented, "The way she said it made me feel chastened. I know I shall never forget the expression of her face or the tone in which she spoke those five words, 'He was needed at Ulm.'"

As the Indians retreated, Colonel Henry H. Sibley of the U.S. Army — whom some contemporary newspaper reporters called "the snail" — slowly, slowly followed them. He arrived to help the citizen-soldiers only when the battle was over. At last he rescued 260 captives, white and mixed-blood Indians, mostly women and children in wretched condition from repeated molestation during their 40-day captivity. He took into custody all the Dakotas who chose to turn themselves over to the government in exchange for food and shelter. Most of the leaders, including Little Crow, escaped, but Cut Nose, the Indian who had accosted W.W. years earlier on the river, was captured. A military commission tried the Indians, supposedly to determine who had killed non-combatants. They judged 307 men guilty and sentenced them to death.

The Indians had no lawyers, no witnesses in their defense, and no time to prepare their statements. Many of them had fought reluctantly. The tribunal condemned any warrior who admitted he fired a weapon. However, President Lincoln believed the sentences were a miscarriage of justice. He allowed time to pass, so tempers would cool, and upheld the sentence of "death by hanging" for only 38 Indians (including Cut Nose) proven to have committed "rape and wanton murder."

Over a period of six weeks, beginning in August, the

Cut Nose, the Dakota brave

Photo by permission of Mayo Foundation for Medical Education and Research. All rights reserved.

Dakota warriors had killed about 800 whites. (Some estimates are as high as 2,000.) The number of Indian casualties is not known; Dakotas buried their dead immediately and kept no statistics. Twenty-three southwestern Minnesota counties were nearly emptied of their people, both white and Indian.

Before the war, 6,000 Indians lived in Minnesota. Afterwards, only about 200 mixed-blood farmer-Indians, with their full-blood relatives, remained in their homes. All the others retreated or were forced to move west to North and South Dakota, Nebraska, or Canada. The war was very costly to the warrior-Indians.

In October, '62, Republicans in the LeSueur area elected W.W. district committee member and chairman of the party convention. After the New Ulm war, people throughout the Minnesota River Valley knew him to be a man of unusual valor, as well as one of the best doctors in the state.

On December 26, 1862, the 38 condemned Indians were hanged simultaneously in Mankato on a giant platform built for the occasion. It was the largest mass execution in American history. W.W. and other doctors went to observe the event. Afterwards, the bodies were buried in a long hole dug in a river bank. When darkness fell, government supervisors looked the other way as men dug up the bodies and distributed them to doctors to be used for medical education. To W.W. they gave the corpse of Cut Nose.

Mayo carried it home to LeSueur and then invited doctor friends from neighboring towns to come for an anatomy lesson. Carefully, he dissected the body, explaining to his colleagues the various systems of human anatomy. Having studied the subject at medical school in St. Louis, he understood it better than the other doctors and was eager to be of use to them, sharing what he knew.

The dissection completed, W.W. cleaned the bones and placed them in a large kettle. At six foot six, Cut Nose's skeleton was too tall to hang under the low ceiling of the little doctor's office.

Nothing of use was discarded in the Mayo household. As years passed, Mayo used the skeleton to teach his children osteology. Both Will and Charlie learned, before they were old enough to whistle, the name of every human bone from Cut Nose's skeleton.

Chapter 7

Moving to Rochester

"One never knows how much one can stand until one is put to the test.... I contracted [trachoma] and went stone blind.... It was very hard at first – very hard on my husband – but I soon learned to be useful. If one doesn't give in under calamity, but just says, 'I'm going to be useful until I drop,' it helps a lot, my dear."

Louise Mayo

The Civil War continued to absorb the Mayo family's interest. LeSueur became the site of a military school which trained volunteers, including John Smith of the Tenth Regiment, who attended it from January 1 to 25, 1863. The next day, January 26, John's company transferred to Kelso Township. He wrote in his diary that, as they quit the town, "Each member of the Company received a needle book from the Ladies of LeSueur. The Company gave 3 cheers for the Ladies of LeSueur."

On February 9, Smith began boarding with the Mayos while he attended the school a second time, remaining in their home two weeks. On his third day in the Mayo home, he responded to an urgent summons for help from Mayo. A kerosene lamp had exploded and burned the doctor's hand. He sent Smith to the army hospital for chloroform to help relieve the pain.

This is the first mention of W.W. handling chloroform. It had come into use gradually since November 4, 1847, when Dr. James Young Simpson of Edinburgh, Scotland, first experimented by inhaling chloroform in his dining room. He decided it was preferable to ether, which had a disagreeable smell and caused patients to cough. Subsequently, he used it to assist women in childbirth. This innovation occasioned a storm of protest from church people who believed that God's words in the Bible, "In sorrow shalt thou bring forth children," meant pain was God-ordained for childbirth. Simpson responded by noting that God put Adam to sleep when He extracted the rib to create Eve, so He must believe in anesthesia.

In 1853, Queen Victoria praised chloroform, which Dr. John Snow used during the birth of Prince Leopold, enabling her to experience pain-free childbirth. This royal approval silenced the critics, and chloroform came into use in Britain and, in time, in America.

Having unconscious patients was a boon to the surgeon; no longer did people measure his expertise by the speed with which he cut. Before the widespread use of ether and chloroform, many surgeons were renowned for fast amputations. Dr. James R. Wood of New York, for instance, took only nine seconds to amputate a leg at the thigh.

On April 24, 1863, President Lincoln appointed Dr. W.W. Mayo examining surgeon for the Union army, first Minnesota district, a very large and populous area made up of the southern half of the state. Mayo's good reputation in the Minnesota River Valley had helped him secure the appointment.

Several weeks into May, Mayo left home, wife, and children for Rochester, which was the headquarters of the Union Army enrollment board, first district. This town of about 2,600 people appealed to him. It was more developed than LeSueur, with two newspapers, a bank, an impressive courthouse, two churches, eight hotels, two breweries and seven saloons. Because it lay along the route planned for the railroad to take west from the Mississippi, W.W. believed the town would grow and offer him and his family opportunities for work and education.

He bought two lots on Franklin Street in Rochester and hired people to build a comfortable log house. In January, 1864, Louise, Trude, Phoebe, and Will joined him in the new home. Louise, who had endured an eight-month disruption to her family life, decided that Rochester would be their permanent home. "We're not moving again," she announced. This is the reason why today people from all over the world travel to a town in Minnesota which is so cold in winter that subways have been built to allow patients comfortable passage from hotel to clinic. Louise said, "No more. We're not moving again."

On January 27, W.W. annnounced in the Rochester newspapers that he was opening a private practice of medicine in copartnership with Dr. W.A. Hyde. The *Rochester Republican* noted that both doctors "are known to be men of ability and skill, and we should think that where they are baffled, medical skill would be of little avail." The doctors promised, "All calls answered by day or night." They opened their office over the Union Drug Store on Third Street.

By June 15, Dr. Hyde had separated from Mayo and moved his office to his home, across from Dr. Cross on Broadway.

A surge of new life and hope lifted W.W. in 1864, after his family joined him. He began making notes in *Rerum* again. In '64 he read articles on the anus, bile, burns, croup, diptheria, the surgical history of the Crimean War, and "pulsating tumors of the abdomen."

That he found time to study at all is surprising, since he was working nonstop examining volunteers and draftees for the Union army, assisted by Dr. Hector Galloway. Some fit men tried to trick doctors into believing they were unfit. W.W. used chloroform on

Dr. W.W. Mayo with other Civil War examining surgeons (Mayo is #153)

Photo by permission of Mayo Foundation for Medical Education and Research. All rights reserved.

draftees who pretended their legs were too stiff for walking. If the legs could be manipulated while the man was unconscious from chloroform, he was judged able to march.

Some time after Louise and the children moved to Rochester, disaster struck the family. She became almost blind from trachoma, an infectious eye disease, after assisting W.W. in caring for a trachoma-afflicted patient. For several years, she was blind.

Early in '65, the U.S. Congress decided that examining surgeons should travel about their districts, so they could examine more men. They were instructed to officially exempt those physically unfit to serve. In January and February, W.W. set up offices in Preston, St. Peter, Mankato, and Faribault. In St. Peter, more than 2,000 men stood waiting outside the board office when he arrived, all hoping to be exempted. It was a scene ripe for cheating. Throngs of lawyers and doctors circulated in the crowd, taking fees to write certificates – from the lawyers, papers saying a man was overage or an alien; from the doctors, papers declaring physical disability. A doctor was allowed to do an examination for five dollars; these street doctors were charging as much as two hundred per exam, saying they had influence with the surgeons inside. Even the guard who admitted the men to see Mayo was accepting bribes to take men in speedily.

Meantime, Mayo and Galloway examined up to 600 men a day, sometimes at a rate of a man a minute. Mayo did some extra exams in his hotel room in the evenings, and for these exams he charged the legal five dollars each.

An observer of the St. Peter scene wrote the newspaper to complain about hordes of doctors and lawyers working the crowd of waiting men. He said this was not an "examination of fitness or unfitness for the service, but merely a buying and selling of exemption certificates." His letter started a storm of protest from other readers.

A newspaper editor from Faribault warned its citizens not to be taken in by the charlatan doctors outside the board offices. About Mayo, he said, "From what we have heard of him, we would not believe him a man guilty of any such baseness."

In a later newspaper, however, he wrote that most of the men Mayo had examined in the evening he later exempted, implying that Mayo, too, was corrupted. This became a topic of great interest throughout the state. The *St. Paul Pioneer* defended Mayo, stating "In the Minnesota Valley, where Dr. Mayo has been known for years, no charge of official corruption would for a moment be entertained by the people."

Nevertheless, the firestorm of suspicion prompted an investigation, ending the Faribault exams. W.W. was ordered to St. Paul, and the doctors who had circulated through the crowd outside his office were arrested. Mayo testified to the examiner, Colonel John Averill, that he had done exams at night, charging five dollars each, for men who could not spend two days or more waiting in line. If he noted physical problems which would entitle the man to exemption, he told him to report back for another exam before the board to receive his exemption papers. If he found the man fit to fight, he sent him home to save the examining board's time. Therefore it was true that men Mayo examined privately who then came before the board were usually exempted, because his exams eliminated the physically able men. He had done nothing illegal to obtain this result.

Colonel Averill was not convinced. He ordered Mayo taken under arrest back to Rochester. Averill sent a report to Washington and then asked another doctor, J.D. Wheelock, to reexamine the men Mayo had exempted in Faribault. Of 153 exemptions by Mayo, Wheelock agreed with only 105. He did not consider missing teeth which might make a man unable to chew, varicose veins which might interfere with his marching, or heart disease to be sufficient grounds for exemption.

In late February, even before it received the Wheelock report, the War Department in Washington dismissed Mayo "for receiving fees for private examinations" and appointed Dr. Edwin C. Cross of Rochester the new examining surgeon.

Mayo, knowing he had done nothing wrong, was relieved to be free of the post and the impossible man-a-minute exams. His reputation seems not to have suffered from the event. The *Mankato Union* wrote, "No one who is acquainted with Dr. Mayo will for a moment question his honesty and good intentions."

He returned to private practice with zest and in March advertised his new office over Woodard & Ells' Drug Store. The *Rochester Republican* stated, "Dr. W.W. Mayo ... is one of the best physicians in the State, and will command his share of practice." Subsequently, he bought a plot of ground on Third Street and had a small office built there. His pithy business announcement once again ran in the local papers: "DR. MAYO/ Office on Third Street/ Rochester, Minn."

On April 9, the Civil War ended at Appomattox Courthouse, and on April 14 President Lincoln was fatally shot at Ford's Theater in Washington. Mayo bought a plaster bust of Lincoln, the man who had appointed him examining surgeon of the first Minnesota district, and placed it in his office.

In a bedroom of the Mayo home on Franklin Street, Louise gave birth on July 19, 1865, to their sixth and last child. They named him "Charles Horace," choosing his middle name in honor of their first baby, the son who had died at the age of six weeks. Will was already four when Charlie was born; Phoebe was nine and Trude twelve.

As a father of four, W.W. settled into his new community, making friends, seeing patients, and seeking every opportunity to mold the town into a place beneficial to his family. In early January, 1866, he met with six other persons as founding members of the Rochester Library. He gave 50 dollars, making him a life member of the library association. They decided to buy non-fiction books at first, especially histories of the state and county. Opening a public reading room over the First National Bank, Mayo and the others in time selected and purchased 1,500 volumes.

They also sponsored a series of lectures each year for the town's amusement and edification. With another man, Mayo chose celebrities to speak. One of these was Horace Greeley, editor of the *New York Tribune*, the man who said the famous words, "Go west, Young Man. Go west!" He has been called "spokesman for the plain people of the entire North" and the man who "exerted a larger influence over public opinion north of the Mason-Dixon line than … possibly any other private citizen in the country." Frederick Douglass came too, an orator so brilliant and eloquent that many who heard him lecture could not believe he had been a slave.

But the speaker who drew the largest crowd for the series was Anna E. Dickinson, advertised as "the best and ablest representative of the rapidly increasing class of women known as the strong-minded." Miss Dickinson, in her mid-twenties when she came to Rochester, began her professional career as a lecturer at age 18 speaking on "Woman's Rights and Wrongs." She was a phenomenon on the antislavery lecture circuit as well as the women's suffrage circuit.

W.W. liked "strong-minded" women. He had married one, and at this time, he needed Louise to be strong, for she was still coping with blindness caused by trachoma. Describing her situation much later to the interviewer Meloney, she said, "One never knows how much one can stand until one is put to the test.… The blow fell just after we moved [to Rochester] from LeSueur.… I contracted … what in the old days was called 'catching sore eyes…' and went stone blind.… Charlie was only a baby in arms. It was very hard at first – very hard on my husband – but I soon learned to be useful. If one doesn't give in under calamity, but just says, 'I'm going to be useful until I drop,' it helps a lot, my dear."

On January 6, 1866, W.W. resumed a habit he had already begun during the late '40s in the *Rerum* book, that of noting baffling cases. This time, he wrote out

Octavia Gray's clinical history in Louise's old millinery accounts notebook, now unused.

Octavia, a child only one year younger than Mayo's nine-year-old daughter Phoebe, had fallen from a horse in October, striking on the hard ground her "head just back of the Ear or from the Mastoid process of the right side extending back." The blow had rendered her temporarily unconscious, bleeding from the ear, eye, nostril, and mouth. Now, three months later, her parents brought her to W.W. for examination, for she was still not well.

W.W. noted: "The right side of the face is fuller and rather puffy with a slight want of expression. The right eye is protruded somewhat and looks much larger than the left." Her vision was blurred and double from that eye. He prescribed use of the Galvanic battery and suggested they call again.

He didn't know how to help the girl and wrote, "Query – where is the injury? It is not in the brain, or the opposite side would be affected and there would be complete paraplegia." He discussed with himself on paper which nerves were damaged, aware, from his anatomical studies, of the function of all facial nerves.

The case of Mr. Johnson from Rock Dell Township also puzzled him. This 50-year old man had been unable to urinate for three days. W.W. introduced a silver catheter "but was perfectly astonished to see that no urine flowed." He checked to make sure the catheter was unblocked, reintroduced it, and "then applied my mouth to the instrument and used suction with considerable force, when a large quantity of thick, clotted pus began to pass...."

W.W. succeeded in helping the patient, but he wondered—-what caused the abscess which produced the pus, and where was it located? After considering various possibilities without resolving the matter, he wrote, "Left open for further thought and research."

On January 11, W.W. attended Ole Nelson, a young man who had fallen into an already dug but unused grave while intoxicated. The temperature was "some degrees below zero," and when Nelson awoke the next morning, his fingers and toes were frozen. Mayo was called to amputate them at the Nelson home, a process he described in detail, noting, "He was kept under the influence of chloroform during the operation."

He examined a 26-year-old woman, Mrs. Ellen Gage, whom he found lying in bed, but from all appearances healthy. This case both amused and piqued him, and he wrote it out in great detail.

"Good morning, Madame, you are feeling unwell, are you?" he asked.

"Yes, Sir, quite unwell."

"How long have you been complaining?"

"About two months, Sir."

"What seems to be the matter with you?"

"I am very much bloated, Sir, about my legs and feet."

"Do you know of any cause for it? Are you regular in your monthly periods?"

"No, Sir."

He discovered her last period was "three months since" and suggested, "Are you in the family way?"

"Yes, Sir, I believe so."

He advised, "Well, Madame, the great probability is that being in the family way is the cause of the bloating, and after a time, when the womb rises higher up into the abdomen, … the bloating will go down."

"Well, Sir, I have got a heart disease …. Dr. Allen told me so. He said I had dropsy of the heart, that the chances were against me getting better, that if I exercised any I might drop down dead, and here I have been for two months, only with great care walking across the floor occasionally."

Mayo examined her pulse and heart and concluded, "You have no heart disease, but … your dropsy is the natural result of your pregnant condition …. Madame, you do not need any medicine."

Mayo concluded the story, "Upon my 'Arise, take up your bed and walk,' this lady is now progressing through her pregnancy without any further trouble."

Later he described the case to another patient, a man whom Dr. J. S. Allen had also diagnosed with "dropsy of the heart." In both cases, Allen charged $40 for his false and alarming diagnosis, which angered Mayo.

"Well, Sir, … I think very little of Dr. Allen's opinion. I am not given to speaking against my co-laborers in the field, but in this case I feel no restraint."

W.W. felt keenly the harmful influence of incompetent doctors. At this date, there was little he could do but correct their diagnoses one by one. Medicine in Minnesota was entirely unregulated, and quacks practiced alongside qualified physicians.

Continuing his journaling on January 22, he described a girl whose symptoms were "shiverings, feebleness, and loss of appetite … Eyes dull… Pulse 100… Thermometer in axilla [under the armpit] shows 102 degrees."

It is his first mention of using a thermometer. He had always looked for fever as an important symptom, but previously his notes had been comments like "skin hot & dry," or "perspiration was just commencing."

Before the Civil War, doctors rarely used the instrument, which was almost a foot long and took half an hour to register. During the war, a pocket thermometer came into use slowly. Not until after 1868, when a German doctor, Carl Wunderlich, published a paper showing how temperature indicates disease, did the thermometer come into popular use. W.W. Mayo was ahead of his time when he used it in January, 1866.

He was called to attend a Norwegian man in June who suffered a severe and bizarre accident. Too drunk to drive his horse and wagon home, Nels Oleson had asked a neighbor to drive, while he lay atop his load of lumber. When the running gear of his wagon separated, Oleson was thrown off and under a wheel. It passed over his forehead, crushing his skull and exposing part of his brain. There was little Mayo could do but remove some pieces of bone from the wound, which he probably did using his bone forceps. Everyone expected Oleson to die.

He was in excruciating pain. Mayo kept watch, and one afternoon he noticed odd movements under Oleson's blanket, which was drawn up over his head. Removing the blanket, Mayo found that his patient held a knife to his throat and was in the act of feeling for the right place to slit his own throat. Mayo took away the knife and prevented the suicide.

The wound healed with no inflammation. Five days after the accident, Oleson, against Mayo's advice, was "put into a lumber wagon and jolted home," according to a newspaper reporter, who added, "That Norwegian will have to dry up and blow away. Nothing can kill him."

During his time as medical examiner for the draft board, W.W. had established a consistent routine for examining patients which he continued now in his private practice. To facilitate the exams, he designed and used a portable bed made of wood covered by a pad. A detachable board underneath could extend the bed if needed. No matter what the complaint, Mayo gave each patient a complete physical exam, for he had discovered that by so doing he often found problems — and means of restoring health — which the patient had not suspected.

Each patient stripped to underwear and lay down upon the table. Mayo began by careful attention to the head — the hair, scalp, teeth, and especially the tongue. He used a pen to assist the patient in focusing during the eye exam. Then he checked the glands of the neck. With a small wooden stethoscope, he listened to the chest. As the patient sat up and bent forward, then backward, he examined flexibility of the spine. Finally, the patient walked about the room while the doctor observed. A complete exam from head to toes required about 15 minutes.

Describing the competence of W.W.'s two surgeon sons much later, Dr. Donald C. Balfour said, "From their earliest days of practice, the brothers, taught by their father, realized that the chief cause of error in diagnosis is incomplete examination.... The early clinical records of both father and sons are models of careful observation and direct deduction."

Besides his five unaided senses, W.W. brought to his examinations only a few instruments——a stethoscope and the new clinical thermometer. He routinely analyzed the urine of his patients. To do so he carried Fehling's solution and acid in his medical bag; during home visits he would boil the patient's urine and add Fehling's solution to test for sugar, and acid to test for albumen. Further analysis would wait until he returned to the small microscope he kept in a corner of his home laboratory/office.

W.W. was alert to new possibilities which would help his patients. By the middle 1860s, he consistently and frequently noted important journal articles in the *Rerum* book. At last he was practicing medicine full time, which, to him, always included study. He consulted a number of medical journals, among them the *American Medical Journal, Medical News, St. Louis Medical Society Journal, American Journal of the Medical Sciences, Rankins Abstract, New York Medical Journal, British & Foreign Medico-Chirurgical Review, Dental Cosmos, Southern Medical & Surgical Journal, Paris Pharmacologia,* and *Taylor's Medical Jurisprudence*. His most frequently-noted source was a journal published twice a year, The *Retrospect of Practical Medicine and Surgery*, edited by William Braithwaite and later James Braithwaite, which said it was "a half-yearly journal containing a retrospective view of every discovery and practical improvement in the medical sciences."

From all these sources he satisfied his curiosity about such different subjects as dysentery, hemorrhoids, requirements of health officers, insanity, lymph glands, muscular power of insects, medical law, microscopes and germs, nutritive value of food, paralysis, rheumatism, spleen, testes, tumors, urinary diseases, varicose veins, and death from chloroform. He noted them all in *Rerum*.

To say that W.W. was in full-time practice of medicine does not mean that his time was fully taken by it. After a strenuous day of seeing patients, he still had energy for many causes, including improving his town and educating his children.

His election to the Rochester School Board in the spring of 1867 enabled him to do both at once. Olmsted County had, only two years before, elected an outstanding superintendent of schools, Sanford Niles, who was eager to improve the 77 county schools. Inspecting them, he had been dismayed to find 56 with no outhouses and 11 with no blackboards, faults he soon corrected. When Mayo and others on the school board suggested building a new schoolhouse in Rochester, Niles was receptive. By the end of '68, Central School was completed, directly across the street from the Mayo home on Franklin Street. It cost $65,000, more than any other Minnesota school. Made of brick and five stories high, it had 16 rooms, single desks, and even furnace heat. Such a place would be good for Phoebe, twelve, Will, seven, and Charlie, three, when he grew older.

Trude, at fifteen, was already outgrowing the school.

As a school board member, Mayo visited Central School once a year to report on conditions there. A newspaper published his comments. He took this job, as all others, seriously, and did not flatter the children or their teachers. After one visit, he noted "an apparent restlessness, an apathetic indifference to the higher achievements of the school room.... It would seem from the action of some of these children as if they thought our City Fathers had ... erected, at great expense, a gigantic playhouse for very large children with small ambitions, instead of a school house for instruction."

Other parents might trust school personnel alone to educate their children; Mayo never did. He personally watched over everything his family learned at school, and he supplemented school teaching at home. The boys learned chemistry and physics from him at an early age, enlivened by stories of his own former teacher John Dalton. The skeleton of Cut Nose was at this time hanging in W.W.'s home office, to be used for quick reference in anatomy lessons. And W.W. was building his home library, for his children's use as well as his own.

Louise later told her interviewer Meloney, "You know that for many years our income was meager – very meager. But we saw to it that the children received good educations. Only those who have education can render the fullest service.... When the children were young, they had to work as well as study.... As the boys came along, they drove their father when he made his calls. This kept them off the streets and out in the fresh air, especially Charlie, who wasn't very strong as a youngster. If an arm had to be set or a wound dressed, the doctor would press the children into service – Trude as well as the boys. He believed in useful children."

The father was a model of indefatigable usefulness. He visited patients in their homes, both in town and country, and he kept very strict office hours, every day from 11 a.m. to 12 noon, 1:30 to 3 p.m., and 7 to 8 p.m. He allowed no interruptions to this schedule, except emergencies. Some afternoons, after school from 3 p.m. to suppertime, he took Will and Charlie with him to visit patients. Charlie was very young at this time, but he came along because he and Will were inseparable. Mayo's daughters did not come. Trude, though a serious and hard-working person like her father, was by now developing other interests, though she remembered what her father had taught her about how to set broken bones. Phoebe was a quiet, sweet, artistic girl whose favorite pastime was drawing.

On the long buggy rides, father and sons talked about medicine and everything else of interest to boys of seven and three.

Father Thomas O'Gorman

Photo courtesy of St. John's Catholic Church, Rochester, Minnesota, and by permission of Mayo Foundation for Medical Education and Research. All rights reserved.

Chapter 8

Beginning to Give Back At Last

"It was in January, 1866, on a Saturday that I reached Rochester, a raw, inexperienced young priest of 22 years old. It was "Root, Hog, or die" in those days.... Among the men whom I became acquainted with was Dr. William W. Mayo, a serious, sympathetic man ... who took me in hand. He was skilled in life, in human nature.... I loved Dr. Mayo.... He guided me in many ways and his talks were full of wisdom."

Father Thomas O'Gorman

A frequent rider in W.W.'s buggy, along with the boys, was the stocky, good-natured young priest Father Thomas O'Gorman, who became a good friend. While W.W. attended to his country patients' physical needs, Father O'Gorman attended to their spiritual needs, if they were Catholic. Usually they used Mayo's horses, for they were faster.

Father O'Gorman was younger than Mayo by 24 years, but they had much in common. O'Gorman shared with Mayo an immigrant's experience, at least second-hand; his parents had come from Ireland. More important, he had a well-trained mind and loved good books and ideas as W.W. did. His bishop in St. Paul had sent O'Gorman, along with another boy, John Ireland, to France to study. After 12 years there, O'Gorman developed a strong religious and moral conscience as well as a cultivated intelligence in history, language, and culture. He came to Rochester as pastor of the congregation which would build St. John's Catholic Church under his direction.

To discuss important ideas with another intelligent, bookish man was a delicious experience for W.W. He also enjoyed the role of mentor; O'Gorman was the first young person outside his own family whom Mayo befriended and counseled. Previously, he had been totally occupied with his own and his family's survival.

Some people in Rochester, especially those Protestants who were prejudiced against Catholics, considered the friendship between Protestant Mayo and Catholic O'Gorman odd. That made the friendship all the more interesting to Mayo, who was never swayed by popular opinions he considered wrong.

He and his family attended Calvary Episcopal Church, but his primary means of worship was not church attendance. As his son Will put it, "He was an Episcopalian, but he didn't work very hard at it." For instance, on Sundays W.W. frequently left church early, or did not go at all, so he could open his office at noon for patients who came to town only once a week and would consult him after Sunday services.

In the way he lived his life, Mayo was still adhering to his mentor John Dalton's Quaker values. Quakers believed in using scientific knowledge to benefit others, as Mayo did. The most important element of Mayo's religion was service to "the least of these" – poor, sick, or suffering people. Also, Quakers did not value religious formalities, nor did the doctor. "True religion stands neither in forms nor in the formal absence of forms," said a Society of Friends epistle of 1855.

Mayo cared about how other people lived out their faith. If they wanted to serve needy souls, the details of their theology didn't concern him.

Will and Charlie were not even aware they were receiving a lesson when they rode along in the buggy with Father O'Gorman, but they did learn one – to judge a man by his character, not by any prejudice against his affiliations. Many of their early lessons were taught so – unconsciously, by example.

In the early days of their childhood, the boys enjoyed freedom to roam together and amuse themselves. They learned to consider themselves a twosome. "From the very beginning," Will said later, "Charlie and I always went together. We were known as the Mayo boys. Anyone that picked on one of us had the two to contend with."

Being four years younger, Charlie was not able to compete with Will, nor did he need to do so. W.W. and Louise had plenty of time for both sons. Will became Charlie's teacher, and because the younger boy was sometimes sick when he was little, Will learned to nurture him.

Charlie was a stocky, dark-haired, brown-eyed fellow, with a love of mischief. Outgoing and affectionate, some said he resembled his people-loving mother. Will was a fair boy with clear blue eyes and erect posture, serious and able like his father. Though shy, he had a reputation in his school days as a tease. The boys spent many hours together, reading, doing chores, playing marbles, and roaming the neighboring countryside. They enjoyed fishing at Lake Oronoco or Zumbro Falls. An ancient Indian burial ground atop a bluff near Rochester fascinated them; they could dig up an occasional arrowhead there. When the circus came to town, they were sure to go.

As soon as Will was old enough, his parents gave him a pony. When Will was eight, the animal tested his authority. Will was leading the pony under a tree, intending to break off a switch. What happened next brought Will his first newspaper write-up: "The pony, anticipating perhaps his master's purpose, started on throwing the rider. In falling, Willie's arm struck a stone [breaking the arm below the elbow]. Some boys nearby helped him remount and he rode home, about one and a half miles, without any assistance." Will's coolness in emergencies was thus already established in 1869.

Both boys enjoyed the books in their father's collection. Even when the family budget could scarcely stretch, W.W. managed to find money for books. Louise said this was his "one weakness.... He knew and loved good books. Oh, many a time I

Will Mayo and his pony

*Photo by permission of Mayo Foundation for Medical Education and Research.
All rights reserved.*

planned to buy a dress for Trude or something for the boys or the house, only to have a book agent come to town and kick over my bucket of milk."

Part of his book collection was especially for his children, with thrilling adventure stories like James Fenimore Cooper's *Last of the Mohicans* and every book by Charles Dickens. The girls and Louise helped themselves to these books too. Louise's eyesight returned about this time, and she became especially interested in reading medical books. When she had mastered a medical problem, W.W. would ask her to assist him. Charlie later remarked, "Mother was a real good doctor herself."

Mary Anderson, who knew Louise, wrote of her, "She was a very brilliant woman with many strong characteristics, well read – in fact, a continual reader. Consequently, she was well posted on many subjects. Foremost among them was medicine and the treatment of disease. She often took the place of her husband."

One day Louise passed a Rochester doctor's open door, and he called her inside to see a man in great pain from a dislocated shoulder. At once, Louise instructed the man to lie down on the floor. Removing her shoe, she placed her foot in the man's armpit, and taking his hands in her own, gave a hefty pull. The patient rose from the floor, healed.

In Mrs. Anderson's opinion, Louise "should have studied medicine, as she was as good as many doctors who were in general practice."

In the late 1860s, W.W.'s medical practice, which had been one of "physician and surgeon" ever since he graduated from the Indiana Medical College in 1850, began to change a little in character. More and more women with gynecological problems consulted him, so that he gradually developed a specialty in that area.

Deaths of women in childbirth were not uncommon. The primary cause was infection caused by dirty hands, clothing, or instruments of the midwife or doctor. Because the germ theory of disease was not yet accepted, these helpers were, of course, ignorant of causing harm.

Dr. Ignaz Philipp Semmelweis, an inquisitive Austrian contemporary of Mayo, solved the problem of high mortality in his maternity hospital. It was as high as 30% some months, when medical students delivered mothers of their babies. He noticed that, by contrast, only 3% of mothers died when midwives assisted them. By careful observation and deduction, he concluded that medical students, having come directly from post-mortem exams, carried infectious materials from dead bodies to the mothers. The fingers of the midwives were not so contaminated, and therefore, their patients lived. When Semmelweis required all doctors and medical students to wash their hands with chlorine water and scrub their fingernails with a brush before examining women, the mortality rate fell within two months to 1.27 percent.

In Olmsted County, where the Mayos lived, one midwife had even better results. Jane Twentyman

Graham delivered 240 babies between 1857 and 1895 without any deaths for mothers or babies. Like the Austrian midwives, she was a clean person.

W.W. was habitually clean too. He took pains with his appearance because he wanted to build public esteem for his profession. Going about his work, he wore professional business clothes – a Prince Albert double-breasted coat which extended into tails in back. Upon his head, he wore a black top hat. His tendency with these good and expensive clothes was to keep them – and himself – immaculate.

Though when W.W. used instruments, he did not understand that infection could be carried upon them, nevertheless, his success in helping women was better than average, which encouraged him to learn and attempt more varied surgeries to correct their problems. His operation to drain a woman's ovarian cyst in 1866 was so successful that a *Rochester Post* reporter wrote all the graphic details and concluded with an encouraging note: "We understand that Dr. Mayo gives special attention to this class of female diseases."

W.W. was present on April 15, 1868, when the Olmsted County Medical Society held its first annual meeting. He was beginning to look for forums in which to give back to his community from his accumulated experience and wisdom, and doctors' organizations were good choices for this. At the society's first meeting, the doctors drew up a constitution and agreed on a common schedule of fees. Patients would receive the same bill for service, no matter whom they consulted – for a doctor's exam in town one dollar, with 75 cents a mile extra for country visits. Charges would be double at night. Delivery of a baby would cost $10, treatment of a simple fracture $5 to $25, compound fractures $25 to $75, and "capital operations" as much as $100.

Mayo knew his colleagues in town well by this time. Hector Galloway was the man he respected most. When W.W. was out of town, Louise called upon him if she needed medical advice. Once, after consulting him, she could not resist commenting on his slow, ponderous manner. "Dr. Galloway, you're just like my old rag bag," she said. "There's a lot in it, but it takes a devil of a time to find it!"

The Cross brothers, Edwin and Elisha, were also part of the Rochester medical scene. Both large, impressive men, the older brother habitually hunched forward as he rode his big black horse around town, so that he acquired the nickname, "Monkey Cross." Mayo preferred the gentler younger brother.

When the society met for its second annual meeting in 1869, Mayo addressed the assembled doctors on "The Character of the Earth's Elements, Its Formation, Development, and Ultimate Destiny, and

Its Inhabitants," – a treatise on evolution. Mayo liked controversy and was so successful in causing it on this occasion, that the society continued to meet bi-weekly for the next six months, usually at his home, to continue talking about Darwin's theories as well as other matters, such as "Philosophy of Disease" and "Electricity and Lightning Rods."

In the autumn of 1869, Dr. Harriet Preston opened her office in Rochester as "physician and surgeon." W.W. welcomed her to town. She had graduated from the first (1850) American school dedicated to training women doctors, the Women's Medical College of Philadelphia. Its founders had to overcome resistance from the all-male Philadelphia County Medical Society, which earlier declared women unfit to be physicians "due to their delicate organization and predominance of the nervous system."

Since Mayo found Dr. Preston competent, he proposed in 1873 that the Minnesota State Medical Society admit her as a member. Its doctors voted her down because her "feminine delicacy would make impossible the frank discussion of certain matters that inevitably arise in medical practice."

Many sick women in Olmsted County preferred Dr. Preston to any male doctor. As her practice grew, Preston began consulting her friend Mayo about difficult cases, especially those requiring surgery.

In November, '69, Louise agreed to another separation from her husband. He wished to travel east to observe the latest medical and especially surgical techniques practiced there. The *Rochester Post* for November 6 announced that Dr. W.W. Mayo had left to spend the winter in New York City "in attendance on medical lectures and is perfecting himself, especially, in the practice of surgery. The Doctor already has a large practice and a high standing in the profession and will return in the spring with still better claims upon the confidence of his patients."

During his absence, W.W. gave Louise his account books, listing patients who owed him money. (He was notorious for not collecting from his patients.) She busily set out to collect what was justly owed the family, and they ate better than usual during the months her husband was away. Mayo's son Charlie later answered an interviewer who asked why the family had a hard time financially for so many years.

"He never collected," Charlie said. "If he wanted to do something, such as someone crowding him for payment, he would crowd the people. He hated to ask for money."

"Was his failure to collect fees a matter of good will or a matter of carelessness, or both?"

"It was half and half."

In New York, Mayo's first destination was Bellevue Hospital, an improved place since his brief stay in

1846. The most famous doctors in New York instructed at the bedsides of their patients, and, in an amphitheater open to students, surgeons demonstrated their skills. However, no one practiced antiseptic methods of surgery, and the post-operative mortality rate was high. W.W. would not have considered this unusual; the situation was the same in all the hospitals he visited.

He was impressed with Bellevue's horse-and-buggy ambulance corps, the first in the world. To the people back home he sent letters from New York, which the newspaper printed on page one. "When an accident occurs in any part of the city," he wrote, "there is a dispatch sent from the police ... and the ambulance is on the ground in a few minutes after. The injured are picked up, and at once taken to the hospital. Truly this is quite as astonishing as any of the fairy tales."

W.W. visited churches and wrote of the gifted Mr. Corbett, "an out and out Methodist Preacher, no halfway about him. If you do not believe his teachings 'the Devil will catch you and plunge you into Hell.'"

Another Sunday he attended Plymouth Congregational Church in Brooklyn to hear the Rev. Henry Ward Beecher preach to a packed house of nearly 3,000. Beecher believed in both evolution and the authenticity of Biblical miracles.

What especially pleased W.W. in this church was the music, which he described at length:

"The organ began to peal forth its notes, and these were just as clear as so many silver trumpets in unison and were really enrapturing. The choir now stood up and one manly voice began to proclaim in song the goodness of God. This was continued for a few stanzas in solo, then there was a confirmation of the statement in chorus. Then a beautiful young woman with a sweet angelic voice sang of what this goodness consisted. Then again chorus and then a big, manly voice in bass sang in solo a paean of joy for the goodness, and again the chorus, and then a sweet singing alto in solo gave thanks to God for all his goodness, then a chorus and sudden silence.

"The whole thing was of magic effect, and I almost involuntarily clapped my hands.... In fact, music of this kind is a little heaven here below, and I suppose a foretaste of the seraphic voices above."

From New York, W.W. traveled to Lancaster, Pennsylvania, to observe a difficult new surgery to remove diseased ovaries, the ovariotomy. Two brothers in Lancaster, Drs. John and Washington Atlee, had been making medical news since 1845 by performing the ovariotomy and writing about it. Washington Atlee had performed almost 300 such surgeries, averaging a 30% mortality rate, when W.W. visited him.

This operation was first performed by an American doctor, Ephraim McDowell, in 1809 upon Jane Crawford, who had called him to assist her in what she

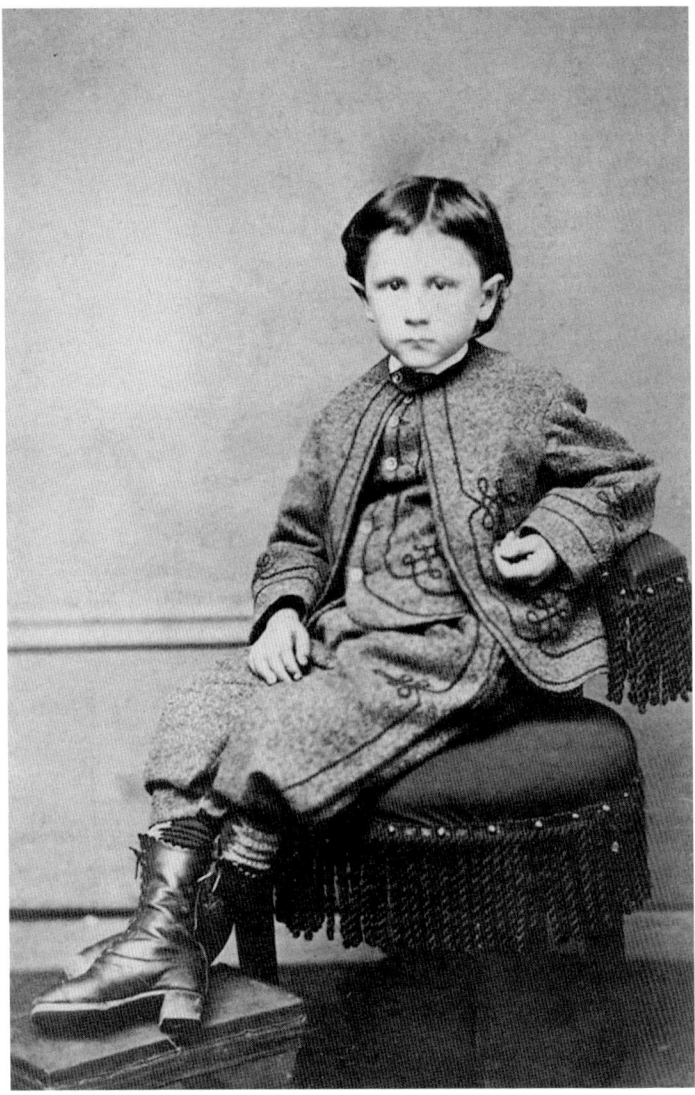

Charlie Mayo at about 5 years old

Photo by permission of Mayo Foundation for Medical Education and Research. All rights reserved.

thought was to be the birth of twins. Instead, he found her cumbered with an enormous ovarian tumor. Since doing nothing meant certain death, Mrs. Crawford chose surgery. The family wrote that "she occupied herself" singing Psalms during the 30-minute operation on McDowell's kitchen table. (This was before the use of chloroform or ether.) He tied off the ovary where it attached to the uterus with a silk ligature, snipped out the gland and the tumor, deposited them in a bucket, and sewed his patient back up. It was several years later, having made sure of Mrs. Crawford's complete recovery, that he dared report his feat to the medical world.

Because McDowell practiced medicine in the backwoods of Kentucky (in Danville), his report was not accepted for publication until 1817. It was rejected as preposterous by the first doctors to read it. In fact, they judged too quickly. McDowell was an example of the preceptor system of education at its finest. His bold surgery was based on nearly three years' apprenticeship under an outstanding Virginia doctor, Alexander Humphreys, who had graduated from the University of Edinburgh, Scotland. McDowell himself studied at that renowned university for two years, one of them with the famous Dr. John Bell, who discussed the theoretical possibility of ovariotomy.

Very few doctors tried the operation until 1842, when Dr. Charles Clay, a surgeon in W.W.'s hometown of Manchester, England, succeeded in removing a woman's ovary and 17-pound ovarian tumor. He performed four more such operations the same year, with a mortality rate of 40%. It is possible Mayo, who was 23 in 1842, knew something of Clay's work, since he was interested in medicine and living in Manchester.

In 1870, the ovariotomy was still not an accepted surgery. Most doctors considered those who did it "belly rippers who ought not to be at large." (When Clay operated on a woman, he made a 24-inch incision across the abdomen.) Despite observing the Drs. Atlee at work in Pennsylvania, W.W. did not perform the operation right away when he returned home in late January. He continued to practice the less-risky method of draining tumors and kept the ovariotomy in the realm of "further thought and research."

Research was very much on his mind when he arrived in Rochester on an early morning train. His sons and Trude met him at the station with the horse and buggy. Their excitement was high at being able to see their father again after his absence of almost three months. Will and Charlie had cleaned his office especially carefully to please him, and when he suggested they stop there before proceeding home, they were glad. In the office, W.W. admired the boys' work, then picked up the little 12-inch microscope he had been using for more than 15 years, and suggested they go on home.

Louise served a big, home-cooked breakfast, and the

doctor distributed presents to his four children. Then, at the right moment, he placed the old microscope on the table and produced from his pocket a color brochure about a wonderful new microscope. It could tell them many important facts about diseases which the old microscope couldn't reveal, he said, but it was expensive. It cost 600 dollars, and he had spent all his money on the trip east.

"The only way we can buy this new microscope is to mortgage our house," he said.

Amazed silence greeted his remark. The children didn't even understand the meaning of the word "mortgage." Louise did, though. Her father's family came from Scotland, and she had inherited his Scottish thriftiness. Louise thought about it and asked W.W. to tell them more about what the new scope could do which the old one couldn't. At last, she said, "Well, William, if you could do better by the people with this new microscope, and you really think you need it, we'll do it."

Dr. Will told this story at a Mayo Clinic staff meeting 68 years later. He had often told the story before. Concluding, he observed, "The circumstances under which the new microscope was bought perhaps gave Charlie and me an especially keen interest in microscopy."

A year after buying the new tool, W.W. bought a pathology book to help him and the boys use it more effectively. The book was somewhat difficult for boys of ten and six: *A Textbook of Pathological Histology: an Introduction to the Study of Pathological Anatomy* by Eduard Rindfleisch, translated from the German by William C. Kloman.

In the spring of 1870, Lila Jones consulted Mayo about her ovarian cyst, which was too large to be tapped and drained. Instead of proceeding to operate, he consulted Dr. William H. Byford of Chicago, a skilled gynecology surgeon, about a possible ovariotomy, but Byford decided the surgery was too risky and refused to do it. Nor did W.W. venture to remove Mrs. Jones' ovary.

His educational trip to the East had emboldened him somewhat. One of his patients, Harriet Fowler, had been troubled for many years with headaches, backaches, and many other symptoms. Examining her earlier, W.W. found a problem apparently caused during childbirth – a rectocele or small hernia of some rectal tissue through a tear in the vagina. He had already tried twice to solve the problem and thought he had succeeded, for Mrs. Fowler had been doing well for two years. Now she was back, consulting him again about the same problem.

With Dr. Byford already in town to see Mrs. Jones, Mayo asked him to look at Mrs. Fowler also. Byford suggested a remedy. W.W. tried this, but it failed. So, heartened by Mrs. Fowler's faith in him, W.W. decided to try a surgery of his own devising. He used ether to sedate Mrs. Fowler. Then he "emptied [the hernial bag] of its contents,… fastened a clamp behind it to shut off the circulation, carefully put in the necessary sutures, and cut off the rectocele close to the clamp. Quickly he seared the cut surfaces with an iron he had heating … near by. The bleeding was very slight."

Cauterization by hot iron stopped the bleeding and also sterilized the wound, so it was a wise strategem. Surgeons had been using the cautery since before the 17th century without understanding its benefits, only knowing they could achieve good results with it. Being able to anesthetize patients before burning their wounds was a major advance in humane treatment.

W.W., in all his years as a citizen of Rochester, expressed his opinions freely on political subjects. In the fall of '70, he tried to rally Republicans and Democrats behind a third party "people's candidate" who would be anti-railroad monopoly, anti-monopoly in general, and pro-free trade. He failed. So he left the Republicans and joined the Democrats shortly after. To his new political party he gave his best efforts, working with his old friend from LeSueur days, Harry Young, now editor of the local Democratic paper, *Federal Union*. W.W. gave speeches almost nightly throughout the county, vigorously urging people to vote for Democrats and against evil railroad owners. "If I could treat this railroad company in my profession," he said, "I would give them such a puke as would bring their corns from their toes through their stomachs."

When Olmsted County, usually strongly Republican, elected the Democratic ticket in November, 1870, Mayo and Young were the heroes of a celebration party.

Early in 1872, Mayo was elected third president of the Minnesota Medical Society, which he had helped organize several years earlier. His reputation in the state was growing. Encouraged by the doctors' vote for him, he addressed them, "Gentlemen, I hope each one of you, by these yearly gatherings will feel that you renew your strength for the labor of life…. By these meetings we open up the best side of our social natures, and from isolated enemies we become fast friends. By this contact of intellect with intellect,… the truths of science [become] more firmly fixed in our minds."

Under Mayo's leadership the society passed a resolution calling for the legislature to establish a state board of health. They did so, and when Mayo reconvened the society the next year, he "gratefully acknowledge[d]" the new Minnesota board as a work brought about by the doctors' prompting. He then spoke on the need for malpractice laws to protect doctors from "these needless, expensive and vexatious suits." One way doctors could protect themselves, he said, was by backing a law to require plaintiffs in malpractice cases to pay all court costs and damages when judgements went against them. Thereby, he said, "the profession would be relieved from a system of blackmailing."

Soon after, W.W. was called as defense witness in a malpractice case against the elder Cross brother, Edwin or "Monkey Cross," whom he disliked. Dr. Cross won the case in district court, so the plaintiff appealed to the Minnesota Supreme Court. In both suits, Mayo testified that Dr. Cross had acted responsibly in splinting and bandaging a broken arm. He said the eventual need for amputation was not Cross's fault but was caused by an artery injured in the original break. Bolstered by this testimony, Cross won.

Expressing the curiosity of many, one man asked W.W. why he defended a doctor he detested. "I did it for the profession," he said, "not for him, damn him."

On another occasion, the two doctors disagreed about how to treat one of Dr. Cross's patients, a man with a badly injured hand. Cross had called on W.W. for a second opinion, to back up his decision to amputate.

"No, the hand does *not* have to come off," Mayo said. The two argued about it, but W.W. won out, and 50 years later, the man still had his hand.

Friends from St. Paul encouraged W.W. to move his practice from Rochester to the capital, where his patients would benefit from established hospitals and a medical school. He could develop his specialty in women's diseases better in a large city than in his present small town, they said. It sounded promising to him. When Dr. Charles Hill of nearby Pine Island told W.W. he was moving to St. Paul and looking for a partner, he agreed to go too. On May 3, 1873, the *Rochester Post* reported that the Olmsted County Medical Society passed a resolution expressing "regret at parting with Dr. W.W. Mayo." By his departure, the society said, we "sustain a loss and this community a scholarly and successful practitioner."

W.W. packed his clothes, medical supplies, and some books and traveled by train to St. Paul, where he opened an office with Dr. Hill. Louise and the four children did not follow. She had said almost ten years before that Rochester was to be the family's permanent home. She had meant it.

Chapter 9

The Boys' Education

"If the love of surgery is a proof of a person's being adapted for it, then certainly I am fitted to be a surgeon: for thou canst hardly conceive what a high degree of enjoyment I am from day to day experiencing in this bloody and butcherly department of the healing art."

Dr. Joseph Lister

Throughout the summer, autumn and winter of '73, W.W. continued trying to make a go of his new medical practice in St. Paul. He joined the Ramsey County Medical Society and was elected its vice president. As often as he could, he came home to Rochester to see Louise, his daughters, who were already 20 and 17 years old, and the boys, now 12 and 8. Winter travel was sometimes difficult in snowy Minnesota, even though he went by train. In early March, '74, Mayo got off the train at Kasson on a Friday to see a patient, intending to reboard it in the morning and continue on home. He awoke Saturday morning to see the results of an overnight blizzard. Two to eight feet of snow covered everything, including the railroad track. No trains were running, so he decided to wait.

The *Rochester Post* reported, "The Doctor possessed his 'soul in patience' as far as practicable until Monday, and then his patience gave out. Although a small man, he is nevertheless exceedingly plucky, and off he starts on foot to Rochester, a distance of 18 miles through the solid trackless snow. He accomplished the feat in due time, but was pretty thoroughly exhausted when he got through."

One week after Mayo's strenuous walk from Kasson, the *Post* announced "with pleasure" his plans to return to Rochester "with the view of permanent location and the resumption of the practice of his profession." He established his office over Geisinger & Newton's Drugstore.

Within months he was engaged with an old adversary, John Edgar, in a hot series of letters to the *Post*, challenging Edgar's attempt to make Rochester an alcohol-free city. Edgar had defeated Mayo for his fourth term on the Rochester school board in 1870 with charges that the doctor was "an infidel and a friend to Demon Rum." Both charges were untrue. Mayo considered himself a Christian, but the same mindset which led him into trying new surgeries also led him into trying new ideas, like fitting evolution into his religion, which some believers considered impossible. His mentor John Dalton, whom he deeply admired, believed that the truths of science would not contradict the truths of God, since God made all truth. Mayo showed no evidence of thinking otherwise.

On the issue of "Demon Rum," he was against drunkenness. He believed the alcoholic should be pitied and helped, but to legislate morality by prohibiting the sale of alcohol rankled his freedom-loving soul.

Edgar was an ex-minister who now sold reapers for McCormick Brothers at inflated prices, in W.W.'s opinion, thereby cheating the poor farmer. He felt no qualms in attacking Edgar on his own turf – religion. On May 30, Mayo wrote the *Rochester Post* of Edgar, "He is not a producer and so far as the interest of the city is concerned, if McCormick Brothers should call him away tomorrow he would never be missed. For ourselves, … we choose yet to worship at the shrine of Jesus Christ, and reverence him for that act, flowing from his good and great soul, of turning water into wine so that the young folks of Cana of Galilee might have a good time at the wedding feast, and we yet think, with the Apostle Paul, that a little wine is good for the stomach."

Edgar, irritated, responded the following week with a long letter. "I remember when he (W.W. Mayo) was away at St. Paul for nine or ten months, Rochester still lived.… We … call to mind a little man who walks our own streets with strutting gait, very erect, with a tall hat, and who looks important, and attempts with seemingly great confidence to teach his neighbors in politics, in morals and religion."

Like a terrier with a juicy bone, W.W. fought back: "In reading his [Edgar's] wordy communication, the idea presented itself.… What a low thing the Reverend John Edgar would have been if Yale College had not partially lifted him out from the gutter.… I have received a statement from the Reverend John Edgar's family physician … that he is insane; therefore I shall forbear to take notice of his verbose ravings … and bestow upon him that pity which all such unfortunates demand at our hands."

W.W. must have enjoyed his final bite. He accused Edgar of lying and said, "I would suggest to the Reverend … Edgar, that if you cannot totally abstain from falsehoods, do at least be temperate in their use."

In time, the matter quieted down. The town did not become "dry."

Meantime, the doctor was busy mentoring a new young man in town, Henry Wellcome, who had worked as a prescription clerk at Geisinger & Newton's and was close to Trude in age. The two men shared memories of the Dakota uprising of 1862. Then Henry had been living in Garden City, Minnesota, about 10 miles southwest of Mankato, in the path of marauding Indians. Only nine years old at the time, he had helped his doctor uncle care for refugees. The event deeply impressed the boy, making him want to help dispossessed peoples and indeed, all of suffering mankind. Wellcome was barely supporting himself with his pharmacy wage when Mayo first became his friend.

A frequent visitor in the Mayo home, Henry learned chemistry and physics from the doctor and borrowed his books. When W.W. judged the time was right, he urged the young man to hope for something greater than remaining a small-town druggist. Wellcome took W.W.'s advice, and in 1874, at the age of 21, he graduated from the Philadelphia College of Pharmacy. Mayo had helped pay his fees.

In time, Wellcome joined a classmate, Silas Burroughs, in moving to London, England, where they established Burroughs and Wellcome & Company, the first firm in Great Britain to sell medicines in pill form. When Burroughs died of pleurisy, Wellcome became, at age 32, sole owner of the company, which expanded to become the largest pharmaceutical firm in Britain. He acquired great riches, and with them, he set out to do good by means of an interest he had learned from Mayo – research. He created the Wellcome Bureau of Scientific Research, for which he was knighted. He also established the Wellcome Tropical Research Laboratories in Khartoum, Sudan, which became a world leader in the study of tropical diseases.

Henry Wellcome returned to Rochester often over the years and always mentioned gratefully Mayo's friendship. Speaking to a group of doctors once, Wellcome called Mayo "one of my most valued preceptors, and the one who, in my youth, inspired and guided me in my studies, and insisted upon my qualifying myself for a career in the field of science." Wellcome's obituary notice in the *Rochester Post Bulletin* on July 25, 1936, carried another of his commendations, "I owe whatever success I have attained in the world to Dr. William W. Mayo, who took an interest in me and gave me my start."

In the traveling classroom, his horse-drawn buggy, W.W. continued educating his sons. At each patient's bedside, he would conduct his routine physical exam under the boys' watchful eyes. Then on the ride home, he helped them draw conclusions from what they had seen.

One time, Charlie mentioned that a certain man was looking better.

In Charlie's words, "Father asked, 'You noticed his tongue was dry in the center, and also at the sides?'

"'Yes,' I said.

"'Well, he will be dead within 24 hours.'"

Charlie said his father talked of everything during the long drives, "for he was interested in everything: nature, botany, geology, and especially … chemistry."

W.W. educated his sons at deathbeds as well as sickbeds. He took them along when he did autopsies, because he wanted them thoroughly familiar with the inner workings of the human body. Will was so small when he first accompanied his father to an autopsy that he couldn't see while standing on the floor, so W.W. placed him on the table, where Will could hold onto the corpse's hair while leaning forward for a closer look. No doubt, later W.W. did the same with his second son.

As Mayo dissected, he was careful to instruct his boys in what he saw and what he did and why. He taught them to think like a detective – the question was not "who did it?" but "what did it?" to bring this person to an autopsy table.

W.W. supplemented lessons and demonstrations with practical experience for the boys. He expected them to study pathology using the family microscope. With great patience he taught them to take tissues he had removed during surgery, cut them, mount them, preserve them in alcohol (a slow process requiring several days' work), and examine them.

To assist his sons, he provided *Lectures on Surgical Pathology* by Sir James Paget, a famous English surgeon and pathologist. Paget cataloged 13,000 pathology specimens which Dr. John Hunter had collected a century earlier. In his book, Paget applied pathological information to clinical cases in a writing style so terse and informative that Dr. Will could still quote from it 40 years later.

Having "the atmosphere of books" at home was one of the most important contributions W.W. made to his children's education, in Will's opinion. The Mayo living room held shelves from floor to ceiling along all four walls. Will remembered 60 years later the thrill of reading treatises by Charles Darwin, Thomas Henry Huxley, and Ernst Heinrich Haeckel, all promoting the new ideas of evolution. W.W. wanted the boys to read these authors, to think about, and discuss them too.

Dr. Will wrote, "I well remember Dickens' works ... and those fascinating books of [Sir Walter] Scott.... How much better it is to have the walls covered with books with which we are establishing friendly relations, than with pictures of passing interest.... Books never lose their fascination."

Besides heroes from books, the boys met men they could look up to as heroes in person as their father took them to Olmsted County and Minnesota Valley medical society meetings. Dr. Will recalled that, by watching the doctors, "Even at that early age, we learned the value of medical conferences."

They met Dr. Asa Daniels, who had served as one of the New Ulm surgeons in 1862 along with their father. And they met Dr. N.S. Tefft of nearby Plainview (Minnesota), a vigorous and courageous surgeon who loved to express his opinions on politics and everything else, and who commanded a large practice despite being partially paralyzed by polio. He needed crutches to walk and was helpless in snowy weather if his horse and buggy suffered an upset. The local liverymen had standing orders to search for him if he didn't return at a certain time, for he might be trapped in a snowbank, unable to stand and rescue himself and his horse.

In 1874, W.W. was elected chairman of the Minnesota State Medical Society committee on gynecology. Only six Minnesota doctors were specialized enough to be called "gynecologists." At this time, he was still draining his patients' ovarian tumors rather than excising them. Five ovariotomies had been performed in Minnesota, and all five women had died.

Young Charlie received his initiation into anesthetics when his father operated to drain a large ovarian tumor. He was standing outside the patient's house, minding his father's horses, when a man whom Mayo had hired as anesthetist ran from the house, vomited in the yard, and collapsed on the grass. Charlie heard his father calling him urgently. He ran into the kitchen, where his father had kicked a cracker box to a position under the woman's head. W.W. and Will stood nearby, in the process of draining fluid from the tumor into a tub. Material which W.W. was pulling through the incision made an odd sucking noise.

As Charlie watched, the woman began to move on the table. W.W. ordered his youngest child to stand on the cracker box and drop chloroform onto a cloth over her nose.

Charlie said later, "When she stopped wiggling, Father would tell me to stop, and when she started, I would drop some more. I did fine. After that I used to help quite regularly. Women used to think sometimes I was a little young, but I felt quite old. It was tremendously interesting."

This story was a favorite of the Mayo sons. Charlie's age was said to be somewhere between nine and twelve.

Henry Wellcome moved away from Rochester, but W.W. found another worthy young man to mentor, Frank B. Kellogg, who was six months younger than his daughter Phoebe. Kellogg had grown up poor on a farm about 15 miles from Rochester, and he dreamed of making something of himself. When he came to Rochester to serve an apprenticeship in a law office, W.W. became his teacher and friend, loaning him books and giving him advice and encouragement. Kellogg taught himself law, history, Latin, and German. He became an attorney for the city of Rochester and for Olmsted County and, in time, a famous trustbuster. His values as a lawyer reflected Mayo's teachings – sympathy for the non-unionized, poor, common man. He won antitrust cases against General Paper Company for restraint of trade and against Union Pacific Railroad and Standard Oil Company for monopolistic practices. Secretary of State under Calvin Coolidge, he was awarded a Nobel Peace Prize for sponsoring the Kellogg-Briand treaty.

When W.W. advised young men that they could and should make something of themselves, they tended to listen.

The teaching of his sons was always tempered by gentle discipline. When someone told W.W. his sons were misbehaving, he answered, "They're no worse than I was."

Charlie was the more mischievous of the brothers, and he sometimes got into trouble at school. But his father's mild discipline led him to expect the best of other disciplinarians too. Once Charlie acquired so many black marks at Central School that his teacher sent him to the principal. After lecturing him on why he should be a good boy, all the while fingering the stick he intended to use to beat him, the principal asked Charlie if he had any comment to make.

"Yes," he answered. "Please, if you could wait until this afternoon, I'd like to get my other [thicker] pair of pants."

The principal struggled to keep from laughing, but could not resist. "And that was the end of that."

Will was less likely to get into trouble at school. But he did get sick after smoking a cigarette for the first time.

"Why did you do it, Will?" W.W. asked.

"The other boys were, so I did too," he answered.

"Listen, Will. Don't ever do things because other people do. Do them because they're right."

This gentle admonition was enough to correct Will. The source of discipline which shaped the boys' lives was inherent in the lessons their father taught them. Nobody could serve the best needs of sick people without a good deal of self control. Mistakes were inexcusable to W.W. He expected excellence of himself and of his boys, and they knew it. Because they shared his concerns for patients, they wanted to do well.

Louise played an important part in shaping the boys' characters too. She once said she believed in corporal punishment "as the doctor believes in the future," but her boys did not remember her as a disciplinarian. She was the steadying influence in the family, counteracting her husband's enthusiasms with her prudence. Her children admired her ability to understand and love their neighbors. Dr. Will said, "I never knew her to say a hateful word about anyone."

Mayo continued buying the fastest horses he could get for his own use, not only because he liked the thrill of speed, but also because he wanted to reach sick and wounded patients in a hurry. Once when his team passed a young Rochester attorney, Burt Eaton, on the road to a nearby town, the rented cutter, driver, horses and lawyer slid off the road into a snowy ditch.

"Why did you pull over?" Eaton asked the driver.

"Rochester liverymen always give Dr. Mayo the right-of-way," he answered. "He is making a sick call."

On another snowy day, W.W.'s daughter Phoebe, 18, took his horse and cutter for a ride with two friends. The *Rochester Post* reported, "Miss Phoebe Mayo with two other young ladies took a lively whirl with the Doctor's horse and cutter last Sunday, resulting in a turn over and runaway.... Fortunately, no injuries to the ladies or the horse."

W.W. returned to Rochester on August 20, '76, from

a nine-week trip to England. The paper reported, "He has had good health and a most pleasant time."

He stayed home in September and attended his patients.

While he was doing this, the International Medical Congress, a gathering of 480 outstanding doctors from around the world, met in Philadelphia. Their featured speaker was Dr. Joseph Lister, who spoke on his new method of surgery – antisepsis, which was also called "Listerism."

In 1865, Lister had for the first time applied carbolic acid dressings to a wound. He believed the acid would kill germs, whose existence he had discovered by experiments in his laboratory – one of the first scientists after Louis Pasteur to do so. His patient was a 12-year-old boy, James Greenlees, whose lower leg bone was fractured when the wheel of a horse-drawn cart rolled over it. A compound fracture such as James suffered became infected as a rule in 1865, which often led to amputation, sometimes followed by reinfection and death. Instead, the boy left the hospital healed six weeks after surgery.

Eleven years after this healing, when Lister spoke in Philadelphia, he was one of the best-known and most controversial doctors in the world. Listerism had become a complicated ritual involving wet antiseptic sprays during surgery and layers of specially treated dressings afterwards.

American doctors were uncertain about this new technique. The day before Lister's speech, W.W.'s former anatomy teacher from Missouri, Dr. John T. Hodgen, spoke to the surgical section on "Antiseptic Surgery," offering a learned summary of published articles on the subject. His speech was that of a scholar, not a scientist. He gave no references to his own experience and offered no rationale to judge the conflicting claims made for different methods of handling wounds.

In summarizing his findings, Hodgen said he was convinced that "living germs" are everywhere. "The atmosphere of hospitals seems to be pervaded by living germs, and the walls and ceilings seem to be encrusted with them." He mentioned a large number of antiseptics, "chlorine, bromine, iodine, and the alkaline sulphites…permanganates and manganates….quinine, salicylic acid, salicine, benzoic acid and boracic acid…carbolic acid, creasote and thymic acid." Hodgen was so convinced of the ubiquitous nature of germs, he despaired of ever conquering them: "We cannot but realize the utter impossibility of protecting wounds from the contact of catalytic germs." He even reported that Dr. E. Fischer had found bacteria under Lister's dressings.

If the auditors of this report were not already confused about how to prevent wound infection, they next heard more of their number giving diverse reports. Dr. Addinell Hewson said he relied upon earth dressings, because he said "water produces germs rapidly, and it is impossible to prevent this even with powerful antiseptic agents." On the contrary, Dr. William Canniff found it "impossible to entertain the doctrine of germ putrefaction." He described a case of "contused wounds of the leg. Cold water dressing was employed; and [the patient] made a rapid recovery."

Even after hearing Lister describe his method and his successes in detail, the American doctors reached no consensus on the subject of antisepsis. Probably the well-read Mayo was aware of his teacher Hodgen's speech, but he stopped using *Rerum* in the late '60s, so there is no record of his reading on Lister or antisepsis. Based on the Hodgen report, he would not have begun the complicated carbolic acid process, especially when he had no hospital in which to use it. The big city doctors at the Philadelphia meeting, including Lister, practiced their surgery in hospitals.

Also, older doctors who were achieving what they thought were satisfactory results by simply washing their hands with soap before surgery were not easily convinced to change their habits. Nor were they eager to accept the idea that when wounds became infected, they themselves had been the agents by which harm was done.

A happy event for the family took place on Phoebe's 21st birthday, June 26, 1877. Trude married Dr. David M. Berkman, a veterinary surgeon, in the living room of the Mayo farmhouse. The Reverend W. C. Rice performed the ceremony in the presence of family and friends. Trude was three weeks shy of 24, her husband 26.

When the wedding notice was taken to the *Rochester Post*, the family sent with it "a bountiful supply of nice wedding cake." The reporter exclaimed in print, "Our best wishes to the happy couple, and may their married life be long, happy, and harmonious."

The same year, another reporter gave a glowing description of the 35-acre farm which W.W. had purchased in 1875. The farmhouse, he said, afforded "a beautiful and magnificent view of the city, Zumbro Valley, and the towering bluffs, together with portions of the far stretching prairie." Mayo was building a "large and elegant" addition to the farmhouse. It will make "one of the most convenient and imposing residences in the city."

Part of the addition was a 40-foot-high tower with an observatory for Louise to use in her studies of the night skies. She mounted a 4-foot telescope on a tripod and used it to inspire in her children a delight in the heavens.

The Mayo Farmnhouse after 1877

Photo by permission of Mayo Foundation for Medical Education and Research. All rights reserved.

One reason W.W. said he bought the farm was to keep his sons away from town boys (who might distract them from their medical studies). With Will already 14 and Charlie 10, he wanted to accelerate the training he was giving them. "Our father taught us" was a phrase often used by both sons over the years.

For their general education, W.W. sent the boys to Central School, and then Will went to the public Rochester High School. In '76 W.W. removed Will from high school and put him into Miss Finch's private school until the Niles Academy opened on January 2, 1877. It was run by Sanford Niles, the man who had ably superintended the Olmsted County school system for 11 years. When he was defeated for reelection, Niles and his wife Priscilla opened the school with the object of "Fitting [students] for college." Courses offered included English, Latin, Greek, German and French. (Science was not taught at Rochester High, the Niles, or the Finch school.)

Having worked closely with the superintendent while on the Rochester school board, W.W. appreciated Niles' superior ability. Therefore, even though the tuition fees put so much strain on the Mayo budget that Louise advertised for boarders, Will attended the academy as one of the original 113 students.

After finishing his work at Central, Charlie's education followed the pattern set by Will: high school, private tutoring, and the Niles Academy. During their school years, the relationship between the brothers changed. Charlie grew less dependent on Will and more able to find his own amusements and friends. Albert Younglove helped him do this, by becoming his companion in fun and mischief. Younglove said of their school days, "Dr. Will, being older, did not have much in common with us younger fellows."

Another factor in Charlie's growing up from willing subordination to Will was the discovery of his own unique abilities. He began to see that Will was better able to do some things than he, but he could do some things better than Will. For example, when it came to mechanical problems, he could fix anything——a pump, a churn, or any gadget. When Charlie was 10, he and Will earned some money hoeing corn, and with it, as Will later reported, "under Charlie's able leadership, we purchased a steam engine. Charlie became the engineer, and after a time I was promoted to the honorable job of fireman. I never did understand that engine and didn't understand how Charlie made it go. But he did, and he is still making things go."

When they became doctors, Will and Charlie at first operated together, one assisting the other in the same surgery, but they soon developed different surgical specialities. Charlie's son Dr. Chuck said the secret of their life-long trust and cooperation was these complementary abilities: "Some psychologists believe that marriages succeed best when each partner has superiority in some area, recognized by the other. I think that's part of the reason Father and Uncle Will got along so smoothly: their areas of superiority weren't conflicting and they were certainly recognizable."

By the time W.W. bought the farm, the boys were developing different personalities too. Whereas Charlie enjoyed the chores his father gave him on the farm, Will detested them. As soon as he could, Will left the farm and got a summer job in Geisinger & Newton's drugstore, located underneath his father's office, taking the same job Henry Wellcome had once held. Here he labored sweeping the floors and scrubbing bottles from seven in the morning to six at night, eleven hours a day, and sometimes three hours more into the evening. He earned four dollars a week for this work. It was enough – he had a plan.

For a month, Will saved every penny of his earnings. Then he spent all 16 dollars on a single item. Louise had been dressing Charlie in his father's hand-me-down suits, and at this time, Charlie was wearing a cut-down version of his father's double-breasted Prince Albert coat.

"Charlie looked so funny," Will said, "in that coat, long-waisted, and with little tails. So I bought him a new suit, a store suit, and he was so happy."

An important person in the W.W. Mayo story, Mother Alfred Moes, moved to Rochester in '77. Without her, there would be no Mayo Clinic. Mother Alfred was nine years younger than W.W. Since she stood five feet three and a quarter inches tall to his five feet four, she could look him eye to eye. Her biographer, Sister Carlan Kraman, O.S.F. [Order of St. Francis], said of W.W. and Mother Alfred, "They were two of a kind. They were both visionaries." She added, "It's like she [Mother Alfred] could see head and shoulders above everyone else. It was a gift. When she got an idea [snap of the fingers], she did it."

Her face was pleasant but its expression could be commanding, for she was an extremely able administrator, an entrepreneur who had already financed the building of a number of schools, and a Christian woman who had promised God she would serve him and intended to keep her word. She covered her black hair with a white cloth and dark brown headcovering and wore a brown wool habit with white ties, a large cross and rosary beads – the Franciscan mode of dress. Glasses covered her large dark brown eyes.

Mother Alfred moved to Rochester at the invitation of Father Thomas O'Gorman, a fact which commended her to Mayo, since he valued Father O'Gorman's good opinion of others. Unlike some men of his generation, W.W. held neither her gender nor her Catholic theology against her.

The priest had asked Mother Alfred to build a convent and teaching academy, and he himself was the first to contribute money. He gave $25, leading others to give until they collected the sum of $2,800, enough to buy land. Mother Alfred bought eight lots and hired architects from Winona to design the school-convent building, which she paid for from funds from the Sisters of Saint Francis, an order she had originally founded in Joliet, Illinois. The new convent in Rochester became the motherhouse for a second congregation of her sisters.

On December 1, the Academy of Our Lady of Lourdes welcomed its first students, both Catholic and non-Catholic. The academy was a secondary school for girls, primarily boarding students, called a "Select School" by Mother Alfred because its curriculum was better than the public high school's. In a short time, the sisters opened a day school as well, for boys and girls.

Another accident involving horses occurred on September 7, '77. Phoebe was riding with Mr. J. Nevil in a buggy when a man from Greenwood Prairie ran into them with his team and wagon. The *Rochester Post* stated, "The buggy was badly smashed, the horse thoroughly frightened, and the occupants were thrown out onto the hard earth. They were considerably stunned and bruised, but escaped without serious injury."

The next year Phoebe was not so fortunate. She was driving W.W.'s horse and buggy, and Louise was a passenger. The horse began turning too sharply into the driveway at the farm, threatening to throw both women from the buggy. Courageously, Phoebe held tightly to the reins, and only she was thrown. The horse dragged her to the house, injuring her spleen. Never again was Phoebe completely healthy. The surgery which could have healed her was not yet developed; much later Dr. Will mastered it.

A happy event occurred in '78: Trude gave birth on April 7 to Louise and W.W.'s first grandchild, Daisy Louise Berkman. A second granddaughter followed on May 9, 1880, Martha May Berkman.

The Mayo family was growing, and it grew by unofficial adoption as well as by birth. One day W.W. brought home to Louise four children whose mother, his patient, had just died. They had no one else to care for them, so Louise gamely took them into her house and heart. In time, relatives asked to adopt the two younger children, but the two older girls stayed with W.W. and Louise until they married. They became like siblings to the Mayo children. A photo of Will taken in his early forties is inscribed to one of them, "Eda Nichols, With the kind regards."

By this time, Louise had gained some weight and was beginning to look grandmotherly. She wore her gray hair pulled tightly back in a bun. During the years when trachoma blinded her, she had lost her eyelashes, and they never grew back. Her expressive brown eyes seemed even more striking without them.

W.W. remained lean all his life. He gradually lost his hair until he was bald on top, with white hair on the sides of his head. At one time he experimented with a goatee, but by the late '70s he had settled on his trademark luxuriant mustache. He wore glasses for reading only.

It was news when Rochester's first telephone connected W.W.'s farmhouse with his office in

W.W. Mayo with goatee and reading glasses about age 59

Photo courtesy of Barbara Berkman Withers

December 1879. Charlie, 14, helped rig it, according to a family story. To phone the doctor, a patient was instructed to go to Geisinger & Newton's drugstore, where either the druggist or a night watchman, depending on the hour, would walk upstairs to the office and ring Mayo's home.

In the fall of 1880, W.W. and Louise sent Will off to medical school at the University of Michigan in Ann Arbor. They chose this institution after much inquiry, thought, and research – W.W. had helped author a report to the Minnesota State Medical Society on the condition of American medical schools. Because Michigan had just begun a more-rigorous-than-average medical program requiring three years of study, with a nine-month term each year, they judged it the best place for Will. They also expected him to receive excellent chemistry instruction, since the university's lab was the best of any American medical school. A newly-built university hospital for 150 patients included an amphitheater where surgeons could demonstrate their work.

When he arrived at the university, Will was already well grounded in anatomy and microscopy, thanks to his father's patient instruction over the years.

Meantime, back at home, W.W. was about to attempt the most difficult surgery of his career. A neighbor and wife of a blacksmith, Mrs. Jacob Waggoner, consulted him about a fast-growing tumor which did not respond to being drained. Knowing she was facing death, W.W. decided to attempt his first ovariotomy. Mr. Waggoner helped by fashioning instruments according to W.W.'s design, involving teeth from an old mower which were used to clamp onto the 20-pound tumor and pull it out through the incision, after it was first drained into a tub. An untoward event complicated the process: an abscess behind the tumor ruptured, spilling toxic materials into the abdomen. Mayo used soft sponges to remove as much pus as possible, then placed a drain in the wound, and sewed his patient back up.

The surgery took place on December 14. Charlie was present, watching. Assistants were Louise, Dr. Berkman (Trude's husband), Dr. Seth Gould (Mayo's partner at the time), and Dr. Jacob E. Bowers from the local state hospital, who administered the chloroform. Mrs. Waggoner suffered severe shock, but she rallied. The *Record and Union* newspaper stated that, a week after the operation, "Mrs. Waggoner … was doing well and out of danger…. The citizens of Rochester must feel equally glad with us that there is one amongst us … who has the nerve and courage to undertake to relieve suffering humanity from this dangerous disease."

Dr. Charlie later said that W.W. tried to get all the surgery patients he could. He "had the equipment and was out for everything – broken leg, collar bone, and whatnot. That was the one thing he wanted to be known for – surgery."

In the ten years after the Waggoner operation, W.W. became Minnesota's leading ovariotomist, performing 36 such surgeries, with a mortality rate of 25%, which was considered good at that time.

His courage as a surgeon served him in private life as well. In March of '81, W.W. experienced what the newspaper called "a severe accident and lucky escape." His team of horses began to run away with him. To slow them down, he guided them into a woods, but instead of stopping, they ran near a large oak, causing the buggy pole to strike it. This unloosed the horses. Then the buggy itself struck the tree and threw the doctor forward, so that he hit his face on the tree and was knocked unconscious. The newspaper further explained, "His nose was broken and his forehead badly bruised, and the only wonder is that he was not killed. If he were a preacher instead of a doctor, we would suspect Providence of having gotten up a special interposition for his benefit…. Notwithstanding his injuries, which would have laid most men up, the doctor was around attending to business in the afternoon. We are glad it was no worse."

W.W. didn't give up driving fast horses after this; instead, he designed and used a seatbelt in his buggy. His grandson Dr. Charles W. Mayo said of him, "Grandfather was a bull about pain."

One day W.W. noticed a lump on his lip which he believed was cancerous. He took a big gulp of whiskey, asked an assistant to cut it off, "hollered a while," in Charlie's words, then sat before a mirror and stitched the wound himself.

Chapter 10

Cyclone

"The course [at medical school] is hard, but some are peculiarly adapted to this kind of a life, and I guess I am one of them.... I am in love with my profession and with hard study and work with plenty of time, hope to make a success, but do not expect to do it in a day."

William J. Mayo

W.W. had what he said was "the greatest surprise of my life" on May 31, 1881. Unknown to him, Louise had planned a big party to celebrate his 62nd birthday. Late in the afternoon, a friend asked W.W. to take her for a buggy ride, so that Louise, Trude, her husband David, Phoebe, and Charlie could receive the guests without his knowledge. Will came home a day early from medical school, arriving on the six o'clock train just in time for the festivities.

W.W. drove up his driveway to find 250 ladies and gentlemen "swarm[ing] in the house and spread over the pleasant grounds." The Rochester Cornet Band, lighted by torches, greeted him with a rousing welcome and played more selections throughout the evening. Later, W.W., encircled by his family, stood on the front lawn while a friend, Walter L. Brackenridge, delivered a speech of appreciation. Almost everyone there had at one time been W.W.'s patient, and they wanted to thank him for "the robust health that all present seem now to possess." Brackenridge went on, "The great physician of mankind,… when he sent his disciples to preach the gospel of the Kingdom,… commanded them to heal the sick. You, sir, … have faithfully followed their divine example. Is it not, therefore, eminently meet and proper that we, who have been healed … by your efforts, should in some way manifest our gratitude?"

Brackenridge especially noted W.W.'s dedication to serving anyone who needed him, no matter the inconvenience or the patient's ability to pay. "By night as well as by day, through darkness and storms you have visited the poor and destitute sick in their cheerless cabins, from whom you have never expected to receive any pecuniary remuneration."

After more such praise, Brackenridge presented Mayo a gift from the guests, the deluxe edition of Wilson and Bonaparte's five-volume *Natural History of the Birds of the United States*. W.W. was thrilled with the books and with the occasion. It took him some time to compose himself to speak, since in the reporter's opinion, "the victim … was as completely non-plussed as anyone that we ever saw under such circumstances."

At last W.W. thanked his guests for their attentions, saying "I have endeavored to do my duty as a physician in a manner satisfactory to myself and to the public, and never thought my efforts were so far appreciated by the community as to bring out a public expression of this character." Then he thanked them for the beautiful books: "Nothing could be so acceptable to me as books.

For years they have been my companions and friends; from them I have learned all that I know of use to others."

The later part of the evening was spent in "exchange of sociability" and "disposing of the abundant refreshments." The reporter concluded with satisfaction that the "well merited tribute to a worthy citizen and beloved physician" was "a perfect success" and "one of the pleasantest social gatherings ever held in Rochester."

Another surprise followed the next year. W.W. was elected mayor of Rochester by a majority of 66 votes from a total 888 votes cast. He ran as a Democrat, the minority party in Rochester, and all but one of the other eleven persons elected were Republicans. The principal issue was "the alleged railroad and wheat trade discriminations." Mayo's opponent for the mayor's post was Samuel Whitten, a wheat buyer, who favored the status quo.

Minnesota wheat farmers struggled against railroad and grain elevator monopolies to make a living. Because the Winona and St. Peter Railroad was the only rail carrier passing through Rochester, it could and did raise its freight rates there to make up for lower rates it charged in more competitive areas. Also, the railroad owned a grain elevator, and it could and did refuse to service competing elevators, and thus could charge whatever it pleased for storage in its space. The result, over time, was impoverishment of farmers.

Mayo and others led an "agrarian crusade" during more than 20 years, in an attempt to protect farmers through political action. He explained in 1890 his reasons for standing with the farmers: "I have in a professional way ridden over this county for more than 25 years. Having seen a generation grow up to manhood, I have personally known of the struggles and privations of many families in their efforts to attain a medium competence.... I have seen men robbed of their earnings by combinations of wheat and coal rings and a railroad which has given them the opportunity to plunder, and to carry away their plunder."

He didn't mention another of his motives – painful memories from his childhood in Salford-Manchester, England. English representation in parliament in the early 1800s favored the landed gentry, not citizens of newly-industrialized cities. The year W.W. was born, 1819, a crowd of workers calling for reform of parliament's "rotten boroughs" gathered in St. Peter's Field near Manchester to protest. Soldiers sent to disperse the crowd attacked them, killing two women and nine men and injuring 400 in what came to be called "the Peterloo Massacre." Memories of this injustice incited talk for generations afterwards, which no doubt Mayo heard as a child and youth.

In the Reform Act of 1831, when he was 12, Parliament widened the franchise, eliminating what the historian Sir George Clark called 56 "despicable little boroughs," and enfranchising 44 "populous places, hitherto unrepresented, many of them busy industrial centres."

Thus in his youth W.W. observed the anguish of unrepresented poor people, but he also saw that by political action they could find relief. As Mayor Mayo, he was unable to control the monopoly powers in wheat and railroad, but he did not forget the issue.

He had plenty of ideas to improve the city, such as a new city hall. (It was completed two years after he left office.) He wanted Bear Creek dammed and the area cleaned up and turned into a park where the creek joined Zumbro River near the center of town. At present, it was an eyesore — frequently flooding its banks, and, at low ebb, full of rubbish. (In time, Dr. Will and Dr. Charlie bought the property and turned it into "Mayo Park," named for their father.)

W.W. wanted the city to buy 80 acres of property, which it did, including a rock quarry on a hill southwest of the city. The crushed rock was slid down the hill, then used to pave city streets. Cost of the land was $25 an acre; the city later sold it for $50 an acre.

For many years, Mayo fought for various public health measures. He worked with the Rochester Board of Health collecting statistics on disease and promoting vaccinations and quarantine restrictions for contagious diseases. He bought a book from England to learn what public health officers should do: C.B. Fox's *Sanitary Examinations of Water, Air, and Food: A Handbook for the Medical Officer of Health*. From it he learned how to analyze food and water for the community's benefit.

He was also continuing his reading on medical subjects and receiving a mixed and mostly negative report on the new antiseptic surgery. At the same time, in medical school, Will was receiving a mixed report on Listerism too. He had the advantage of studying with a brilliant surgeon, Dr. Donald Maclean, who had worked with Dr. Joseph Lister in Edinburgh. Their association predated Lister's great discovery of antisepsis, but Maclean kept up with Lister's written reports on it and practiced Listerism during the 1870s. However, the carbolic acid spray was too toxic for his skin, and he discontinued its use before he became Will's teacher. The biographer Helen Clapesattle said, "On the whole, it is safe to say that Will Mayo finished his course at Ann Arbor with only an incidental introduction to the revolutionary theory that was to create his own great opportunity."

Because of the solid work Will did in anatomy, he won the position of underdemonstrator in dissections during his junior and senior years for the professor whom he called "the great anatomist Corydon L. Ford. From him [I] obtained a lasting love of anatomy and embryology." Meanwhile, his work in surgery was so outstanding that he was chosen to assist Dr. Maclean at the operating table during his senior year. (Will was one of the best students in his U. of M. class of 1883.)

Medical school confirmed his love of the doctor's calling. Shortly before graduating, he wrote his sister Trude a letter: "A good many [medical students] do not learn easy – in fact should never have entered a profession. The course is hard, but some are peculiarly adapted to this kind of a life, and I guess I am one of them as I have never been sick a day or missed a meal and have worked right along and have had a good time too.... Don't let Father work too hard – and when I get home I will give him more time to run the farm and rest, for I am anxious to get out and put my shoulder to the wheel for our common good. For I am in love with my profession, and with hard study and work with plenty of time, hope to make a success, but do not expect to do it in a day."

Will received his doctor's degree on June 28, 1883, at a ceremony attended by his sister Phoebe, representing the family. They returned home immediately afterward, and Dr. Will joined his father in medical practice.

Happily preparing for Will's return, W.W. had rented a new office in the Ramsey Building which the Rochester newspaper described as a "large reception room and consulting rooms, and an operating room. All rooms are light, airy and cheerful, nicely furnished. There is no pleasanter office in the city." W.W. had missed working with a partner. He had enjoyed working with Dr. Deming in Lafayette 30 years earlier, and he had tried partnering with Dr. W.A. Hyde, Ole Anderson (a druggist), Dr. Seth Gould, and Dr. Elisha W. Cross (the younger Cross brother) over the years, but not until his son joined him did he find anyone he could partner with as pleasurably.

One of the first things Dr. Will did, working with his father, was make sure medical bills were sent to patients on time. He continued excusing people who were too poor to pay, agreeing with his father that nobody should ever mortgage a home to meet the Mayos' bill. And he never charged any pastors, fellow doctors, or their families for medical care. The charities which W.W. instituted remained in place, but Dr. Will did not agree with his father that bills should be sent out in a haphazard manner or not at all. As a result, for the first time in her married life, Louise began to receive enough income to enjoy occasional travel to visit her brother and his family in Michigan. Speaking later to Mrs. Meloney about this, Louise said, "We were getting to be real old people before we came to know most of the actual comforts of life."

W.W. was now the best-known surgeon in southern Minnesota. He did little eye surgery though, so he encouraged Will and Charlie to master it. Dr. Will operated on three cataract patients at the county poorhouse. One was found to have an atrophied optic nerve after the cataract was removed, but the other two enjoyed perfect results.

It was eye surgery that took Will and Charlie to the slaughterhouse north of Rochester on the afternoon of Tuesday, August 21, 1883. To learn more about cataracts, they spent the afternoon dissecting the eyes of some freshly-slaughtered pigs and sheep.

Since morning, the day had been oppressively hot, the sky overcast with leaden gray clouds. About 4 p.m. it grew very dark. The butcher went to the door and returned to the young men, excited, saying he was leaving at once because a great storm was coming. He jumped into his wagon and took off for home.

The brothers worked several more hours, until it became too dark to see. Then from the door they saw a huge funnel cloud about two miles away to the west, moving toward them, gobbling up houses, barns and trees, and spewing out their fragments in all directions. They jumped into their buggy and whipped their horse to a gallop. Barely, they managed to flee the mile-wide tornado. Moments after the Mayos crossed the North Broadway bridge over the Zumbro River, it fell to the twisting winds.

As they continued south on Broadway, they saw large grain elevators tipped over and traincars skittering down the tracks like giant toys. Just as Will and Charlie arrived at the corner of Broadway and Zumbro Streets, a 16-foot cornice blew loose from the big Cook House Hotel and struck their carriage, breaking the shafts. This freed their terrified horse, which fled down the street, turned into a little alley, and sought shelter against the stone wall of a blacksmith shop. The young men ran after the horse and hugged the wall too, as the tin roof blew off into the alley. In a moment, the violent wind ceased. A clock, stopped at exactly 6:36, set the time of the storm.

Charlie and Will started towards home, but they encountered so much debris they couldn't get through. Hearing news of people hurt north of town, they went to their father's office to assist in caring for the wounded.

No trace remained of the slaughterhouse they had just left. The cyclone destroyed all houses, trees, animals and people in its path. Most of North Rochester, which people called "Lower Town," was wrecked.

The *Rochester Post* described the catastrophe: "We have never driven our pencil up to so hard a task as it becomes our painful duty to do in attempting to describe the indescribable storm that passed over this city and county on Tuesday evening.... Trees bent down as wax candles in a furnace; chimneys, roofs, spires, cupolas, fences, barns, and houses sank before its awful force as men sink down in battle.... But worse than all the rest was the news that flew from lip to lip that in North Rochester many lives were lost and many were wounded, while hundreds were without shelter." In all, the storm killed 31 people in Olmsted County and seriously injured 50 more. In Lower Town, 157 houses were destroyed.

W.W. responded to the emergency by setting up a temporary hospital in Buck's Hotel, near the railroad station, where he worked through the night. His sons continued their ministrations in his office rooms.

Next morning at 8:30, the mayor appointed a relief committee and named Dr. David Berkman (Trude's husband) steward of improvised hospitals in Rommel's Dance Hall and the nearby German Library Association. The committee also organized distribution of beds, supplies, clothing, and food offered by generous citizens. By 11 o'clock that morning, 34 patients were residents of Rommel's Hall, attended by all the local doctors.

That day Mayo sent for Mother Alfred Moes. He knew and trusted her and the Sisters of Saint Francis, so he asked if the sisters could house wounded people at the convent.

"We have room for a hundred beds," Mother Alfred answered decisively. "The beds can be made ready immediately."

As a result of this offer, 40 less badly-wounded people were taken to the motherhouse, where the sisters used common sense, compassion, and prayer to guide them in what to do. They had been trained as teachers, not nurses.

Very soon, contention arose among the doctors at Rommel's Dance Hall. One doctor ordered an emetic

Mother Alfred Moses, O.S.F.

From Saint Mary's Hospital archives and by permission of Mayo Foundation for Medical Education and Research. All rights reserved.

given to all the patients, which would cause them to vomit. He had heard somewhere that this was prudent for accident victims. W.W. was outraged by this idea and told the relief committee, "Either he gets out or I do."

The committee responded by naming W.W. chief doctor at the makeshift hospitals. His first concern was to find dependable nurses. Good-hearted local housewives in the first days cared for the patients, but they tended to disappear around suppertime to cook for their own families. So Mayo called again upon Mother Alfred.

"There ought to be a sister down there to look after these fellows," he said. "Could you send some to the hospital to supervise the nursing staff?"

Mother Alfred hesitated. Should she allow her young sisters into a dance hall? But eager to help in the emergency, she agreed to send two women with Dr. Mayo at once and another two that night. In the next few days she arranged for three shifts of sisters to nurse in the hospitals until the patients were released.

W.W. later said of the sisters' help: "They came to us like soldiers ready for duty and stood to duty firm and constant as rocks."

The relief committee assisted 233 families and 101 men. They built 51 new houses, helped 106 families rebuild and 69 more families repair homes. More than 225 families were given bedding and 570 persons clothes.

Money poured into the city from nearby and far-away sources, including Chicago, which sent $10,000, St. Paul, Minneapolis, Stillwater, and St. Cloud. In all, $75,293.85 was received in cash and goods such as lumber, furniture, and coal in what was called "a grand outpouring of benevolence."

After the dead were buried, the wounded cared for, and the destroyed homes rebuilt, Rochester settled in for the winter, trying to forget the tragedy. But Mother Alfred could not forget. She had a waking dream, which she believed was from the Lord, telling her to establish a hospital and to ask Dr. W.W. Mayo to direct it. It would become "world renowned for its medical arts," she said.

Accordingly, Mother Alfred went to W.W. and said, "Doctor, do you not think a hospital in this city would be an excellent thing?"

He answered, "Mother Superior, this city is too small to support a hospital."

He warned her of the great cost involved and the slim chance that a town as small as Rochester would make a success of it after all the money had been spent. (He knew that the hospitals he had seen – full of patients with infected and foul-smelling wounds – were not used by people with money. They were places where poor people went to die.)

But Mother Alfred was not dissuaded. "Very true," she said.

"Besides, I'm too old," he added.

"But you have sons," she said. "You just promise me to take charge of it, and we will set that building before you at once. With our faith and hope and energy, it will succeed."

He asked, "How much money would the sisters be willing to put into it?"

"How much do you want?" she replied.

"Would you be willing to risk 40,000 dollars?"

"'Yes,' she said, 'and more if you want it. Draw up your plans. It will be built at once."

Mother Alfred had spoken with such assurance because she was eager to do God's will, and she was positive the hospital was His will. Sister Carlan Kraman, said of her, "What gave her confidence was that she prayed."

Mother Alfred also believed in the ability of the sisters whom she led. Sister Carlan explained of the Rochester Franciscan order, "Our vow of poverty means that any money we earn or inherit goes to the community." Mother Alfred and her biological sister, Sister Barbara, both had given to the order all the money they had inherited from their wealthy family. Teachers in Mother Alfred's 20 schools in various states charged students fees and returned this money entirely to the motherhouse. From school funds, Mother Alfred paid all school expenses, including the sisters' food, clothing, books, etc., but there was a profit, which went into the Rochester motherhouse bank account.

Even so, the hospital was not built "at once," as Mother Alfred had so positively declared. The money flowed in slowly, while the sisters – in the entire community, not just those in Rochester – followed Mother Alfred's lead, living sparingly and working incessantly. They wore two-dollar shoes and cheap clothes made from rough wool. Mother Alfred's own leather shoes cost only $1.50, and at home she saved more money by wearing 50-cent cloth slippers.

The sisters' meals were wholesome but sometimes meager. For 50 people – sisters and academy boarding students – a day's allotment of meat was only one and a half ounces of beef each, cooked with a 15-cent soupbone.

To earn more, the sisters, in addition to teaching, crocheted doilies, embroidered linens, made wax flowers, and painted pictures for sale at the annual fair, and they offered music lessons. Besides these tasks, they labored as required for living – shoveling snow, chopping wood, making their own soap, cleaning, washing clothes, baking and cooking.

What sustained the spirits of the laboring sisters, in Sister Joseph Dempsey's words, was the fact that "it was all for God." She and others tried to keep their parents ignorant of some of the sacrifices they made at the convent, for fear this knowledge would cause anxiety.

Less than two months after the cyclone, Trude gave birth to her third daughter, Helen Phoebe Berkman, on October 9. The baby's middle name was given in honor of Trude's sister Phoebe, now becoming an invalid from her spleen injury.

Returning to normal life for W.W. meant continuing his preceptor relationship with Dr. Will, whom he urged to join county and state medical societies. He arranged for Will to be named to the Committee on Surgery of the state medical society.

Will continued his practice of spending an hour a day reading and taking notes on medical literature. When, much later, Dr. Will spoke to graduating doctors of Rush Medical College in Chicago, he advised them to

— develop regular habits of study, reading one hour a day, every day;
— take vacation time to visit clinics and hospitals to see first hand the work done there;
— attend medical society meetings and ask questions, and
— write scientic papers, at first to broaden one's own knowledge, and then to contribute to others' knowledge.

Above all, he stressed "honesty in every conception of the word; let it enter into the details of your work; in the treatment of your patients and in your association with your [colleagues]."

All these things he learned from his father.

Meanwhile, W.W. began serving on the Minnesota State Board of Health, encouraged to do so by his friend Dr. Charles Hewitt of Red Wing, who had given up his surgical career to devote his life to public health.

By the end of '83, Joseph Lister was experimenting with asepsis, a technique more radical than antisepsis. In "anti-sepsis" the doctor comes against septic (germ-laden) materials with a counter or "anti" agent; in "a-sepsis," he sterilizes the surgical site and everything that touches it, making it not septic, or "a" septic.

In September, 1884, Dr. Will traveled to New York for a two-month course in the New York Postgraduate School, an institution only two years old. His favorite surgeon there was Dr. Henry B. Sands. One stormy evening, Sands invited Will to come along with him to examine an interesting emergency case. The patient suffered from an abscess in the right lower quadrant of his abdomen, a condition we now call "appendicitis." After opening and draining the abscess, Sands asked Will if he had ever seen a similar case, and Will remembered a slim barber with the same symptoms who had come to W.W. for relief while Will was still his father's office boy. W.W. had introduced a needle to find the place of infection, then used the needle as a guide for a later incision to drain the pus.

"That big needle trick is a good one," Sands said. "Your father is a wise surgeon." He said before he learned the needle trick he had more than once been

Hattie Damon Mayo

Photo courtesy of Barbara Berkman Withers and Olmsted County Historical Society

humiliated when he removed the needle too soon and was then unable to find the abscess.

A week after Will returned home, while W.W. was out of town, a young Swedish man consulted Will with symptoms of what was called "perityphlitic abscess" (appendicitis). Dr. Will's treatment followed Sands' example, and the man recovered.

Shortly after, on November 20, 1884, Will, now 23, married 20-year-old Hattie May Damon, a local girl. They had been friends since his Rochester schooldays. "The ceremony [in the home of the bride's parents] was performed by Rev. Mr. Bradshaw in his happiest style," said the local newspaper, "and after many hearty congratulations came the call to the dining room. Here was displayed a table laden with all that could constitute a feast, and 'mid the fragrance of fruits and flowers the bride for the first time sits as a guest at her father's board. Happy pair! Happy evening."

The next spring, Phoebe Mayo grew sicker, and on Friday, May 15, 1885, she died at the age of 28. The *Rochester Post* said, she "suffered a great deal. All that could be was done for her, but without avail, and death came to her relief. She was a lady of rare excellencies."

"It is seldom," the reporter continued, "that the announcement of a death elicits such an expression of deep and general sorrow. She was especially remarkable for her earnest and unaffected piety, and her faithful observance of all Christian duties, as well as for her cheerful, genial, loving spirit."

In July, W.W. and Will bought a microscope which had been exhibited at the Minnesota State Medical Society. It had been made in England, and the *Record and Union* found it of sufficient importance to announce its purchase, "the finest instrument in the state, costing them $350."

Dr. Will returned to New York in the fall to observe Dr. Arpad Gerster at the New York Polyclinic. It was from Gerster more than any other man that Dr. Will learned the importance of aseptic and antiseptic surgery, and to him he owed, he said, "a debt of gratitude."

Two years later, when Gerster published his book *The Rules of Aseptic and Antiseptic Surgery*, both Will and Charlie learned it by heart. It was a very practical little book, giving precise directions to doctors who operated in kitchens or bedrooms, telling them how to arrange their equipment to transport it, and how to rig the operating theater with antiseptic solution suspended from a bedpost or light fixture.

Father and son, the Drs. Mayo worked together to

Phoebe Louise Mayo

Photo courtesy of Olmsted County Historical Society

remove a large tumor from Edwin Jacobs' armpit in December, 1885, and the *Rochester Post* remarked, "The operation, which was one of the first magnitude, required the greatest skill."

They also went to Spring Valley to operate on a three-month-old girl, taking flaps of her skin to fashion lips and a nose, for the child was born without them.

W.W. began traveling more often in these days. He attended the American Medical Association meetings every year without fail from the mid '80s on, no matter where the meetings were held. He also took Will on a tour of eastern hospitals, so they could note every useful feature which would make the proposed Rochester hospital a good place for patients. Together they studied administration offices, lighting, floor plans, and especially surgery rooms and accoutrements. All this information went into the hospital plans which, under W.W.'s direction, were not finalized with the architect until his third attempt at drawing them.

Mayo indulged his taste for political activity too. In 1886, when he was elected to the first of two two-year terms as city alderman, the Rochester city band came to his home to give him a victory serenade. In '87, he went to Minneapolis as part of the official Rochester party to greet President and Mrs. Grover Cleveland during their visit to the Minneapolis Exposition. During the four years W.W. served as alderman, he effectively promoted a gasworks and a new railroad line from Clear Lake, Iowa, to Duluth by way of Rochester. The *Record and Union* congratulated him on "our excellent waterworks, now admitted to be an inestimable public blessing ... for the consummation of which [Mayo] fought persistently against organized and powerful opposition during many weary months."

During this time, he ran for state representative twice too, losing one election by 200 votes and another by only one vote.

Louise and W.W. welcomed their fourth grandchild, David Mayo Berkman, born to Trude in 1886. Less than one year later, in March '87, Hattie gave birth to her first baby. She and Will named her Carrie Louise Mayo. All five of Louise's grandchildren lived in easy access to her home and gave Louise great satisfaction.

Charlie had now completed his first year at Chicago Medical College, a nominal part of Northwestern University, the school which the family had chosen after joint discussions. They especially liked the chance Charlie would have to observe surgeries at more than one hospital, including the clinics of Drs. Charles Parkes, Christian Fenger and Nicholas Senn. The course was for three years, each session six months long.

Charlie's forte was not so much the academic side of school, though his grades were nothing to be ashamed of, ranging from 10, the highest possible, to 7. His greatest skills lay in his physical and mechanical aptitudes. Some people have said he was a mediocre student. (Surprisingly, the 7 grade was in surgery.) But his real proficiencies were untested and so ungraded. He scouted and found the best surgeons and their most interesting cases, and these he attended, arriving early for each one. He selected the best seat (in the center, up close), so he could memorize the surgery and describe it precisely in the evening to his friends. Years later, he could repeat what he had observed. If physical aptitude for surgery had been measured, his grade would have been 10.

Charlie had the advantage of studying public health under Dr. Oscar DeWolf, who, as Chicago's first public health commissioner, fought hard to improve sanitation. Having also observed his father working as a Rochester health officer, Charlie later volunteered for the same work.

Another advantage of Chicago Medical College was its belief in antiseptic surgery and in using the trained nurses essential for helping doctors carry out the rigorous technique.

To graduate, the college required a certification of character. W.W. was happy to provide the needed document, saying in his concise way, "To whom it may concern, This is to certify that Chas. H. Mayo is over 21 years of age and is of good moral character. W.W. Mayo."

On March 27, 1888, at age 22, Charlie received his doctor's degree, with his proud father present in the audience. Minnesota had passed a law requiring candidates for state doctor's licenses to be examined, and early in April, Charlie took the difficult test in St. Paul. Of the 12 who tried, only a few passed it; Charlie was one of them.

The Mayo listing in the *Rochester Post* business directory changed to "Drs. W.W., W.J., and C.H. Mayo, physicians and surgeons, office Cook's Block." From the beginning, according to Will, "It was the practice of Father, Charlie and me to have a common pocket book. Each used what he wanted for his own purposes."

The checks read simply, "Drs. Mayo."

On August 1, '88, Mother Alfred signed a contract with J.D. Billingsley of Winona to build St. Marys Hospital for $16,500 and its heating plant for an additional $2,200. She had already bought nine choice acres, west of the city limits on Zumbro Street, at a cost of $2,200. She especially liked the lovely site, where the hospital would be surrounded by shrubs and trees. The sisters assumed that a peaceful, beautiful, home-like hospital would minister to the patients along with good doctoring and nursing.

Now that Charlie had joined the Doctors Mayo, Will began teaching him all he had learned during his years of practice. Will was proficient in every operation W.W. performed, except his specialty, the ovariotomy. This operation was too difficult for Will, his father said.

One day in November, Dr. Will examined Hannah Worthington in Kasson. She had grown so huge from the ovarian tumor she carried that when Dr. Will asked her to turn to her side on the parlor sofa, she fell off it. Will told his father of the problem, and W.W. said he would perform an ovariotomy the following Sunday morning, when neighboring doctors could come and observe.

But mid-week, W.W. was called to St. Paul by his friend Dr. A. J. Stone, who wanted his advice on a difficult case. He said he would return Saturday night. Instead, he stayed on to help Dr. Stone, planning to bring him to Rochester Sunday afternoon to see the postponed operation on Monday morning.

However, on Sunday morning, arrangements had already been made for the surgery at the Carpenter House on Broadway, which served the Mayos as a hospital in those days. Fifteen doctors had gathered there with the patient and her relatives at the appointed time. Dr. Will felt he could not send everyone home disappointed, so he offered to do the operation, if Mrs. Worthington was willing. She was. So he carefully and successfully performed the difficult surgery, assisted by Dr. Charlie, Dr. Ida Clarke, and Dr. A.W. Stinchfield of Eyota, removing a tumor large enough to fill a washtub.

The patient rallied and all seemed well, but Will was nervous when he met his father and Dr. Stone, arriving on the Sunday evening train. W.W. was especially happy, telling his friend what an exciting surgery he would be seeing next morning.

Will summoned his courage and told his father he had already performed the operation, and Mrs. Worthington was making a good recovery. The older doctor stared at his son in disbelief.

Dr. Stone had no trouble believing Will though. He laughed so hard he cried and had to sit down on the station steps at the thought of the boy doctor stealing his father's patient and performing his father's favorite surgery.

When W.W. recovered from his shock, he, Will, and Dr. Stone went to the Carpenter House to visit Mrs. Worthington and see her tumor in the washtub.

Chapter 11

Battle for the Hospital's Survival

*"Was Dr. William Worrall Mayo in charge, medically,
of the hospital at its opening, at 70 years of age?"
"Yes. He was alert, able, enthusiastic,
young in body and mind."*
— Sister Joseph Dempsey, O.S.F.

Dr. Charlie contracted whooping cough in the months after graduation and took so long to recover that his parents sent him to Europe in January, 1889, for a change which they hoped would cure him. It did. While there, Charlie visited his father's family in Salford, England, and then toured surgical centers in England and on the continent.

W.W.'s sister Sarah, now 65 years old, entertained him, along with her husband, Thomas Thorp, taking him sight-seeing in Manchester. Charlie especially admired the great turn-around basin for ships, built years earlier, which had enabled W.W. to depart from Manchester by boat to Liverpool, instead of by train.

From Britain, Dr. Charlie traveled to Germany to observe surgeries done using the antiseptic method. He was impressed by the large jars containing antiseptic liquids, and by the special operating tables designed to slough off water and other fluids poured on during operations. Charlie noted that the surgeons and their assistants wore rubber boots and carefully scrubbed their hands and cleaned their nails before each surgery. A few of them wore boiled white cotton gloves, for they were beginning to practice asepsis.

Louis Pasteur was a hero to the Mayo family, and in Paris, Dr. Charlie managed to see him and hear him deliver a lecture. Charlie said, "Of course, he spoke in French and I did not understand it, but I saw this great man. He had had a mild stroke, and he came in with a little drag to his left leg…. He sat at a desk while he lectured, and spoke from notes, and most of the time his head was bent forward and down, which greatly muffled his voice and seemed to make it difficult for those present to hear him, for they all listened intently. I felt that to see this man was a great privilege."

Pasteur was a celebrity. Only three years earlier, he had saved the life of nine-year-old Joseph Meister, who had been bitten 14 times by a mad dog. Pasteur inoculated the boy with an anti-rabies vaccine. Success of this treatment brought crowds of people at risk of developing rabies to Pasteur's laboratory, begging for help.

When he returned home to Rochester, Charlie was eager to rejoin the Mayo practice, but, like Will some years before, he had to overcome resistance from patients who considered him too young. As he put it, "Father would go and see what the trouble was, and then he would send me thereafter to some special friends of his. When I would get to the house, I would put my foot in the door, so as to assure my entrance, and would explain that Father was busy or called away and was unable to get there. Could I do something for them? I would, when given the chance, give a thorough examination with all my instruments, and it would take me quite a while, whereas Father could detect the trouble offhand, and consequently by the time I had finished, they would remark that I had given them the best examination they had ever had."

With Charlie home and working with W.W., Will was free to travel and learn. He visited Dr. Joseph Price in Philadelphia, whom he said was "daring, courageous, and aggressive. He aroused the most violent antagonisms and warmest affection. I went to Philadelphia first in '89 with an average mortality of 17% in abdominal work. I came back and brought it to 5% in two months."

As Dr. Charlie continued working with his brother, he soon came into his own, demonstrating his unusual surgical originality and dexterity. He did not copy Will but developed his own way of solving surgical problems. In time, as Will specialized more and more in abdominal surgery, Charlie operated on everything else – the brain, eyes (especially cataracts), nose and throat, joint and bone, blood vessels, spinal cord, chest, amputations, and prostate.

Mother Alfred's faith was severely tested at least twice in the building of the hospital – some of her sisters turned against it, and her contractors cheated her. Yet she persisted in believing Saint Marys Hospital was God's will.

In the summer of '87, she had called an executive meeting of her congregation. It was only at this point that she revealed to them the building project for which they had been working and sacrificing for several years. Mother Alfred asked for a vote on whether or not to build "a hospital for invalids" in Rochester. Of 52 votes cast in all, five sisters voted against it. This one-tenth minority disapproved the idea of changing their purpose from teaching to nursing. (All 52 sisters, on the other hand, voted at the same time to support building an academy in Ironton, Ohio.)

The minority not only voted against the hospital in '87, but they also complained to Bishop John Ireland in St. Paul, saying they thought Mother Alfred was too old to make sound decisions. (She would turn 61 in the fall of '89.) Responding to them, now Archbishop Ireland came to the Rochester motherhouse in the summer of '89 to preside over the election of officers. He declared Mother Alfred ineligible for reelection as mother superior. Against his instructions, the sisters voted for her unanimously, but he nullified the vote and appointed Sister Matilda in her place. Thus, while construction of the hospital was progressing, Mother Alfred was stripped of her nominal authority to superintend the work. She did it anyway, with most of the sisters' approval.

Edith Maria Graham
First nurse and first nurse-anesthetist at Saint Marys Hospital

Photo by permission of Mayo Foundation for Medical Education and Research. All rights reserved.

Her second test of faith came when the original contractor, J.D. Billingsley, left town furtively by night without completing more than half the building, though he had already received $15,700 of the original $18,700 or 84% of the money.

Mother Alfred had been warned that he might do this, and she took legal steps to protect the sisters from claims on their assets. Two men of integrity in Rochester, Granville Woodworth, a building contractor, and George Weber, a pharmacist, had posted bonds on the building, making the possibility of loss theirs. They ordered the workmen to finish the job and managed to stretch the remaining $3,000 to pay them.

So the hospital was completed as planned, without costing the Sisters of Saint Francis anything extra and with no fees imposed on the bondsmen.

A second baby was born to Dr. Will and Hattie in August, '89, and named Worrall Mayo for W.W.'s family. Sadly, he died in November.

Louise was busy with life on the farm and her grandchildren at this time, but she also found time to return to a craft she enjoyed. She sewed all the choir robes for Calvary Episcopal Church's first boys' choir and enjoyed listening to the children singing on Sundays, dressed in her handiwork.

Painting by F.C. Henselmann of an early operation (1889) at Saint Marys From left are Sister Constantine, Dr. W.W. Mayo, Dr. Charlie, Edith Graham, Dr. Will and Sister Joseph

From Saint Marys Hospital archives and by permission of Mayo Foundation for Medical Education and Research. All rights reserved.

W.W. never did embrace antisepsis – he left that to his sons. But he did take a step to help them follow the technique. He hired Edith Graham, 22, in the spring of 1889, after she graduated from nurse's training at Chicago Women's Hospital. She became his nurse, the first professionally-trained nurse in Rochester, and his bookkeeper. When the hospital opened a day earlier than planned with an emergency eye surgery performed by Dr. Charlie on Monday, September 30, she was present. Her special knowledge helped her prepare antiseptic agents, bandages, and everything needed for the operating room, where, in Dr. Charlie's words, "Everything was slushing."

From the beginning, Dr. Will and Dr. Charlie used antiseptic techniques in all surgeries, which they later modified to aseptic techniques. Dr. Will assisted with this first operation, and W.W. delivered the anesthetics.

The one operating room was, the newspaper reported, "a credit to its deviser. Part of the room is built out in the same manner as a bay window, and as it is on the north side, the light will fall upon the operating table from the north and the skylights above. Surgeons unite in the opinion that a north light is the proper light for operating purposes, hence this room must be perfect. The floor of the room is inclined a trifle and is so constructed that it can be flooded with water, which instead of running into the adjacent hall, will run into a waste pipe."

Two gaslights provided illumination at night in the small, square room, each wall 12 feet long. Its wood floor was painted yellow. Along the walls were a radiator, a sink, and a double gas plate, to be used for boiling water.

Dr. Charlie designed and made the wooden surgical table, using ideas he had picked up in Germany. The top was padded and covered with oilcloth, and it had an adjustable headrest. Three boards slanted down on the sides towards long tin pans held in position by stirrup-like fixtures at the corners. This was all to accommodate the "slushing" surgery.

A small journal which Edith Graham kept at this time shows how carefully the Mayos appointed the surgery room. It had a "sponge table" with six granite sponge basins and four pitchers, plus a quart basin, a funnel, and a vomiting bowl. On the instrument table were a large and a small granite dish for the doctors' hand-washings

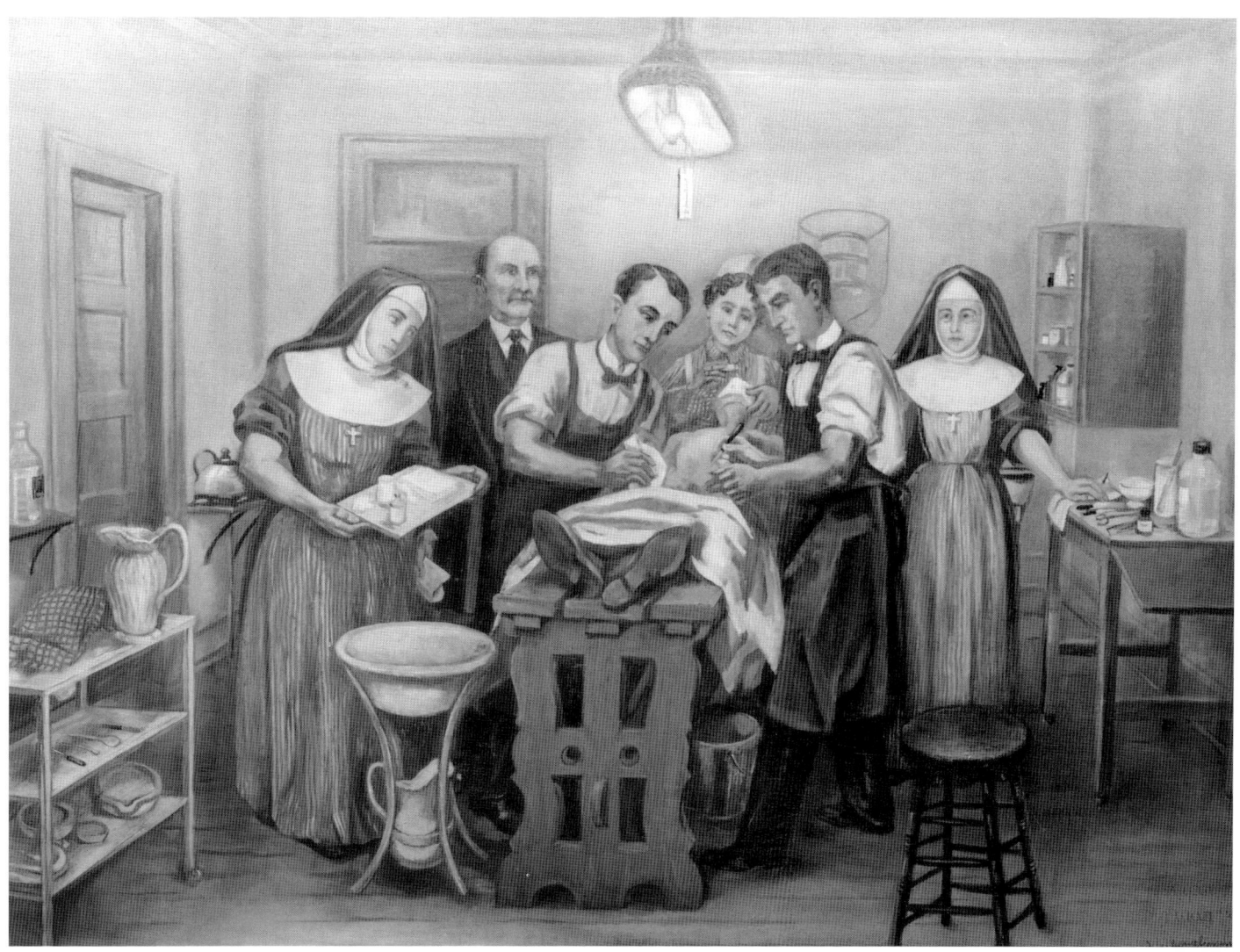

and a specimen dish for pathological material.

On another table lay "dressing table indispensibles" – a large glass container for "inside and outside sponges, airtight tins for absorbent cotton and gauze [which the nurse had prepared in carbolic acid during four days of treatments], an ether cone, iodoform in a shaker, cosmoline, hypodermic syringe, morphine, brandy, alcohol, glycerine, sweet oil, castor oil, spirits of ammonia, aqua ammonia, spirits of camphor,… nitric acid,… iodine (peregoric), laudanum, and antiseptic tablets."

This was much more equipment than W.W. had ever used in his surgery practice. His daughter Gertrude said her father differed sometimes with the boys' opinions, especially concerning the number of accessories and instruments needed in their work, and he always expressed his opinion to them. But in the end, though he was technically chief surgeon at the hospital, he left his sons free to make whatever decisions they wanted about the new antiseptic method. He had, by this time, taught them so well that he knew he could abide by their carefully-made decisions.

The hospital itself was imposing. It had three stories plus a basement and was made of red brick decorated by cut-stone window ledges and curved stone accents. Inside, the first floor held doctors' offices, reception rooms, dining rooms, and a kitchen. On the second floor were the operating room, a ward for women, and several private rooms. A chapel for the sisters was on the third floor, along with a men's ward, and a recreation room. The basement held a laundry room, a room for dispensing medicine to outpatients, storage rooms for food, a huge cistern holding 500 gallons of city water, and a room called the "foul air room," which was part of an unusual ventilating system designed to keep the air pure on the three patients' floors.

The capacity of the hospital was said to be 27 beds, but in fact, the sisters could provide only 12 iron cots on September 30, and several of them had no mattresses. The motherhouse funds were in demand for other building projects, and the sisters refused to give any more money to the hospital. They even turned down requests from Mother Alfred for furniture. She appealed to the public through newspapers, but the only donations were some books and a few heavy quilts.

When more than 12 patients were admitted, the sisters gave up their own beds to them and slept on the floor. There was no furniture in the rooms except the beds and one big black walnut dresser. On the patients' trays were iron knives and forks and unmatching pieces of china and linen.

The Doctors Mayo wanted the hospital to pay for itself. Therefore, they told their patients to pay the sisters' bill at the hospital before paying them, and if there was not enough money, the Mayos would go without. They also asked the sisters to forego putting out alms boxes for the poor, since the free service they gave poor people satisfied the same purpose.

Hospital charges were modest: one dollar a day or six dollars a week for a ward bed, and between eight to ten dollars for a week's stay in a private room. In the first eleven months, the sisters received about $1,100, which they used to meet their expenditures and also to buy things for the hospital. They wanted the rooms to be homelike, because they thought this would comfort the patients and help them get well. So, as they were able, they bought linens and blankets, rocking chairs, pictures, mirrors, and dressers, as well as pretty dishes and some silver knives and forks, which were carefully wrapped up between meals.

At night, kerosene lamps lighted the floors. The night nurse carried a lantern when she moved about the building, and another lantern hung on a tree outside, in case a doctor or patient needed to come to the hospital. At first the building had an open elevator shaft, but no elevator. This was a potential danger at night, so a nurse sat beside it with a light, to keep people from accidentally falling down the shaft.

The three Doctors Mayo, Mother Alfred, and the sisters opened the hospital "to all sick persons regardless of their color, sex, financial status, or professed religion." As Mother Alfred put it, "The cause of suffering humanity knows no religion and no sex; the charity of the Sisters of St. Francis is as broad as their religion." They also opened the hospital for use by all Rochester doctors and their patients.

Mother Alfred asked four sisters to work as the first nurses, Sisters Sienna, Constantine, Fidelia, and Hyacinth. They had no training, and Dr. Will said much later, "The little band of hospital sisters, as untried as ourselves, will never be forgotten."

Edith Graham took over teaching the sisters how to be nurses. Her lectures for their benefit included a glossary of terms they should learn in order to converse with doctors, including "deglutition,… micturition [urination], abrasion, placebo, placenta, puerperal, puberty, tuberculosis [a new term for phthisis],… uremia, vertigo, ureter and foetus." She also lectured them on the psychology of the patient and gave good advice like "Cultivate light touch and step and soft voice. Do not whisper in patient's room. Do not tell patient condition of temp. or pulse, or make him think he is very sick."

On October 25, Father William Riordan of Rochester conducted a blessing ceremony for the hospital. Fifty people came, including Protestant clergy, several visiting priests, a number of Protestant doctors, and Rochester's Common Council. The priests, led by three boys, walked through the hospital and scattered holy water on the walls. After mass, dinner was served to 25 guests.

The big cross atop the hospital marked it as a

Christian organization, and the dress of the nurse-sisters marked it as Catholic. They wore their long hair braided and over it headdresses like Mother Alfred's. Over their heavy brown woolen habits and capes they wore brown striped aprons with flat bibs and sleeves ending in starched cuffs.

This was all quite natural to the Mayos and, of course, to the sisters, but it was unusual for 1889. Sister Ellen Whelan, O.S.F., wrote, "The relationship of the Doctors Mayo and the Sisters of Saint Francis was unique for its own time and beyond. Saint Marys was the only U.S. hospital owned by Catholic Sisters in an exclusive partnership with nonsectarian physicians. Perhaps even more unusual, a handshake sealed this partnership for almost 100 years. Based on trust and mutual respect, their pledge required no written documents or legal agreements."

Originally, the trust and mutual respect of Protestant and Catholic had existed only between Dr. W.W. Mayo and Father Thomas O'Gorman. It gradually widened to include the two young Doctors Mayo, Mother Alfred, and many sisters who came to work in the hospital over the years. Decisions between the Mayos and Saint Marys' executives were commonly made at the hospital's kitchen table.

However, not all Protestants in Minnesota were favorably disposed towards Catholics. Some local people raised objections to being cared for by Catholic sisters in a Catholic institution. Therefore, local Protestant doctors did not, at first, use the hospital. W.W. tried to solve this problem by appointing his good friend John Willis Baer, a prominent Presbyterian, to be superintendent, at least in name. When Baer spoke at the Old Boys and Girls Reunion in Rochester 32 years later, he surprised all the sisters with his remark that he was the first superintendent of Saint Marys. None of them knew he had ever been associated with the hospital. Baer explained it was only for a month or so that he "came frequently to the hospital to be observed rather than to observe; and while he was most unobtrusive within the building, outside of it he was very ostentatious of his office."

The real, practicing superintendent of the hospital after November 5 was Mother Alfred, appointed to this position by the new mother superior, Mother Matilda. With characteristic energy, Mother Alfred threw herself wholeheartedly into hospital work, not only directing activities, but also doing menial chores – enough to wear out a much younger person. She sometimes worked 40 hours straight without sleep, carrying water upstairs from the basement to the third floor, delivering trays of food from the first floor kitchen to patients on the second and third floors, and shoveling coal for the furnace. As she had always been, she was an exemplar to her sisters of serving God by serving needy people.

The sister-nurses followed her example ardently. All the water needed for cooking, cleaning, baths and toilets, they carried up from the basement reservoir. When the sewer backed up, as it often did, the sisters cleaned the mess, and until it could be made right, they carried out all sewage by hand. It was 10 years after Saint Marys opened that the hospital sewer was connected to the city sewer system, at the sisters' expense.

An ordinary day for the sister-nurses was entirely devoted to patient care, and it started early – at three or four in the morning. Often they worked until eleven at night, and sometimes, when a patient was critically ill, a sister sat up all night with him or her, going more than 40 hours without sleep.

The location of the hospital, though quiet and beautiful, and so advantageous to patients, was an inconvenience to the sisters. Each day they had to walk one mile to Rochester to buy food and other provisions for patients and nurses, and then they had to carry it back.

Some nursing duties were at first difficult for sensitive women trained to spend their lives teaching children. For instance, they gave enemas and inserted and supervised catheters. One young nurse, called for the first time to assist in examining a nude male patient, objected strongly. She ran to a corner of the surgery room and stood there, shivering with shame, her eyes to the wall. Edith Graham dealt with her

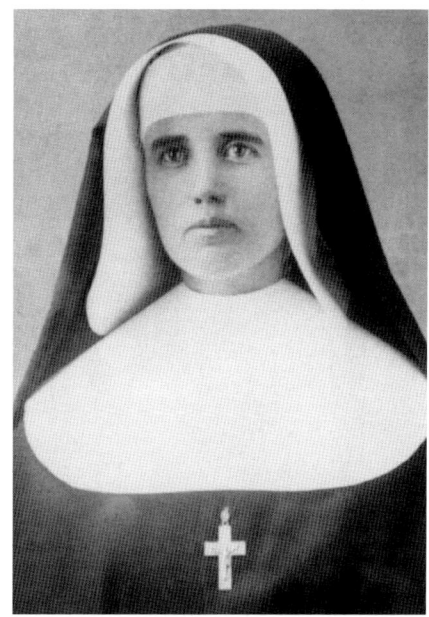

Sister Joseph Dempsey, O.S.F.

From Saint Marys Hospital archives and by permission of Mayo Foundation for Medical Education and Research. All rights reserved.

kindly and firmly, explaining that the examination was absolutely necessary for the patient's treatment.

This sister heeded Miss Graham's words. She went on to become a dedicated nurse, then first assistant to Dr. Will in surgery (the best assistant he ever had, he said), and supervisor of the hospital for 47 years. She was Sister Joseph Dempsey, 33 years old when she arrived to work in Saint Marys Hospital, November

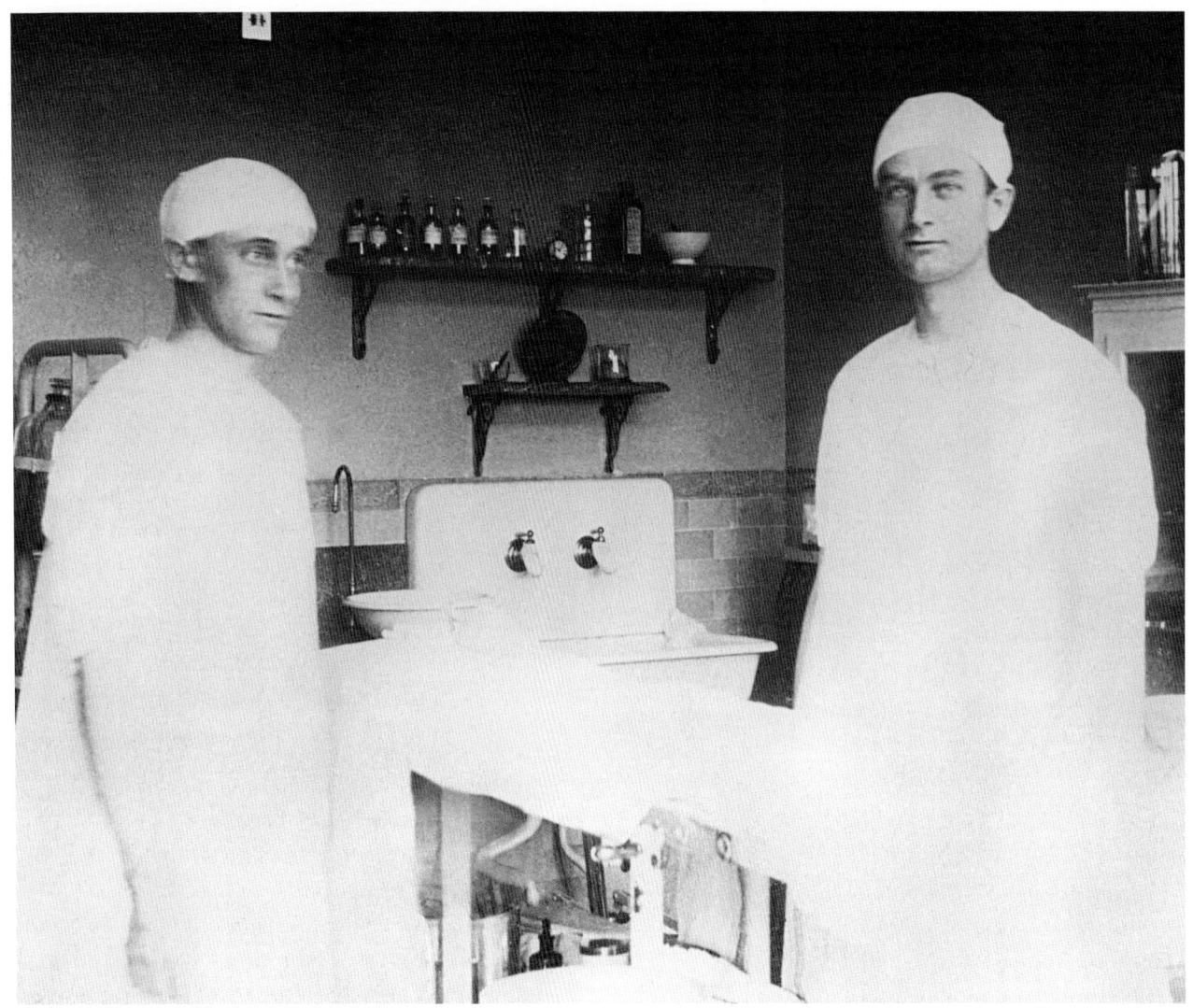

Dr. Will and Dr. Charlie in the first operating room, Saint Marys Hospital

Photo by permission of Mayo Foundation for Medical Education and Research. All rights reserved.

1889. In the early years, Sister Joseph continually prayed for strength and for God to bless the work of her hands. She and the other sisters prayed also for their patients' recovery. This spiritual element in the care they gave was supported by the Drs. Mayo.

After a particularly difficult operation on a patient, Dr. Will said to Sister Joseph, "I know she can't live, but you burn the candles and I will pay for them." ("Burning the candles" implied prayer for the sick woman, who did recover.)

After several months of teaching the sisters to be nurses, Miss Graham, with the Mayos' assent, judged them competent to continue without her, and she returned to work for W.W. He decided he would train her as a nurse-anesthetist; she became the first to serve in this capacity at Saint Marys Hospital.

For a long time, W.W. had been aware of the dangers of chloroform. Male interns at this early time sometimes inadvertently caused the death of patients when they became so absorbed in watching interesting surgeries that they forgot to monitor their patients' vital signs. A nurse, he reasoned, would care more about the patient than the procedure. He taught Miss Graham to watch the patient's breathing, pulse, blood pressure, and dryness of the skin and eyes, and adjust the chloroform dose accordingly. At first, since the petite 22-year-old looked so young, W.W. always stood beside her while she administered the anesthetic, to reassure the patient until sleep came.

Though he was 70 years old, W.W. continued working long hours as a doctor, but he did not perform surgery in the hospital – he left that to his sons. He did see patients at the hospital though, where it was he, not Dr. Will or Dr. Charlie, who in those early years commanded the confidence of the public. He also saw them in his office in town, and he continued his obstetrics-gynecology practice, delivering babies in private homes, some of which he reached by horse and buggy, as he always had. Mothers at this time resisted the idea of giving birth in a hospital.

For the first three years, Dr. Will and Dr. Charlie worked tirelessly, like the sister-nurses. They saw hospital patients early each morning and performed surgery from 7:30 a.m. until at least 1 p.m. After lunch, they went downtown to their medical offices to see patients there. They were on call after dinner and sometimes tended emergency patients at night. During the first years, Dr. Will and Dr. Charlie also undertook night nursing for male patients whose care might distress the sister-nurses, such as those with genito-urinary disorders. They took turns sleeping at the hospital, using an alarm clock to wake them for their nursing duties.

Even with so much work and prayer, the first year was difficult, and the hospital's survival in doubt. Some of the teaching sisters continued to oppose the project, and some Catholics in the area objected to a hospital staffed by Protestant doctors. And even with John Baer's act at superintending, some Protestants remained leery of being cared for by Catholic sisters. Dr. Will later said, "By the greatest effort, we obtained 300 patients in hospital the first year. It was impossible to close the hospital at the end of the year, because there were 30 patients in bed in it, and we had been self supporting."

All along, the Right Reverend Joseph B. Cotter, Catholic bishop of the new Winona diocese, had been giving his support to the work. Dr. Will described him as a "broadminded man, beloved by Protestant and Catholic…. Bishop Cotter's tactful handling of the local situation poured oil on the troubled waters, and we soon had a united sisterhood and a united community behind the enterprise."

From the beginning, the success rate for surgery at Saint Marys was phenomenal. Of the first 400 surgeries, only two people died, a mortality rate of one-half of one percent. This was far superior to what was happening in other American hospitals.

Non-Mayo doctors began using the hospital, but some of them brought highly-contagious patients with terminal disease into it, which threatened the well-being of surgery patients. Consequently, the sisters made and stuck by a rule that one of the three Drs. Mayo must examine all in-coming patients and could exclude anyone who might endanger others. In the first 39 months at Saint Marys, 22 patients died of 1,037 admitted, a mortality rate of only two percent. These early reports of low mortality were so uncommon that experienced surgeons in other cities refused to believe them at first.

News began traveling out of Rochester from people treated there, who told their friends – patients at Saint Marys Hospital do not die; they get well. As a result, three years after the hospital opened, patients were coming from Minnesota, Wisconsin, Michigan, Ohio, Illinois, Iowa, Missouri, Kansas, Nebraska, North Dakota, South Dakota, Montana, and even as far away as New York.

Twenty years later, they came from Europe, South America, Asia, Australia, and Africa.

Mayos' Clinic Grows

The sisters' "overwhelming gratitude and admiration ... went to the Mayos. They would never forget how the Mayos endured public abuse with steadfast courage on their behalf; the Mayos' unswerving loyalty had almost certainly saved the hospital."
Sister Ellen Whelan, O.S.F.

One day, according to Dr. Charlie, "a pretty good-looking tramp came along, and the sisters [at the hospital] were feeding him." The elevator shaft was still a gaping hole. When the tramp described a hydraulic elevator he had seen in Paris, France, the sisters called Dr. Charlie to hear his report. Figuring he could rig a similar device, Dr. Charlie asked a mechanic friend, Fred Livermore, to cast pipes in the shaft, which they dug forty feet deeper; the pipes would carry water under the elevator platform. It was, Charlie said, "nothing but a big syringe."

They flooded the pipes with city water, and "it pushed the thing up. I hated to see the water all wasted, so I ran a pipe up the corner of the elevator so that when the elevator went down, it pumped the water up [into a water tank on the roof], and it ran all the toilets."

The elevator had one deficiency. It was operated from within the car. If the elevator car was on one floor, and the person wishing to use it on another, a sister had to use the stairs to fetch the car.

For fifteen years, this elevator ran at the hospital with no cost to the sisters except for some grease. Dr. Charlie said, "We figured every way to make the hospital pay."

About this time, Dr. Charlie also built the first telephone line for Saint Marys, connecting it to the Mayo offices downtown.

The Mayos' practice, known now as "Mayos' Clinic," soon grew too large for the three doctors to handle it all. After Edith Graham's sister Dinah graduated from nursing school at Chicago Women's Hospital in the spring of 1890, the Mayos hired her. She nursed for them in their downtown offices, visited country patients, and kept their account books, relieving Edith of this task.

In February, 1892, they hired Dr. Augustus W. Stinchfield as their first partner. He was 49 at the time, but looked older. Dr. Charlie explained why they chose him: "W.J. and I looked young, although we were capable, and we felt Father should have a little rest.... We also felt that we should have an older man with us." They knew Stinchfield's work well. He had assisted the Mayos at times, as on the occasion of Dr. Will's first ovariotomy. Also, they noticed patients rarely came to them from nearby Eyota, where he had been a doctor for 19 years. Apparently, he was satisfying them with his care.

In selecting Dr. Stinchfield, the brothers followed their father's dictum——always choose the best possible person to fill a need. Dr. Will later said of Stinchfield,

Dr. W.W. Mayo at a Farmers' Alliance Meeting about 1890
Mayo is sixth from the left in the front row

Photo by permission of Mayo Foundation for Medical Education and Research. All rights reserved.

"He was a good diagnostician, a loyal and energetic colleague. Our association was most happy."

At Saint Marys, the sisters began adding helpers too – nurses increased to eleven from the original four, and two Rochester girls were hired as maids.

W.W. now felt more free to indulge his non-medical interests. The Farmers' Alliance nominated him in '90 for a four-year term in the Minnesota State Senate, and two months later, the Democrats nominated him too, which assured his election. As Senator Mayo, he sponsored three major bills – two to regulate railroads, and one to regulate medicine – but none passed. He also shared sponsorship of a law which regulated unfair grain-grading practices. This bill did pass, so W.W. succeeded in helping farmers at least this much.

W.W. had provided wise and pacific counsel during the early years of Saint Marys Hospital, which was highly effective, but when he stood to give a political speech, he couldn't resist releasing what he called "a dynamite bombshell." He described one of these, quoting from memory his speech to the Minnesota Senate on January 17, '92, in a letter to Edith Graham: "I wish I could stop hurting folks, but then there is nothing but a pitchfork will go through some people's hides."

Senator Dean was asking for a tax on farmers to benefit the Republican party, which W.W. disliked. He compared the Republicans to Judas and the poor farmer to "Christ…crucified," explaining, "The money to pay these unnecessary expenses for party purposes cannot be swept from the streets. To get it, you must go down deep into the farmers' pockets and with wheat at 43 cents per bushel…, you will have to go so deep into his pocket you will be likely to pull out his bread and butter along with the few coins which are left. It is the labor of the farmer that makes us all great. His ardent toil makes your gold from the soil….

"I am now ready to vote on Senator Dean's motion. Let us have a chaplain at once, that Divine Providence may watch over us. Let us have the ministrations from the Gospels so that our Republican friends may be impressed with the fear of God in their souls before any more business shall be done…. I shall vote against this resolution."

The following year, W.W. again wrote Edith Graham from St. Paul, saying, "This has not been a very interesting week in the Senate." The upcoming World's Fair in Chicago was the topic of discussion. Senator Ignatius Donnelly spoke on it, and W.W. also, though he did not mention the substance of either man's remarks. Closing the letter, he said affectionately, "Now what a pack of nonsense I have written you. You must take it home, and some night when you cannot sleep, read it, or commence it, and you will be asleep in one moment. Love to you and [to] all good night. W.W. M."

The doctor had by now made friends with the gifted orator Senator Ignatius Donnelly, who shared his devotion to farmers' welfare. Donnelly had, just the year before, drawn up the platform for a third political party friendly to farmers, the People's Party, and run for Vice President of the United States under its banner. One issue he fought for was controlling rates charged farmers for railroad and warehouse use, an issue dear to Mayo's heart. It was through Donnelly that W.W. had been able to join the Farmers' Alliance in the first place, after proving to him that he was a farmer. When Donnelly endorsed Mayo's right to be in the Farmers' Alliance, he in effect empowered Mayo to be elected to the Minnesota Senate, as a Farmers' and Democrat candidate.

J. J. Hill of St. Paul renewed his friendship with Mayo about this time. They had first met in 1860, when both men worked on Minnesota River steamboats. Now one of the wealthiest men in the state, Hill had built the Great Northern Railroad, which reached Puget Sound, Washington, from St. Paul in 1893. W.W. went up to St. Paul for the big celebration of this event and met Jim Hill at his home. They recognized each other. Shaking Hill's hand, Mayo said, "You are the old Jim Hill on the River."

Hill answered, "And you are the little Dr. Mayo on the

Portrait of Dr. William W. Mayo at about age 73

Photo by permission of Mayo Foundation for Medical Education and Research.
All rights reserved.

Louise Wright Mayo

Photo by permission of Mayo Foundation for Medical Education and Research. All rights reserved.

River." They then went off together, to talk of old times.

When W.W. was not in St. Paul doing Senate business, he continued seeing patients in Rochester, both at Saint Marys Hospital and in the Mayo office in town. The fact that he was now in his seventies didn't slow him down.

He liked to travel to observe surgeons at work. His sons established a travel pattern early – one of them visited surgical centers in the spring, the other in the fall, so that one brother was always on duty at Saint Marys Hospital. W.W. liked traveling with his younger son.

In November, '92, Dr. Charlie wrote the popular Miss Graham from Chicago; his father was with him. Charlie said they rose at four to visit Dr. [Nicholas] Senn at St. Joseph's Hospital. In the afternoon they watched him operating at Presbyterian Hospital, and in the evening, they went to a play. "Father goes everywhere with me," Charlie said.

Four days later, Charlie wrote Edith again: "We are having a very good time here yet. Each day we spend from 5 to 6 hours with Dr. Senn. He has taken quite a fancy to us. We are invited to go with him on Monday to the Practitioners' Club, have a banquet and general big time."

Over the winter of '92-'93, Dr. Charlie fell in love with Edith Graham, and in February, he proposed to her. Charlie was now 27, Edith had just turned 26. They were married April 5 in the Graham family home in Rochester. The Reverend W.W. Fowler of Calvary Episcopal Church performed the ceremony, which the *Rochester Post* called "one of the neatest and at the same time one of the most quiet home weddings that has occurred in some time."

Following the ceremony, W.W.'s oldest grandchild, Daisy Berkman, played the wedding march on the Grahams' piano just before the family served "an elaborate supper." The reporter predicted, "The happy couple deserve and will receive all of prosperity and connubial bliss that can fall to the lot of mortal."

Immediately after the wedding meal, Dr. Charlie and Edith left on the evening train for New York and other eastern cities, where they spent their eight-week honeymoon touring surgical centers. When they returned to Rochester, they moved right in with Dr. Will and Hattie on College Street, while their own home, an exact replica of Will and Hattie's, was being built next door.

The Grahams managed to produce Edith's serene wedding in the midst of vexing events in Rochester which might have distracted them all. A rival hospital had opened and was threatening to destroy Saint Marys. Bigotry against Catholics, which had seemed to abate, came back in full force after 1890, a negative reaction to increasing numbers of Catholic immigrants in America.

The American Protective Association, a secret society dedicated to promoting Protestant institutions and working against those of Catholics, grew rapidly in the Middle West. Being secret, the extent of A.P.A. involvement in Rochester in the early '90s is uncertain, but it is probably one of the reasons why several homeopathic physicans, led by Dr. W.A. Allen, decided to remodel a house on Line Street near the river and open it as a hospital friendly to Protestants. Riverside Hospital has been called "an institution that Protestants and patriots could enter without doing outrage to their convictions by furthering an agency of the hated and alien Catholic Church."

The *Rochester Post* wrote an enthusiastic article, making it clear that Saint Marys Hospital held no privileged place in their hearts. "The new Riverside Hospital is now nearly ready for occupancy and is one of the most complete of its kind in the northwest.... Dr. W.A. Allen has had an experience of about 30 years and has already one of the largest medical practices in the northwest.... The Riverside Hospital is an institution of which this city may well be proud, and Drs. Allen and Granger deserve much credit for their efforts in establishing so excellent a hospital."

Apparently unworried, Senator Mayo set off in early May, '93, with another Minnesota senator, Jay LaDu, to attend the World's Fair in Chicago, where W.W. was the official surgeon from his home state. This was the Columbian Exposition, an event which attracted nearly seven million people during its months of operation. Here Nikola Tesla conducted spectacular demonstrations of a new form of power, electricity, ushering in an age of technological innovation which W.W. enthusiastically welcomed. Tesla introduced AC power at the Chicago fair, lighting the various displays with it.

W.W. wrote later of the fair, "I think it was one of the grandest events of the last century.... It was a great school on the whole, on the questions of industry, and has apparently stimulated the whole world toward general advancement."

What he especially liked was the religious tolerance he witnessed in Chicago, contrasting greatly to the current bigotry against Catholics in Rochester: "We all met together in common as brothers and sisters of the human race.... Men who had hatred for each other came together and discussed their ideas of religion and of God in a spirit of fairness.... So if we did not Christianize the whole world, we have humanized it, making all more tolerant of each other's opinions. In this alone the Chicago World's Fair has done more good to people than all the missionaries that ever existed."

W.W. did not mention whether he tasted a hamburger or cream of wheat for the first time, or rode on the new Ferris wheel. These were introduced at the fair.

While in Chicago, the Mayos purchased an up-to-date set of glazed enamel operating room equipment and brought it back for use in surgery at Saint Marys Hospital.

In 1894, Edith Graham Mayo's brother Dr. Christopher Graham, 38, became the first intern at Saint Marys. He had earlier trained as a veterinarian; then, encouraged by the brothers Mayo, he earned his doctor's degree at the University of Pennsylvania. Dr. Will said that Graham was "one of the keenest diagnosticians I have ever known.... I would rather have his opinion on the medical aspects of a surgical case than of any man I ever had the privilege of working with."

Even with rivalry from Riverside Hospital, the Mayos' patient load at Saint Marys kept growing, so they asked the Franciscan sisters to finance a hospital addition. Encouraged by Sister Joseph Dempsey, now hospital superintendent, the sisters awarded a contract to builders for $17,338.95. As with the original hospital, the plans for this building were drawn up under W.W.'s direction. On April 4, '94, the addition was dedicated in a ceremony attracting 800 guests. It enlarged the hospital's bed capacity from 40 beds to 70.

At this time, Riverside Hospital was at its height of popularity, and the Mayos were out of favor with local anti-Catholic people. When asked to perform surgery on two Presbyterian patients at Riverside, Dr. Will and Dr. Charlie, with their father's approval, refused to do it. They said they would "never hold the knife outside of Saint Marys Hospital." Because of their refusal, Protestant clergymen vigorously criticized the Doctors Mayo from their pulpits.

W.W. was unruffled by this opposition; in fact, he and his sons ignored it. At the dedication ceremony, as chairman of the event, W.W. gave a speech praising the Sisters of Saint Francis for their vision, energy, and sacrifice in building and maintaining the hospital: "The building has sprung up and developed into its present magnificent proportions almost without your knowing it," he said to the listening audience. "To many of our people it is as a grand and useful gift dropped from the clouds. It has cost you not one cent of money, not one hour of labor, not one moment of anxiety, and there it stands without a peer in the Northwest.… Its equipments are surpassed by no hospital in the United States. The Sisters of Saint Francis have done this for us out of their goodness and charity, and I thank you in their name for your appreciation of their efforts."

In his speech, W.W. especially praised Mother Alfred, who had retired from hospital work and moved to St. Paul. He told in detail how she had first presented the hospital idea to him, and how he had resisted the idea at first: "She was, I think, a wonderful woman, so full of hope and energy."

Playing to his audience, he remarked, "I cannot pride myself on my faculty of hope, but I believe I have the name of being a very mild manner of man."

Laughter followed this remark, so he continued, "I am the mildest man in the world, provided I have my own way, and in passing along through the world, I have had my own way pretty thoroughly, and where I don't get it, I fight for it." Laughter greeted this explanation too.

W.W. concluded his speech with a totally irrelevant, but, he hoped, useful suggestion – the city should institute a public works program to give employment to "a great many men willing to labor and even asking for employment [who] are to be met about the streets, idle and needy."

By the summer of '95, Riverside Hospital was losing money. Its success rate in healing patients through surgical intervention did not compare to the Saint Marys rate, and patients stopped electing to have their surgery done there. In mid-September, Dr. Allen, founder of Riverside, announced that he was moving his practice to St. Paul, and the hospital, opened three years earlier, closed its doors on December 17. Mysteriously, Allen was back in six months, practicing medicine in Rochester again.

Many years later, Sister Joseph Dempsey was asked what caused the opposition to Saint Marys Hospital. She answered mildly, "The people of Rochester were strongly religious though of various sects; Catholic ascendency was not desired by them."

"What did you attribute this to?" asked her interviewer.

"The earnestness of their faith in their own churches," she responded. "The Mayos and their highly intelligent friends allayed and finally effaced it.… [It was finally overcome through] the splendid influence of the Mayos [and] … the good work of the Sisters.… Within three or four years, there was no trace of it."

Chapter 13
Travels and Celebrations

Thomas Spillane praised Mayo "not so much ... because he established Saint Marys Hospital, ... but rather that he was a man, a genuine, hearty man, whose entire forgetfulness of self in the assistance of others made him friends, friends to whom he was a counselor and adviser, a man whom all respected and loved."

from the Rochester Post and Record

W.W. at age 77 was still the first of five doctors listed under the Mayo practice in the *Olmsted County Democrat*. They were, in all, Mayo, Mayo, Mayo, Stinchfield, and Graham. Every afternoon between 1:30 and 4 p.m., W.W. saw patients in his downtown office.

In '97, the Mayos purchased their first ambulance to carry patients to Saint Marys Hospital. It was a horse and buggy, like the one W.W. had seen at Bellevue Hospital in 1869.

During these years, the doctor brothers and their wives experienced the grief of four infant deaths. Hattie and Dr. Will lost three babies – Worrall, Helen Phoebe, and William Damon – all before their first birthdays. Edith and Dr. Charlie's daughter Margaret died when she was five days old.

It was, then, with great joy that both couples welcomed healthy daughters born within two days of one another in 1897. Edith gave birth first, on January 23, to Dorothy. Hattie followed on January 25, giving

W.W. Mayo about 1897

Photo by permission of Mayo Foundation for Medical Education and Research. All rights reserved.

birth to Phoebe Gertrude, named for Dr. Will's two sisters. Hattie and Will's other daughter, Carrie Louise, was now ten, old enough to help care for her little sister. To make life especially enjoyable, the two families were next door neighbors, Dr. Charlie and Edith living in "the red house" on College Street beside Dr. Will and Hattie's house, which was identical except for color. It was "the yellow house."

W.W., as well as Louise, enjoyed the grandchildren. He built a close relationship with Carrie and, when he was away from home, wrote to her in tones appropriate to a child: "All children['s] lives should be made happy and filled 'chock' full of sunshine.... Sometimes children cast a cloud over their own sunshine.... These black clouds come over ... when they get cross, and 'do things they ought not to do.' Then the little bright fairies of good sense and good manners leave them. They take away with them all the beautiful and bright flowers that belong to life.... Then ... the bad fairies come in. They are named Sulky, Talk Back, and Cry, and ugly Talk Back is the worst of all."

When he was 79, while climbing a ladder to check on a shed roof, W.W. suffered what might have been a serious accident. He was almost atop the ladder when "it slipped and precipitated him upon the ground with considerable force." A *Rochester Post* reporter said the doctor "sustained bad bruises on his face and neck, and was badly shaken," but the injuries were not permanent. The writer concluded, "The doctor is strong and capable of resisting much hardship, but had the accident happened to one less inured to hard blows, it might have been a serious affair."

In 1898, two grandsons were born, Dr. Charlie's son Charles William (Mayo), and Trude's son John Mayo Berkman. As the boys grew, Chuck and Johnny became fast friends.

Because she was lonely in the country when W.W. traveled, Louise moved into town and was living with Trude and her family in a new house on Franklin Street, built on the site of the original Mayo home. W.W. often stayed there too. It was natural, then, that both grandparents developed an especially close friendship with Trude's son Johnny over the years.

The Mayos maintained and continued to enjoy their farm home also. Their granddaughter Daisy Berkman, now 20, liked to go out to the farm to browse in W.W.'s library, which numbered 3,000 volumes.

About this time, the Mayo brothers, because of the extraordinary success of their surgical practice at Saint Marys Hospital, were, in Dr. Will's words, "now coming to the idea of a greater institution." They made several decisions to promote this possibility.

For one, they decided to do what they could to make Rochester a city which would attract the caliber of doctors and other medical persons with whom they wished to work. They began to see the importance to the Clinic of good schools, parks, and places of amusement.

Another decision involved their handling of money. By 1898, both brothers had paid for their homes and were carrying enough life insurance to protect their families. With a total in their joint bank account of slightly less than $30,000, they decided to spend ten percent of their earnings each year to improve Rochester. They turned over to Burt Eaton, a capable lawyer and businessman, whatever money they earned in excess of what they needed to live. (They purposed at this time to begin living on half their incomes.) Asking Eaton to invest the money safely for them, they began building a fund which, Dr. Will said, "should be returned to the people in a way to do them the greatest benefit."

"We never took back a dollar of principal or interest," Dr. Will said, "and in a little less than twenty years, the total fund amounted to one and a half million dollars."

The impetus for this saving and investing program came from lessons W.W. had taught his sons. According to Dr. Will, "Father was looked on as a radical, but he believed that if a man had greater physical or mental powers or superior opportunities, he owed proportionately more to his fellows. We had been thoroughly infused with that doctrine during our youth."

W.W., meantime, was busy traveling. He went to St. Paul in January '99, and joined a group which included Governor Lind. They went on to St. Louis, Missouri, to help plan the 1903 Grand Centennial celebration of the Louisiana Purchase. The *Rochester Post* reported that in St. Louis, W.W. was elected to represent the state at the fair as Vice President of Minnesota: "We are glad to note that Dr. Mayo was recognized. The honor is deserved and could not have been better conferred."

W.W.'s comment was, "I never had a more pleasant time in my life."

Less than two months later he was traveling with Charlie. The two men visited Dr. Alfred Ochsner at Chicago's Augustana Hospital and watched him operate on March 15; in the evening they dined with him at his home. The next day they observed Dr. Christian Fenger at work. In Baltimore, Maryland, Charlie observed surgeries by Drs. William S. Halsted and Harvey Cushing at Johns Hopkins Hospital, but, as Charlie reported to Edith, "Father had other business." The two men saw "a fine play" with Anna Russell, and another night they went to a boxing match.

By March 24, they were in Philadelphia, observing surgeries. Charlie wrote, "Father is going to New York to stay a short time and then possibly to Boston, he says. I rather hate to see him go so far alone now, but would not say anything."

His trip completed, two months later W.W. celebrated his 80th birthday at home.

Asked the date when his father retired from medical practice, Dr. Charlie said, "He never did actually retire." But about this time, ten years after the hospital opened, W.W. officially stopped seeing patients. *Souvenir of Saint Mary's Hospital*, published after his death, tells that he gave up "routine professional duties to devote himself in a more social way to the patients and their friends and to the visiting physicians."

Each morning he was in Rochester, W.W. visited, without fail, every single patient in the hospital. He checked on the diagnosis of each person and the treatment ordered by the doctor, and if he did not believe the patient was progressing well, he offered his advice to the attending physician. In the afternoons, he received callers in his office, near the front door of the Mayo downtown clinic. He welcomed old friends, famous people, visiting doctors and surgeons. "He was affable and he had leisure. Every one who wished to see him was welcome, particularly those who were interested in Saint Marys Hospital and his two sons. His health and vigor were remarkable."

Also in 1899, Dr. Will became a member of the American Surgical Association, which was, he said, "the proudest day of my life. I sat in that august assembly, one of the youngest men to achieve the distinction." (Will was 38.)

By now the Clinic was drawing near the end of what Dr. Will later called "the developmental period." The brothers had agreed from the beginning that Will should be head administrator, since they did not consider the leadership position something that could be shared, and Dr. Will's personality was much better suited to administrative work than Dr. Charlie's. In the words of Dr. Charlie's son, "Father didn't care for the executive end of things. It never appealed to him.... Uncle Will was the executive, the man with the drive, the man who put the ideas through, though they sometimes came from Father.... You can't ever have two executives. One person has to have the final say-so. In this case, that was Uncle Will."

Did Charlie feel slighted by this arrangement? His son said, "No, I don't think Father ever resented Uncle Will's dominant position. They really got on remarkably well together. They might argue out the best way to do things, but fundamentally, they always agreed." Dr. Chuck said that all "major and serious decisions" were always discussed between the brothers until there was complete agreement.

In November, 1900, the Mayo practice moved to larger facilities across the street in the new Masonic Temple building. W.W.'s name was no longer listed with the other doctors, though he continued his friendly visits with interested people in his own Clinic office. The practice was now Mayo, Mayo, Stinchfield, Graham, Millet, and Booker. Dr. Melvin Millet had been hired for his special interest in gastric problems, including kidney disease. Dr. Gertrude Booker joined the Mayo practice to assist Dr. Charlie in treating diseases of the eye, ear, nose and throat. She eventually took over optometry work. (The Mayos had always sought to associate with the most qualified doctors, showing no prejudice in favor of males.)

The new office was large enough to accommodate a persistent interest of the Doctors Mayo – research. They had reception rooms, a library, a business office, consulting rooms, a dark room for "eye cases," and a small laboratory. They had hired Dr. Isabella Herb in January, 1900, as an anesthetist at the hospital and a pathologist in the Clinic lab. There Dr. Herb tested blood, urine and sputum.

Trude somehow managed to bring off a surprise party on February 2, 1901, to celebrate W.W. and Louise's golden wedding anniversary.

"Twenty-five elderly friends," according to the paper, "spent [the evening] most delightfully." At the party, "the conversation naturally drifted back to old times, the doctor and his wife telling many pleasing and touching stories of their early days in Minnesota. The company brought with them an abundance of edibles, all of which helped to make the evening more enjoyable."

Later that same year, Dr. Will did what he called "the best day's work ever done for the Clinic." Dr. Albert Plummer of Racine, 30 miles south, had called his old

Dr. Henry S. Plummer

Photo by permission of Mayo Foundation for Medical Education and Research. All rights reserved.

Dr. W. W. Mayo and Johnny Berkman in 1904

Photo courtesy of Barbara Berkman Withers

friend W.W. in consultation on a difficult case. Since W.W. was out of town, Will went instead, but, upon arriving, he found Dr. Plummer sick and unable to leave his home. Plummer asked his son Henry, 26, a graduate of Northwestern Medical School, to take his place at the patient's bedside. Dr. Henry Plummer at this time was "a slender, eager boy, dreamy appearing, full of ideas and ideals," Dr. Will said, "his thought rushing ahead of his language, which, one or two sentences behind, was attempting to keep up. He had a microscope with him."

The two doctors diagnosed the patient with pernicious anemia, using young Plummer's microscope, and on the ride home, Plummer talked about "all kinds of things about the blood, most of which I knew nothing of," said Dr. Will. When he reached home, Will told Charlie that Plummer "was needed in the Clinic and needed badly."

Within a week, they had hired him, "the best brain ever connected with the Clinic," said Will.

Dr. Plummer made good use of the little laboratory in the new Mayo offices, and, at his urging, they set another room aside for x-ray technology.

W.W. spent the summer of 1901 traveling in Italy and Spain on a leisurely ship excursion sponsored by the *Literary Digest*. He enjoyed the shipboard dinners,

Gertrude Mayo Berkman

Photo courtesy of Barbara Berkman Withers

"elegant in the extreme," and his companions – lawyers, a poet, a woman preacher. He liked the "dining room… flooded with electric lights."

In Naples he admired the milkmen, who brought their cows or goats to the customers' doors and milked the animals "while you wait."

"Everything so far," he said towards the end of his four-month trip, "has been wonderfully charming and fascinating. I wish you could get from my letters as much as I feel and dream."

Often when W.W. traveled, his good friend, the lawyer Charles C. Willson, went along, but sometimes the two men came back separately, having quarreled along the way. They returned to Rochester from a six-week trip to the Pacific Northwest in September 1902, by chance arriving within three hours of each other, though they had parted in San Francisco some weeks earlier. Mr. Willson said his dread of the Utah heat had kept him from accompanying the old doctor to Salt Lake City. According to the *Olmsted County Democrat*, "The outing was a delightful one for both, and each is satisfied that he had the better time."

A month before he turned 85, W.W. returned from a two-month tour of Mexico, California and Salt Lake City. The newspaper said, "Dr. Mayo is a little tired from his journey, but it has apparently been of real benefit to him physically."

According to a family story, passed down four generations, W.W. was thrown out of a Mexico City bullfight on this trip – for cheering the bull.

The Rochester *Post and Record* headline describing W.W.'s 85th birthday party on May 31, 1904, read: "A Fitting Tribute to a Gentleman Who Has Done so Much for the Good of Rochester." On that day, 110 gentlemen friends gathered at the Cook Hotel to honor the old doctor. They sang for him, gave speeches praising him, and ate delicious food – roast suckling pig with many side dishes, champagne, ice cream and cake, followed by coffee and cigars. The Kahler brothers (who were hosts) "certainly have reason to feel satisfied," said the paper, "…every dish being a triumph of the culinary art."

The general desire was to "in some way show the doctor that his worth, his high character, the many benefits which have accrued to Rochester from his efforts, are appreciated, and that as friends, the residents of Rochester wish him happiness and good health in his evening of life."

The first speaker, Mayor A. C. Stevenson, praised W.W. with a short poem:

Words are but breath,
But when great deeds were done,
A power abides
Tranferred from sire to sons.

"Our Irish Wit," Thomas Spillane, said Mayo was "a genuine, hearty man, whose entire forgetfulness of self in the assistance of others made him friends, friends to whom he was a counselor and adviser, a man whom all respected and loved."

W.W.'s special friend C.C. Willson presented a sterling silver three-and-a-half-pint loving cup as a symbol of the doctor's sterling worth, "protesting that it did not, and that nothing could adequately, typify the respect and esteem which they all had for him."

When W.W. was asked to speak, he was so overcome with emotion, he could say nothing, so Dr. Will and Dr.

Charlie thanked the company on his behalf. At length, W.W. did manage to say a few words to his friends. Then they sang a hearty round of "For He's a Jolly Good Fellow," and, following a toast to "Our Honored Guest," the party ended. It was, the paper said, "the most successful reception and banquet ever held in this city."

Next morning, in an effort to overcome his speechlessness the previous night, W.W. took to the *Post and Record* a hastily written item, which they published directly under their news account of the event. What troubled the old doctor was that he had received too much praise for the founding of Saint Marys Hospital; he felt the praise more properly belonged to the Sisters of Saint Francis: "It is to them that the citizens of Rochester are indebted for this grand and successful institution. This much and more I wish to say personally in behalf of these good and grand women who have their home in our midst. To me they have always been true and good sisters." He went on to explain how their confidence in him had "urged me on to higher planes of effort for the progress not only of the hospital but the whole city.

"To Mother Alfred, dead and gone to her rest, is the tribute due that she was untiring in her efforts for the benefit of humanity in general." He praised also Mother Matilda, Mother Augustine, the priests of this diocese, and "worthy Bishop Cotter."

"Now," he continued, "relieved of all active work by my sons in the hospital, what greater pleasure than to go there every morning and see the sisters' pleasant faces and receive their warm greetings to 'Father Mayo.'"

At the end of his written remarks, still emotionally moved by the birthday celebration in his "evening of life" and his memories of the sisters' goodness, W.W. broke his life-long rule of privacy on personal and religious matters. He said, "during a long intimacy with [Catholic] people, whom I highly respect, not one of them has ever asked me what religion or what church I belonged to."

Then he begged to "make a public confession under cover of the name of the great Chancellor of Germany, Prince Bismarck," who had revealed his most private thoughts shortly before death. The chancellor had said, "I never felt the need for any [religion], and therefore never had any."

Now W.W. spoke "under cover" of Bismarck in the sense that if such a prominent man could break his code of privacy when close to death, then so could he. W.W.'s faith, however, was quite unlike the chancellor's: "My own religion has been to do all the good I could to my fellow men, and as little harm as possible."

This was the faith Mayo had learned 70 years earlier, while studying under the tutor he respected as a father. John Dalton had lived out the Quaker ethic of serving God through serving other people so consistently before his young student that W.W. formed his own life in a similar mold.

W.W. Mayo stands by his horse and buggy about 1904

Photo by permission of Mayo Foundation for Medical Education and Research. All rights reserved.

Chapter 14

Last Years

The end was "quiet and peaceful, closing a life of unusual activity in the city of Rochester and state of Minnesota. Few men have passed out of the history of this city surrounded by more loyal friends, a wider acquaintanceship, a more useful life, and whose death will be more mourned."

The Post and Record, March 6, 1911

W.W. was on the road again in early July, 1904, as a delegate from Minnesota to the Democratic national convention in St. Louis. The delegates attacked trusts and monopolies in their platform and selected Judge Alton B. Parker for Presidential nominee. Parker lost in November to Theodore Roosevelt.

When John A. Johnson won the Minnesota governorship in the same election, W.W. traveled to Johnson's hometown, St. Peter, and rode as guest of honor in the victory parade, thrilled that a Democrat was governor for the first time since the Civil War.

Louise never accompanied her husband on his many travels. She was not addicted to sight-seeing, as he was. The sight which pleased her most was the faces of her grandchildren, with whom she spent many happy hours. She had 11 grandchildren now — Trude's five, Will's two, and Charlie's four. Little Edith was born (and named for her mother) in 1900, and Joseph Graham, named for Edith's father, was born in 1902.

Louise's oldest grandchild, Daisy Louise Berkman, married Dr. Henry Plummer on October 4, 1904, the "slender, eager boy" Dr. Will had hired three years before.

Saint Marys Hospital was now the site of more surgical cases each year than any other hospital in the United States, even Johns Hopkins. The Mayos continued to develop their interest in research, and they added to their staff Dr. Louis B. Wilson, an assistant professor of pathology at the University of Minnesota. "With his rare ability as an organizer," Dr. Will said, he "solved many problems for us which by nature and training we had been unable to set right ourselves.... Louis Wilson [was] tremendously brilliant. I have met few men his intellectual equal."

Dr. Wilson's value to the Clinic was immediately apparent. Within weeks of coming to Rochester in 1905, he solved an important problem which Dr. Will put to him: "I wish you pathologists would find a way to tell us surgeons whether a growth is cancer or not while the patient is still on the table."

Using knowledge he had picked up studying botany, Dr. Wilson used methylene blue to stain fresh tissue, after first freezing it on his lab windowsill. Since this was January in Minnesota, the freezing was quick. By dying the quick-frozen tissue, Wilson was able to report to Drs. Will and Charlie within five minutes, sometimes less, whether excised tissue was malignant or not. This fast diagnosis of surgical problems through tissue analysis has become a distinctive feature of the Mayo Clinic.

To care for their burgeoning load of surgical

Dr. Will at age 44, taken for his presidency of American Medical Association, 1905. This photo he inscribed to Eda Nichols.

Photo by permission of Mayo Foundation for Medical Education and Research. All rights reserved.

patients, Dr. Will and Dr. Charlie told Sister Joseph in 1905 that they needed a fourth addition to Saint Marys Hospital. She said she would pray about it.

Next morning she told them, "God did not approve of expansion just yet."

Dr. Will disagreed. "That's odd," he said. "Charlie and I consulted God too, and He told us to go ahead and build."

In time, the sisters agreed to build again.

In the spring of 1905, at age 39, Dr. Charlie became president of Minnesota State Medical Society. Several months later, Dr. Will, at age 44, was unanimously elected president of American Medical Association. The Philadelphia doctor who nominated him called him "one of the ablest, one of the cleanest, one of the best loved of the western profession," adding, "living in a small town, he has made it the surgical Mecca of America."

Dr. Will was the first Minnesota doctor to be honored with the A.M.A. presidency. Accepting the presidency the following summer, he revealed his attitude towards his profession, learned from his father: "To realize that one has devoted himself to the most holy of all callings, that without thought of reward he has alleviated the sufferings of the sick and added to the length and usefulness of human life, is a source of satisfaction that money cannot buy."

Trude's second child, Martha May Berkman, married Ralph Van Blethen, a lawyer, in June, 1906, and moved to northern Minnesota, the first in the family circle to leave Rochester. Besides W.W. and Louise, the family now numbered twenty – three children and their spouses, twelve grandchildren (including young Louise, born to Charlie and Edith in 1905), and two of their spouses, Dr. Plummer and Mr. Blethen.

Louise was 80. She had established Rochester as the family home 42 years earlier, and she didn't like any of her family moving away. Martha Blethen said Louise's letters "show clearly how her heart yearned over me."

Louise wrote Martha news tidbits. Charlie, the first person in Rochester to own a car, had now bought "two autos from the East. One is a fine runabout and the other is large enough to hold eight, I think…. It was fine looking and made quite a showing up the street." Charlie and W.W. went to an Irish banquet "in honor of Father Riordan who has been saving souls … for the last quarter century here."

Louise's longest story was about Martha's little brother, Johnny Berkman. He had eaten lightly at supper and then "he is off out of sight. At eight o'clock the band was in the park and popcorn hot in plenty and John without a cent." The little boy begged from his Mama, but she had no change, "and his tears rolled down his cheeks and still no nickle." Louise remembered a dime upstairs, retrieved it, and slipped it quietly to the boy. He came back from the park later with two bags of hot popcorn.

W.W. was probably indulging the boy at this time too. Johnny at age seven was the last person his 87-year-old grandfather mentored. W.W. often took Johnny along in the horse and buggy to visit people in the country who weren't patients anymore, but would still discuss their health with the old doctor. In this way, he taught Johnny to love medicine as, 35 years earlier, he had taught Will and Charlie. John Berkman grew up to be a doctor of internal medicine at the Mayo Clinic, a person so skilled in helping young women with anorexia nervosa that other doctors asked him how he did it. Part of his secret was the attitude of intelligent concern he learned as a boy from the old doctor.

Some people say W.W. was irascible in his later years; others disagree. His grandson Chuck Mayo wrote, "I won't forget how [Joe and I] hid whenever we decently could from Grandfather, whose good nature in his declining years was in scant supply and did not extend itself to encompass a tumble of hearty grandchildren."

Johnny Berkman said that Chuck "just didn't know [Grandfather]." Johnny said W.W. "was really kindly and genial" except when it came to certain matters he disliked, "like whistling or chewing gum." Johnny lived with W.W. and knew him better.

Was W.W. more mellow in old age than in his youth? He himself said he was. At age 87 he wrote this note to the Sisters of Saint Francis: "The gracious privilege is not often accorded mortal man to live to witness the accomplishments, the culmination of his best wishes, his ideals. That this happiness has come to me after many days, fills my heart with the deepest gratitude and peace. Of me it can be truly said: Every yesterday was a vision of hope. Every today is a dream of contentment."

In February, 1907, W.W. returned from a two-month tour of Mexico and the Southwest with C. C. Willson. Weeks later, on March first, he left Rochester again on another ambitious trip. James J. Hill, "the empire builder of the Northwest," planned the journey for him aboard his Great Northern Railway and his ship the *Minnesota*.

"J. J. Hill and I have been warm friends since the early days," W.W. said, "and when he discovered that I contemplated a trip to Japan, [he] asked me to go as his guest."

Mr. Hill also sent a man along to look after the doctor en route. W.W. was so vigorous at this time that no one questioned his going. In Japan he was entertained by Baron Takaki, Surgeon General of the Japanese army. (Doctor Takaki, who had visited Mayo Clinic the previous summer, was a charter member of the International Surgeon's Club, organized during his visit.) For three weeks the baron arranged receptions for Dr. Mayo. The *Olmsted County Democrat* said "the venerable physician was the recipient of so many favors and such boundless hospitality that it is no wonder he feels his heart swell in gratitude toward his new-found friends across the sea."

W.W. continued on to China before returning home in mid-June. He was crossing the Pacific aboard the *Minnesota* on his 88th birthday, May 31. James Hill had given instructions for a birthday celebration in his honor.

The chef baked an enormous cake and presented it to W.W. with 88 lighted candles, which pleased him greatly.

At home, when W.W.'s many friends questioned him about Japan and China, he referred them to his wife, who had read, during his trip, every book on those countries she could find. "I don't know," he would say. "Ask Louise."

The First Baptist Church of Rochester held its 50th anniversary celebration on August 22, 1907, and invited W.W. to speak. Louise later proudly described the event: "He got up – straight and strong as he was at 30 – and talked. About the Indian wars? The hard times? The rough days? No, indeed! He didn't mention the past. He told them what they would be doing 50 years from now – talked water-power, electricity, more and better automobiles, good roads to run them on, and airships. That was the Doctor."

On July 19, 1907, "Mayos' Clinic" began registering its patients by number. Five thousand people registered that year. The Clinic was the first place in the world to store medical data on each patient in closed packets, keeping them "in perpetuity" and indexing them, creating a valuable system for research purposes.

Trude's third child, Helen Phoebe Berkman, married Dr. Edward Starr Judd in 1908. He was a local doctor who had assisted Dr. Charlie in surgery and who so excelled in it that at age 26, he was put in charge of his own Clinic surgical section, the first person besides the brothers with this responsibility.

Dr. Will said of him, "He rapidly developed into one of the best surgeons I have ever known. Good judgment, fine technique, courageous, conscientious, and untiring."

In 1909, W.W. observed his 90th birthday shortly after the birth of his last grandchild, Esther, to Dr. Charlie and Edith.

One day that summer, W.W. went out to his farm to check on what his tenant farmer was doing. Because the doctor foresaw the coming need for a cheap automobile fuel, he was especially interested in a machine at the farm, operated by a little gasoline engine, designed to make ethanol from animal and vegetable waste.

Suddenly, the engine stopped – W.W. thought because a corncob got stuck in it. He forgot that, though the engine had stopped, the wheel inside would keep moving from its own momentum. Impatiently, he stuck his left hand in the machine to free the corncob. The revolving wheel struck his left hand, crushing the soft parts and breaking the bones of his hand and his middle and ring fingers.

The tenant farmer rushed W.W. to the Clinic, where Dr. Charlie bandaged and splinted the injured hand. Next morning, W.W., dissatisfied, asked the hired man to rebandage and resplint it the way he wanted. When the bones didn't heal properly, Dr. Charlie amputated the two broken fingers. The old doctor began wearing a black glove on that hand, cotton stuffed into the glove

W.W. Mayo in Japan, 1907

Photo by permission of Mayo Foundation for Medical Education and Research. All rights reserved.

fingers where his own fingers were missing.

From the time of his accident, W.W. was never free from pain, which gradually wore away his strength. Dr. Charlie operated on him twice more, to remove his left hand at the wrist, and to remove part of his forearm. During his last year, W.W. developed nephritis,

Drs. Mayo in 1910, from left, Dr. Will, Dr. W.W., and Dr. Charlie

Photo by permission of Mayo Foundation for Medical Education and Research. All rights reserved.

inflammation of the kidneys, from constant nervous stress. He occasionally took morphine to relieve his suffering.

Dr. Will's daughter Phoebe, now 12, attended Central School across from where her grandparents lived on Franklin Street. At Dr. Will's urging, she began stopping every afternoon after school to see W.W. She later said, "I enjoyed doing this, and he always gave me a big kiss, which tickled because of his moustache."

On February 2, W.W. and Louise observed their 60th wedding anniversary very quietly. They were the longest-married couple in Olmsted County.

Five weeks later, on Monday, March 6, 1911, William Worrall Mayo died peacefully at ten minutes before four in the morning, in the Berkman/Mayo home. It was two months before his 92nd birthday. Dr. Henry Plummer, his attending physician, gave the cause of death as chronic nephritis, but the cause of nephritis was the terrible accident to his left hand more than a year and a half earlier.

"The end was a gradual decline up to the time of dissolution," said Rochester's *Post and Record*. "Few men have passed out of the history of this city surrounded by more loyal friends, a wider acquaintanceship, a more useful life, and whose death will be more mourned."

His funeral was the next day. "The presence of many friends and a profusion of floral tributes evidenced the sentiment of the living toward the departed," according to *Rochester Daily Bulletin*. The rector of Calvary Church, Reverend W.W. Fowler, read Episcopalian funeral rites in a ceremony which was conducted without eulogy or music, at the doctor's request.

After the service, six physicians bore the casket from the Berkman/Mayo home, one of them Augustus W. Stinchfield, retired from the Mayo practice. Members of Olmsted County Medical Society, which the doctor helped organize 43 years earlier, were honorary pall bearers. W.W.'s body was interred in Oakwood Cemetery in the Mayo plot, near the graves of his daughter Phoebe and five of his grandchildren (Dr. Will's and Hattie's three babies, Dr. Charlie and Edith's baby Margaret and their daughter Rachel, who had died at age two).

Rochester's mayor ordered all public schools closed early on the afternoon of his funeral. City banks also closed. Flags were flown at half mast, and, during the funeral service, which began at 2:30, all businesses and offices of the city ceased doing business.

Sister Joseph Dempsey spoke privately an epitaph commemorating the man she had known well for more than 20 years. She was now 55 and head administrator of Saint Marys Hospital as well as Dr. Will's first assistant in surgery. Of W.W., she said: "He was an alert, able, earnest humanitarian, worthy of all the glory his sons have added to his name."

Chapter 15

The Legacy of Louise and William Worrall Mayo

"The biggest thing Will and I ever did was to pick the father and mother we had."
Dr. Charles Horace Mayo

Soon after W.W.'s funeral, a group of his friends, headed by Burt Eaton, began collecting money for a statue of him to stand in Mayo Park. The family asked that no one contribute more than one dollar.

The Mayos' Clinic-Saint Marys Hospital enterprise was growing fast. Mayo staff in 1912, including support persons, numbered 110. Saint Marys Hospital had grown to a 300-bed capacity and six operating rooms with 5,835 patients that year and 6,835 the next year. Six doctors were in partnership – Dr. Will, Dr. Charlie, and Drs. Christopher Graham, Henry S. Plummer, E. Starr Judd, and Donald C. Balfour. All were related to the Mayo family, but no Clinic policy had ever favored family: Drs. Stinchfield and Millet had been partners, and they were not family. The policy was always to hire the best person possible to fill a Clinic need.

Once a person was hired, he or she was expected to emulate the brothers as they followed their father's three-fold approach to medicine: patient care, research, and education working together, so that the needs of the patient came first. The brothers were still working long hours, as their father had always done.

Dr. Will said, "We never brought a man in as an assistant, but as a colleague and an equal. We were the first to reach the hospital in the morning and the last to stop work at night. We never took vacations except those incidental to travel for knowledge."

About a doctor's continuing need for education, Dr. Charlie commented: "Whenever some new thing in surgery or medicine came up ... we would go out to see them do it, to see if it was really as it was written up. Some things that read to look pretty good are not much, for the man in his enthusiasm forgot to put down the hard luck side of it. So we were always going."

They were always teaching too. Both brothers had been rudely treated in their youth by some doctors in other cities. This bad treatment made them resolve to be courteous when their turn came to teach others. "Will and I said that if we ever had anything, we would fix it so that every doctor coming could see and have everything explained to him, and there would be no charge to the doctor...," said Dr. Charlie. "If we had any operations that were unusual, we would send word out."

Like their father, the sons enjoyed teaching. Harry

William Worrall Mayo reclining

Photo by permission of Mayo Foundation for Medical Education and Research. All rights reserved.

Four generations in 1912. From the top, clockwise: Martha Berkman Blethen, Gertrude Mayo Berkman, Joan Blethen, Louise Mayo

Photo courtesy of Olmsted County Historical Society

Harwick, who knew them well, said, "Perhaps second only to their own surgery, both men found their greatest satisfaction in teaching. Busy as they always were, both could always somehow find time to give wise and sympathetic counsel to the young on personal and professional problems."

Less than a year after W.W.'s death, his son-in-law, Dr. David Berkman, died of cancer on February 13, 1912, at the age of 61, leaving Trude a widow at age 58. Their son Johnny was only 13.

Trude took a trip to Cuba to try to recover from her loss. While she was gone, Louise wrote Martha Blethen about Johnny's activities. One night he was away from home, staying with his cousin Chuck, "and I missed him so much.... I am so old and feel so uncertain."

Dr. Will encouraged Phoebe to pay extra attention to her grandmother. Every Sunday, Phoebe used to go with her father to visit Louise. Grandmother Mayo would be sitting in her rocking chair reading, although her eyesight was poor. Beside her, always, was a small table holding a cup of coffee.

One day there was no coffee. Will said, "Ma, where is your coffee?"

Louise answered, "Will, I have decided that drinking as much coffee as I have been drinking is a bad habit, and I am not going to let any habit get the better of me."

She never drank coffee again.

Phoebe admired Louise and called her "a real pioneer woman, with a very strong character.... I think Father inherited from her, as well as from Grandfather, his strong character, his determination and perseverance in following any path he set for himself."

Another of Louise's grandchildren, Chuck Mayo, admired her too, though he was less admiring of W.W.: "In my opinion, [Grandmother] deserves an honored place in the family history. Her life was a long trial and her patient endurance of my grandfather's moods and disappearances was nothing short of heroic."

Others have also said that Louise's marriage was one of patient endurance. This was not, however, her own view. Three years after W.W. died, Mrs. William Brown Meloney, in her interview with Louise, wrote, "I wish it were possible to put in type just the way 'The Doctor' came from her firm lips. Capitalizing the pronoun *him* might convey a faint idea of the way she spoke of the husband who, [three] years ago, died in harness."

Meloney continued, "I expected that she would speak first of her two sons. But not this mother. 'I think Dr. Mayo, my husband, was the greatest man – the most useful man – I ever knew,' she said.... 'And I often think ... that the secret of The Doctor's usefulness was that he never looked backward. Looking backward is not a good thing for one's soul.... The Doctor thought nothing about the past, very little about the present, but always about the future.' She paused and then, with a really wonderful smile, added: 'To be happy, my dear, never look backward. Never!'"

Louise, as she spoke to Meloney, sat gazing out the window of Trude's home at a new, impressive building next door. It stood on the site of the Franklin Street house in which her husband had died. Her sons bought the house from Trude, to whom W.W. deeded it, and had it torn down. Then they built the Mayo Clinic Building on the site. Now the fountains in the lobby played directly over the spot where Charlie was born.

Two years of careful planning, supervised by the perfectionist Dr. Plummer, resulted in this building – the first in the world to house in one structure a private group practice dedicated to patient care, research, and education. On the first four floors, the building held a cheerful lobby, business offices, reception desks, examining rooms, a pathology lab, x-ray rooms and dark rooms, an auditorium for teaching, a library, art studio, and workshops. The top floor was reserved for experimental labs where research animals lived, and on the roof, runways for their exercise.

The first telephone intercom system in America was designed by Plummer so that the doctors and staff could communicate within the building. An ingenious system of lights and a telegraph ticker system made it easy to call doctors wherever they were needed. The medical record packets, begun in 1907, could be moved in minutes from their storage place in the basement file room to any doctor who requested them, thanks to a conveyor belt system Plummer also designed.

It was with the opening of the Mayo Building on March 6, 1914, – three years to the day after the old doctor's death – that the practice became officially "Mayo Clinic."

About this time, the brothers got the idea of changing from a partnership to a corporation. The idea originated with President George E. Vincent of the University of Minnesota. He wished to affiliate the university's new medical graduate school with Mayo Clinic, but to do so, he needed the Clinic research and education functions organized into a corporate entity. Dr. Will, a member of the university Board of Regents, agreed with the wisdom of this plan. On February 8, 1915, incorporation papers were signed by the Mayo partners, creating a new entity, which is now called "Mayo Foundation for Medical Education and Research."

The day after the papers were signed, Dr. Will and Dr. Charlie endowed Mayo Foundation with all the money in their savings fund, one and a half million dollars at this point, and gave control of it to three trustees, Harry Harwick, Burt Eaton, and Judge George Granger. This was step one in the process of creating Mayo Clinic as an entity which would survive its founders' retirements and deaths.

Judge Granger was there only because W.W. Mayo had intervened dramatically in his life many years earlier. The doctor had been visiting someone else at the Granger farm when little George came to him and answered a friendly question W.W. put to him. Immediately, W.W. reacted to the strange garble which passed for speech from the little boy. "That child is tongue-tied," he said. Then the doctor invited George onto his knee, took a small pair of scissors from his pocket surgery case, asked George to open his mouth and quickly cut the membrane under George's tongue. When the wound healed, George could speak normally. He grew up to become a lawyer, judge, and legal advisor to the Mayo family.

An audience of hundreds stood for an hour in the rain at Mayo Park on Friday, June 4, 1915, to see

W.W.'s statue unveiled and hear speeches about him. The program began with a chorus of "The Star Spangled Banner" by the schoolchildren of Rochester. Then two close friends of the doctor spoke. The first was Judge C. M. Start, former chief justice of the Minnesota Supreme Court.

"Doctor Mayo was a man of generous impulses and unique personality," he said. "He may have seemed blunt and intolerant at times to those who did not understand him, but in fact he was a sympathetic and chivalrous man. I never knew a man more anxious to help others."

The second speaker was Father Thomas O'Gorman, now Bishop O'Gorman, who came from his home in Sioux Falls, South Dakota, for the event. He reminisced about the times he had spent riding in Mayo's buggy nearly 50 years earlier. He spoke too, in his humorous way, about how W.W. had consulted him about Will's and Charlie's futures back in '77. O'Gorman had advised the doctor "that the future of medicine was surgery, and that he could do no better than make surgeons out of the boys.… I helped to make them what they are." Concluding, Bishop O'Gorman said, "I loved Dr. Mayo. As I have said, he guided me in many ways and his talks were full of wisdom."

Louise, old and infirm, came to Mayo Park in a wheelchair. During the ceremony she sat in a large

Statue of William W. Mayo, M.D.

Photo by permission of Mayo Foundation for Medical Education and Research. All rights reserved.

armchair on the platform, an umbrella held over her head. At length, the bronze statue of W.W., made by Leonard Crunelle of Chicago, was unveiled. It was a gift from the people of Rochester who had donated, one by one, 5,000 dollars to pay for it. Dr. Will provided the inscription which summed up his father's personality: "A man of hope and forward-looking mind."

Less than six weeks later, Louise Abigail Wright Mayo died early on Thursday morning, July 15, 1915, in the home of her daughter, Trude Berkman. Louise's attending physician was Trude's fourth child, Dr. David Mayo Berkman, who gave the cause of death as old age. The *Rochester Daily Bulletin* said, "Death … came peacefully and calmly, the tired body relaxing, the spirit hovering for a moment and then taking its flight to realms eternal."

Louise's death, like her husband's, was hastened by an accident. She had broken her hip earlier when she slipped off a porch step at night, while calling her cat. Months of inactivity sapped her strength. She was 89 ½ years old when she died.

The *Daily Bulletin* said of her: "Mrs. Mayo … was a remarkable woman, possessing those rare traits of character, that determination of purpose, that stamped the lives of this country's pioneers.… Few people who are privileged to attain the age that Mrs. Mayo reached are possessed of faculties as keen as this unusual lady had until her last hour on this earth.… There are hundreds outside the family who will mourn her demise."

Following a funeral service the next day in Calvary Episcopal Church, her body was buried beside her husband's in Oakwood Cemetery.

The second step in creating an independent and self-perpetuating Mayo Clinic came to pass between 1917 and 1919, but strangely from the perspective of today, not without a struggle. Drs. Will and Charlie had decided to transfer their Mayo Foundation endowment fund to the University of Minnesota regents, in order to fund medical graduate work using the Mayo Clinic facilities and staff in Rochester. The brothers' vague purpose 20 years earlier that the money "should be returned to the people in a way to do them the greatest benefit" had now taken specific shape. They wished to use it for advanced medical education—-for the first American graduate school in clinical medicine.

When their noble idea became known in the world of Minnesota doctors, however, a furor arose. Other doctors, even University of Minnesota doctors, opposed the idea of the university accepting money from a private source. For some, the motive was fear and jealousy of the Mayos' success. Others felt the university could not affiliate itself with a private clinic without giving the clinic too much power to appoint teachers and grant degrees. Opponents united and lobbied the Minnesota legislature to pass a bill preventing any affiliation between the university graduate school and Mayo Clinic. It narrowly passed the state senate too late for the house to act.

A group of friends met with Dr. Will at the home of Fred B. Snyder, President of the Board of Regents, to consider what should be done about the bill. They asked Dr. Will to speak in the Assembly Hall of the legislature. "He demurred at first," according to a witness. But he had learned from his father not only how to give but also how to fight.

Finally, he said, "Well, I am a good soldier, and if you say I ought to speak, I will."

On March 22, 1917, Dr. Will addressed a crowded chamber of Minnesota legislators and citizens, explaining to them the give-back ethic which prompted this gift: "Every man has some inspiration for good in his life. With my brother and [me] it came from our father. He taught us that any man who has physical strength, intellectual capacity, or unusual opportunity holds such endowments in trust to do with them for others in proportion to his gifts."

Why did the brothers wish to give away their fortune? Did they seek more money for themselves? "It seems to be the idea of some persons," said Dr. Will, "that no one can want to do anything for anybody without having some sinister or selfish motive back of it. If we wanted money, we have it. That can't be the reason for our offer. We want the money to go back to the people from whom it came, and we think we can best give it back to them through medical education."

With quiet intensity, Dr. Will invoked the memory of Abraham Lincoln as he quoted the Gettysburg Address: "'That these dead shall not have died in vain.' That line explains why we want to do this thing. What better could we do than help young men become proficient in the profession so as to prevent needless deaths?"

Dr. Will's words were not recorded that night. Notes of only some of his remarks were taken by reporters and reprinted in newspapers the next day, so this talk has become known as "The Lost Oration." It perfectly achieved its object. The bill opposing Mayo Clinic/University of Minnesota affiliation never became a law.

The Mayo brothers, following their father's benevolent social philosophy, established their clinic as a corporation independent of family and controlled by its own board of governors, a "self-perpetuating charitable corporation" whose charter states that medical care must be for "anyone without regard to financial status, race, color, or creed, all meeting on a common level." When they then established and funded Mayo Foundation for Research and Education, they launched today's Mayo Clinic, a multi-billion-dollar private group practice dedicated to the needs of patients. Their father would have been proud of them. But he would not have given all the credit to his sons.

During his old age, when W.W.'s visits with patients were more social than medical, he sat one day with a friend near the entrance of Saint Marys Hospital. A man from overseas came up to him and said, "I cannot leave without congratulating you on your two splendid sons."

The old doctor answered, "Why don't you congratulate me? I started all this."

It's true. That's just what he did.

Thanks to Many Who Helped Me

I could not have written this book without the help and encouragement of many persons. In the family, my husband, Tom Hartzell, is my first and toughest editor, but I also benefited from editorial advice from my son, Andy Hartzell, daughters, Liz Hartzell Reumann and Laura Hartzell Ricketts, and son-in-law Dr. Christopher Ricketts. Jodi Mayo gave me valuable and timely research assistance. Also Karin Rankin Sisk, Dr. John Mayo Hartzell, Barbara Berkman Withers, Waltman and Vern Walters, and Claude Graf provided information and help.

Mayo Clinic people encouraged me throughout the writing, especially Dr. Kerry Olsen. He not only cheered me on during the early stages by reading my manuscript and offering advice, but he also made available to me the invaluable boxes of research notes which Helen Clapesattle used for *The Doctors Mayo*, so that I could use the same primary materials she used. Matthew Dacy read the manuscript and gave excellent suggestions for improving it, and Alexander Lucas II helped me greatly. He found an abundance of source material for me in the Mayo archives and library. Rene Ziemer and Nicole Babcock were a big help with the photos. Others who gave support are Darlene Bannon, Cynthia Nelson, Marilyn Toogood in Rochester and Thomas Bour at the Scottsdale Clinic.

More and essential editorial advice came from Sally Berk, Judy Stevens, Laurie Hamlett, and Nancy Parker and her writers group. I appreciate the encouragement of David, Pat, Ben and Lisa Pennington, Jim Hamlett, and neighbors Jerry Gabbard and Anne Kaplan. (She first heard many of these stories during our early morning walks.)

Persons associated with Saint Marys Hospital helped me find information there: Sister Ellen Whelan, O.S.F.; Sister Lauren Wienandt, O.S.F., and Mona Stevermer. Thanks also to Jeanne M. Klein and Sister Carlan Kraman, O.S.F., for their encouragement.

Some diligent librarians and archivists helped me also: Melinda MacCall at Tippecanoe Public Library, Lafayette, Indiana; Paul Sheeler of Tippecanoe County Historical Association; Susie Richter of LaPorte County [Indiana] Historical Society Museum; Darla Gebhard at Brown County Historical Society [Minnesota]; the Manchester [England] Library; Olmsted County Historical Society [Minnesota], especially Sherry Sweetman and John Hunziker; Dorothy von Lehe and Jean Haas of the W.W. Mayo House in LeSueur, Minnesota, and Carol Lamberg of Calvary Episcopal Church in Rochester. To all these people I am indebted. Any faults which remain in the book are my own responsibility.

End Notes

CHAPTER 1

Page 9:

Opening quote by Dr. William J. Mayo is from a letter he sent to the University of Minnesota, written February 15, 1934, quoted in Appendix 2 of *Aphorisms of Dr. Charles Horace Mayo and Dr. William James Mayo*, collected by Fredrick A. Willius. Rochester, Minnesota: Mayo Foundation, 1997, page 93.

Mayo's sleigh accident is in *Rochester City Post*, March 1, 1873, page 3.

Dr. Will on the give-back ethic, from his speech before the Minnesota Senate Committee on Education, March 22, 1917, quoted in Appendix 1 of *Aphorisms*, page 87. Dr. Will explained his father's philosophy on different occasions and sometimes in slightly different words.

Page 10:

Mayo's comment to Thomas Lang is in Helen Clapesattle: *The Doctors Mayo*. Minneapolis: The University of Minnesota Press, 1941, page 65.

Mrs. Titus' operation is in *Rochester Post*, August 25, 1866, page 8.

Page 11

The quote about Dr. Preston is from Clapesattle, page 131.

"Parasites of our profession," from an unpublished speech by W.W. Mayo, "Inaugural Address of the Minnesota State Medical Society," February 7, 1872, delivered in St. Paul, Minnesota, page 1. I have it from the private papers of Dr. John Mayo Hartzell, W.W.'s great-grandson.

"The impecuniosity of one class," from the same speech, page 3.

Page 13

Dr. W. J. Mayo, "When we were small boys…," *Aphorisms*, page 87.

Page 14

Carolyn Stickney Beck, Ph.D.: *Teamwork at Mayo: An Experiment in Cooperative Individualism*. Rochester: Mayo Press, 1998. Description of the Clinic as the "largest private medical system in the world" is by Dr. Jarrett W. Richardson, III, Chairman of the Mayo Foundation Humanities in Medicine Committee, in an introduction, page 1. Beck's quote, page 22. She was coordinator of Mayo Center for Humanities in Medicine.

Dr. Will's quote is from *The Mayo Brothers' Heritage, Quotes & Pictures*, edited by Thomas M. Habermann, M.D.; Renee E. Ziemer, and Carolyn Stickney Beck, Ph.D. Rochester: Mayo Clinic Scientific Press, 2001, page 100.

CHAPTER 2

Page 15

W.W. Mayo's birthplace is said by some to be Manchester, by others Salford or Eccles. The confusion is easy to understand. Manchester is about one mile east of Salford and was the more dominant community. Mayo was born in the ecclesiastical parish of Eccles and baptized in the parish church of St. Mary's, in the village of Eccles. However, Salford was his birthplace, according to the ecclesiastical register of his birth, now located in the Manchester Library. This information comes from an article, "William Worrall Mayo, 'I Started All This,'" by J. L. Burn, medical officer in the Public Health Department of Salford, in *Postgraduate Medicine*, Volume 5, published in April, 1949. Burn says, "Salford is proud of the fact that she can claim William Worrall Mayo as one of her sons." Matthew Dacy, Director of Mayo Clinic Heritage Hall, verified that Salford is the birthplace; he visited Salford and Manchester in November, 2002, and looked up Mayo's baptismal certificate in the Manchester Library. He has kindly shared his information with me.

James Mayo was 42 at the time of W.W.'s birth, Anne Mayo 34. Information about W.W. Mayo's family, including correct spelling of names, is from a thoroughly-researched article by Dean L. McLeod, Family History Services of Brigham Young University, "The Origins of William Worrall Mayo, A Contribution." It was presented at Mayo Clinic on May 19, 1989. The typescript manuscript is in a folder, "William Worrall Mayo," in Mayo Clinic archives, Plummer Building, second floor historical suite, Rochester, Minnesota. (Whenever I use the term "Mayo Clinic archives" hereafter, I refer to this place.)

Page 16

Names and birth years of W.W. Mayo's siblings and parents are from a genealogy sent me by William Worrall Mayo Berkman, great-grandson of W.W. Mayo.

Average lifespans for Manchester workers, from McLeod, "The Origins of William Worrall Mayo."

Population of Manchester is from Elizabeth C. Patterson: *John Dalton and the Atomic Theory*. Garden City, NY: Doubleday & Company, Inc., 1970, page 48.

Page 17

"Easy walking distance," from an e-mail from the Manchester [England] Library Archives and Local Studies in response to my query. Anne Mayo's house was on the east side of Salford, near Manchester.

Page 19

Mayo on his religion is from Clapesattle, *The Doctors Mayo*, page 92. I discuss it more thoroughly in connection with W.W.'s 85th birthday celebration, the occasion when he made the comment. "As little harm as possible" is not from the Hippocratic Oath, as some have suggested to me. If Mayo took this oath at all, which is unknown, it was the classical version, which does not contain these words.

Page 21

Mayo's trip on the *Oxford*, from Clark W. Nelson's article, "Historical Profiles of Mayo, William Worrall Mayo Arrives in America," published in *Mayo Clinic Proceedings* by Mayo Foundation, 1995; 70:1028.

Page 22

I am in debt to my brother-in-law Claude Graf, a builder of yachts and student of sailing ships, for the information about conditions of travel in 1846 on a three-masted packet boat, including details about food that passengers brought on board.

Samuel Johnson, from James Boswell, *Life of Johnson*, quoting a letter to Lord Chesterfield which Johnson wrote on February 7, 1754.

The *Oxford* was a new type of "flat-floored" ship, measuring "147 feet, 6 inches long with a beam 33 feet, 6 inches and a hold depth of 21 feet, 6 inches," according to Nelson, "William Worrall Mayo Arrives in America."

Mayo's self description, Clapesattle, page 41.

CHAPTER *3*

Page 23

Information about Bellevue Hospital, Clapesattle, pages 14, 15.

Information about Erie Canal and Wabash Canal from Melinda A. MacCall, reference librarian, Tippecanoe County Public Library, Lafayette, Indiana. Her source was Harlan Hatcher's book *Lake Erie*, published in Indianapolis by Bobbs-Merrill, 1945. Similarly, I have population figures for Lafayette and Tippecanoe County in 1850 through Ms. MacCall's kindness. Her source was *Old Lafayette 1811-1853*, published by Tippecanoe County Historical Association, 1988.

Page 24

A copy of Mayo's *Rerum* book was duplicated at Mayo Clinic from their original copy and sent to me through the kindness of Alexander Lucas II, archivist with Mayo Clinic.

The *Wabash Atlas* announcement, Clapesattle, page 724.

Dr. Deming taught pathology at the University of Missouri in 1853; he had to be skilled in microscope use to do this. This information comes from the boxes of notes which Helen Clapesattle used as background material for her book, interviews conducted by herself and others. I refer to them as "Clapesattle notes." This reference is to Box 2, Folder 1, "Dr. William W. Mayo: Notes on His Education in England and America." These materials are in Mayo Clinic archives.

Page 25

Whenever I use unpublished material, as in the case of "Emeline Bates," I have created fictitious names as required by the Mayo Clinic, following their policy of protecting patients' identities. However, if names are already published, for instance, case histories published in newspapers or in the Clapesattle book, I use real names.

Page 26

A copy of William W. Mayo's application for citizenship was sent me by Paul Sheeler of the Tippecanoe County Historical Association, Lafayette, Indiana.

Page 27

Information on Indiana Medical College at LaPorte is from Lafayette County Historical Association, an August 9, 1938, letter on the school's history by Edith J. Backus, depositions and inquests reporter from LaPorte; also Clapesattle, pages 20 and 21.

Joseph Lister's experience in medical school is from Richard B. Fisher: *Joseph Lister, 1827-1912*. New York: Stein and Day Publishers, 1977, pages 48-50.

Page 28

Louise Abigail Wright was born December 23, 1825, the daughter of Horace Wright and Sarah Totten Wright. (Sarah, born in New York state, was the granddaughter of an English battleship commander, Totten, who fought during the American Revolution.) In 1844, Louise traveled to the Galien Woods area of Michigan, a big section of virgin forest stretching for miles around the present-day towns of Galien and Three Oaks. (After Chicago burned in the Great Fire of 1871, it was this forest which provided timber for rebuilding the city. So many trees were cut for this purpose, the woods disappeared and the "Galien Woods" name fell into disuse.) Clapesattle, page 25, uses the name "Galene Woods" as if it were a town. However, her sources of information were oral reports at least 20 years after

W.W. Mayo died. She incorrectly spelled the word "Galene," making a phonetic rendition of "Galien," named after a French explorer.

I located the names of Louise's two uncles through the courtesy of Susie Richter, Assistant Curator of the LaPorte County [Indiana] Historical Society and Museum. She found the names in the 1850 LaPorte City Directory.

Page 29

Information on the Daniel L. Hart drugstore arrangement and the trip to England is from Clapesattle, pages 24, 25.

CHAPTER 4

Page 31

The marriage certificate of W.W. Mayo and Louise A. Wright, in Mayo Clinic archives, names the site of the wedding as "Berrien County, Township of New Buffalo," suggesting this was in Galien Woods but not in a town.

The idea that Sarah Ostrander traveled west for Louise's wedding is from Dorothy Von Lehe and Jean Haas of the W.W. Mayo House in LeSueur, Minnesota. They discovered that Ostrander settled in Michigan early in the 1850's, (Horace Wright, Louise's brother, had been in Michigan long enough by November 19, 1853, to find, fall in love with, and marry Sarah Goforth.) Ostrander's grave is in Sebring Cemetery, about 80 miles east of the Galien Woods near Hillsdale, Michigan. Her name, along with two Ostrander boys and Horace Wright, are in the Hillsdale County census of 1860. Tom Mohr, Hillsdale County Clerk, suggested that Ostrander was probably part of "the back migration" in the 1850's, which accounted for the growth of Hillsdale. During this event, settlers from Illinois (which became a state in 1818) and Indiana (which became a state in 1816) moved back eastward to Michigan after it became a state in 1837.

Page 32

Hart lawsuit is in Mayo Clinic archives in a folder, "William Worrall Mayo."

Dr. Will's quote comes from *Aphorisms*, page 64.

Page 33

Louise's letter, December 4, 1892, to Carrie France is in W.W. Mayo House archives.

Information on Lafayette locations for the Mayo businesses is from an article by Herbert H. Heimlich, "Founder of Famed Clinic Got Start As Surgeon Here Ninety Years Ago," July 8, 1939, sent to me by the Tippecanoe County Historical Association.

Page 34

Dr. Charles William Mayo from his book, *Mayo: The Story of My Family and My Career*. Garden City, New York: Doubleday & Company, Inc., 1968, page 6.

W.W. Mayo tutoring in chemistry and physics is from Clapesattle notes, Maud Mellish Wilson interview of Dr. William J. Mayo, Box 1, Folder 1, page 1.

W.W. Mayo's *ad eundem* degree is from Clapesattle, page 728.

Page 34

The urine analysis paper is in Box 2, Folder 1, Clapesattle notes.

Page 35

Deming's death is from an article, "Focus on Local History: Dr. Mayo," by Bob Kriebel in the *Lafayette [Indiana] Journal and Courier* on April 2, 2000, in the Tippecanoe County Historical Association.

Page 36

The well-known line, "Good-bye, Louise..." comes from an interview Mrs. William Brown Meloney conducted with Louise Mayo, "Mrs. Mayo, Wilderness Mother." *The Delineator [Magazine],* September, 1914, page 9.

CHAPTER 5

Page 37

Newspaper coverage of the Grand Excursion of 1854 is from the website, "Grandexcursion2004" "Overview, Excursionists," pages 1 and 2, and "Overview, The Original Event," page 1.

W.W. Mayo spoke on Minnesota's climate to the Minnesota Medical Society on February 5, 1873. From Hartzell papers.

Page 38

Details on passengers buried by night, Clapesattle, page 35.

Purchases made on all the shopping trips W.W. and Louise made to Chicago and New York City are carefully entered in Louise's millinery accounts book. Alexander Lucas II kindly duplicated it and sent it to me from the Mayo Clinic archives.

Page 39

"To put food on the table" was Louise's answer to Daisy Berkman Plummer's question. From a phone interview with Daisy's niece, Barbara Berkman Withers. W.W.'s walk, Clark W. Nelson, "Historical Profiles of Mayo, Dr. William Worrall Mayo and the Minnesota Territory," published in *Mayo Clinic Proceedings*, 1999;74:210.

Page 41

W.W. is quoted in Clapesattle, pages 38, 39, 41, 42.

W.W.'s attempt to take an accurate census, Clapesattle, page 45.

The county commissioners naming Duluth as county seat of St. Louis County is from Clapesattle notes, Box 2, Folder 1, "Dr. William Worrall Mayo." Other information is from W.W. Mayo's obituary in Rochester's *Post and Record*, March 6, 1911, page 5.

W.W. and the Northwest Exploring Company, Clapesattle, page 44.

Page 42

Louise's ad in the *Daily Minnesotian* is from the W.W. Mayo House archives.

Dr. Charles W. Mayo, *Mayo: The Story...*, pages 7 and 8.

Page 43

"The Story of My Childhood, Written for My Children" by Alice Mendenhall George is unpublished. The typescript manuscript, which Mrs. George completed in Whittier, California, in 1923, is in W.W. Mayo House archives.

Information about Nathaniel Wright comes from a phone interview I conducted July 20, 2001, with Dorothy Von Lehe at the W.W. Mayo House and from Clapesattle, page 48.

The flatboat story comes from an interview with Gertrude Mayo Berkman in a LeSueur newspaper on November 23, 1932, in W.W. Mayo House archives.

W.W.'s agricultural activities are from Clapesattle, page 50.

The trip which Louise and Trude made to Cronan's Precinct is described in an unpublished typewritten manuscript called "W.H. Farm Journal," written by the man who owned and operated the stagecoach between St. Paul and LeSueur in 1856, page 30, in W.W. Mayo House archives.

Page 44

George, "The Story of My Childhood," page 30.

Louise's "hard times" comment, Meloney, *Delineator Magazine*, page 9.

Page 45

The Indian's joke, George, page 25; scalp dance, George, pages 27, 28.

The meeting of W.W. and Cut Nose, Clapesattle, page 56.

The Ohio Life Insurance and Trust Company failure and resulting panic, as well as the value of town lots prior to the panic, is from Dr. Louis B. Wilson, "William Worrall Mayo: A Pioneer Surgeon of the Northwest," in the journal *Surgery, Gynecology and Obstetrics,* May, 1927, page 4, in Mayo Clinic archives.

W.W.'s purchase of two lots in LeSueur is from an interview with Dorothy Von Lehe of the W.W. Mayo House on October 22, 2002.

Louise's letter to Mrs. Lucans, Mayo Clinic archives, millinery accounts book.

Page 46

Minnesota River flood in March, 1859, Clapesattle, page 57.

Page 47

The house built by the Mayo brothers is from "The House That Mayo Built," a three-page description written by the historians at the W.W. Mayo House.

The J.L. Drake and Otis Ayer stories are from Clapesattle, page 58.

Page 48

Census records on James Mayo's death, Clapesattle, page 733.

CHAPTER *6*

Page 49

Diseases Mayo treated, from a transcript, "Tape on Medical Practice Used in Dr. Mayo's Office," W.W. Mayo House.

Louise's herbs, "Mayo House Herb Garden," a two-page pamphlet, W.W. Mayo House. The information is from *American Dispensatory* by John King, M.D., 1878.

The steamboat job is from Clapesattle, page 59.

Page 50

Information about James J. Hill comes from websites about him, www.mnhs.org/places/sites/jjhh/aboutjames and www.railserve.com/JJHill

Exact date and cause of Sarah's death are unknown. The historians at W.W. Mayo House believe she was about 18 months old, from their video, "If Walls Could Talk: the Mayo House Legacy, Part I – The Mayo Story."

The case against Dr. Ayer, Clapesattle, pages 60-61.

Page 51

Presidential election of 1860 is from *Encyclopedia of American History*, edited by Richard B. Morris. New York: Harper & Brothers, 1953, page 227.

Beginning and end of the *LeSueur Courier* are in Clapesattle, pages 61-63.

Page 52

Mayo's letter appeared in *The Henderson Weekly Democrat*, March 2, 1861. Dorothy von Lehe of the W.W. Mayo House kindly sent me a copy from their archives.

Lincoln's inaugural remarks, Morris, page 229.

Page 53

Mayo as examining surgeon in LeSueur County, Clapesattle, page 68.

Page 55

Description of New Ulm on Tuesday, August 19, is from Clapesattle, page 71. Another source is Duane Schultz: *Over the Earth I Come, The Great Sioux Uprising of 1862*. New York: St. Martin's Press, 1992, pages 98 to 100. Statistics in the five books plus Clapesattle I consulted on the Sioux War do not agree, for no one took time to do official counts of participants or victims during those dire days.

Dr. Weschcke's part in doctoring the wounded is from *Charles E. Flandrau and the Defense of New Ulm*, edited by Russell W. Fridley, Leota M. Kellett and June D. Holmquist. New Ulm: The Brown County Historical Society, 1962, page 37. The Brown County Historical Museum also kindly sent me articles about Dr. Weschcke.

The rescue and decision to return to New Ulm are from Schultz, page 153.

Page 56

For the Indians' point of view, I consulted an excellent book, *Through Dakota Eyes, Narrative Accounts of the Minnesota Indian War of 1862*, edited by Gary Clayton Anderson and Alan R. Woolworth. St. Paul: Minnesota Historical Society Press, 1988. The Indians' motives for action and plans for war are in the introduction, pages 8-13.

Myrick's comment, Clapesattle, page 69, and other sources.

Page 57

Conversation of the young Indians, "Big Eagle's Account," *Through Dakota Eyes*, page 35.

Indian leaders in the second attack, "Lightning Blanket's Account," *Through Dakota Eyes*, page 157; and also Schultz, page 11; and Kenneth Carley, *The Sioux Uprising of 1862*. St. Paul: The Minnesota Historical Society, 1976, page 37. Numbers of Indians, *Charles E. Flandrau and the Defense of New Ulm*, page 41.

Page 58

Flandreau's quote, C.M. Oehler, *The Great Sioux Uprising*. NY: Oxford University Press, 1959, pages 129, 130.

The Saturday battle, *Through Dakota Eyes*, page 146, and Clapesattle, page 73. Le Sueur Tigers' bravery at the windmill is from Carley, page 37, and Schultz, page 155.

Mayo's actions are from Clapesattle, page 73. More than 50 years after the battle, Dr. William J. Mayo received a letter from Dr. Asa W. Daniels telling the story of how W.W., the priest, and Captain Dodd spoke courage into the discouraged citizen-soldiers. This letter, dated February 17, 1919, is in Mayo Clinic archives.

Page 59

Flandrau's counter-offensive is from Carley, page 38.

Flandrau's quote on the importance of the New Ulm defense, *Charles E. Flandrau and the Defense of New Ulm*, page 49.

The deserter story, George, page 44.

Meloney interview, *The Delineator*, pages 9 and 46.

Page 60

Dr. Charles William Mayo, *Mayo: The Story...*, page 9.

Louise and Trude feeding the refugees, Meloney, page 9.

Colonel Sibley's pursuit of the Dakotas, Schultz, page 5, and Oehler, page 199.

Unjust treatment of the Indians, *Through Dakota Eyes*, page 221.

Page 62

Numbers of casualties and effect of the war, *Through Dakota Eyes*, page 1, and Oehler, page 235.

Clapesattle says 39 Indians were sentenced to be hung, and this is true, but one of them, Tatemima, was reprieved, so only 38 were hung. Clapesattle, page 77; *Through Dakota Eyes*, page 221, and Schultz, page 221.

W.W.'s use of the skeleton is from a speech by Dr. Charles H. Mayo, "Early Days of the Mayo Clinic," given at the Medical History Club in Rochester, Minnesota, February 5, 1929, page 3. I have it from the private papers of George Mayo Elwinger, W.W. Mayo's great-grandson.

CHAPTER 7

Page 63

John Smith from his unpublished manuscript, *Tales of the Tenth Regiment, Minnesota Volunteers, 1862-1863*, pages 6 and 10, in W.W. Mayo House archives.

Quotes about using chloroform are from Otto L. Bettmann, Ph.D.: *A Pictorial History of Medicine*. Springfield, Illinois: Charles C. Thomas Publisher, 1956, page 259.

Dr. Wood's speed is documented in *The Rise of Surgery, From Empiric Craft to Scientific Discipline* by Dr. Owen H. Wangensteen, M.D., and Sarah D. Wangensteen. Minneapolis: University of Minnesota Press, 1978, page 36.

Page 64

W.W. as examining surgeon for the Union army, Clapesattle, page 78.

Rochester description from Sister Ellen Whelan, O.S.F.: *The Sisters' Story, Saint Marys Hospital-Mayo Clinic, 1889 to 1939*. Rochester, Minnesota: Mayo Foundation for Medical Education and Research, 2002, page 6.

Praise of Drs. Hyde and Mayo, *Rochester Republican*, January 27, 1864, page 3. Dr. Hyde's separation from Mayo is in its June 15, 1864 issue.

Page 66

Louise's trachoma affliction, Dr. Charlie interview, Clapesattle notes, Box 1, Interviews by Dr. Richard Beard (folder 1), page 7.

Events in St. Peter, including newspaper quotes, are from Clapesattle, pages 82-84. Mayo's loss of the examining surgeon job is from page 86.

Page 67

Rochester Republican quote, March 8, 1865, page 3.

Page 68

The meeting of Rochester Library Association is from *Rochester Post*, January 6, 1866, and Clapesattle, page 89.

Horace Greeley and Frederick Douglass are in Morison, Commager and Leuchtenburg, pages 462 and 327. The quote about Anna E. Dickinson is from Clapesattle, 1941, page 89. Other information about her is from "Anna E. Dickinson Biography" by Patricia Chadwick on the Internet at: http://wiwi.essortment.com/annadickinson_rytk.htm

Louise's quotes about blindness, Meloney interview, page 46.

Page 70

History of the thermometer is from *Medicine, A History of Healing: Ancient Traditions to Modern Practices*, edited by Roy Porter. New York: Marlowe & Company, publishers, 1997, page 56.

Page 71

"That Norwegian will have to dry up and blow away...," *Rochester Post*, June 23, 1866, page 8.

W.W.'s method of examining patients is in Clapesattle, page 115.

Dr. Donald Balfour's quote is from his article, "William James Mayo and Charles Horace Mayo," in *Surgery*, August, 1940, page 172, in Mayo Clinic archives.

W.W.'s use of the stethoscope, thermometer, etc., Clapesattle, page 118, as well as from his own notes in Louise's millinery accounts book.

Page 72

W.W.'s election to the school board, Clapesattle, page 90. Sanford Niles as superintendent of schools is from Harriet W. Hodgson, *Rochester, City of the Prairie*. Northridge, California: Windsor Publications, Inc., 1989, page 63.

Page 73

W.W.'s comment on students, Clapesattle, pages 90 and 91.

CHAPTER 8

Page 75

Father Thomas O'Gorman's quote is from a speech he made at the unveiling of Dr. W.W. Mayo's statue, *The Olmsted County Democrat*, June 4, 1915, page 2.

Information about Father O'Gorman is from Whelan, *The Sisters' Story*, pages 13 and 14.

"He was an Episcopalian, but..." is from Clapesattle, page 92.

W.W. treating patients on Sunday from the Beard interview with Dr. Charlie in Clapesattle notes, page 11.

Page 76

"Charlie and I always went together," Clapesattle, page 159.

The Rochester Post on Will's accident, August 18, 1869, page 3.

Mrs. Barbara Berkman Withers of Rochester, Minnesota, inherited the library of her great-grandparents, Louise and W.W. Mayo. I examined the books in her house.

Page 77

"Bucket of milk," Meloney interview, page 46.

"Mother was a real good doctor too," Clapesattle, page 148.

Anderson letter, August 16, 1948, Olmsted County Historical Society archives.

Page 78

Deaths in childbirth from *Medicine, A History of Healing*, page 38.

Semmelweis is from *The Great Doctors, A Biographical History of Medicine* by Dr. Henry E. Sigerist, translated by Eden and Cedar Paul. New York: W.W. Norton & Company, Inc., 1933, pages 354, 355, and from *A Pictorial History of Medicine* by Otto L. Bettmann, page 258.

Jane Twentyman Graham was the mother of Edith Graham Mayo, wife of Dr. Charlie Mayo. Information on J.T. Graham is in Clapesattle, page 362.

Mayo Clinic honors W.W. Mayo by continuing his manner of dressing in professional clothes. The Prince Albert coat and top hat were business dress for professional people of W.W.'s day. Today, Mayo Clinic doctors wear business suits, not lab coats, when they confer with patients in their offices.

Rochester Post article, August 25, 1866. My copy of the article is from the Hartzell papers.

Page 79

Olmsted County Medical Society meetings, Clapesattle, page 120.

Louise's comment to Dr. Galloway, Clapesattle, page 111.

Philadelphia County Medical Society is from Bettman, page 277. The quote about "feminine delicacy" is from Nora H. Guthrey: *Medicine and Its Practitioners in Olmsted County Prior to 1900*. Rochester, Minnesota, page 181. It is reprinted from *Minnesota Medicine*, volumes 32, 33, and 34.

Page 80

Dr. Charlie on W.W. and money, Beard interview, page 2.

Bellevue Hospital in 1869 is from *Walter Reed, A Biography* by William B. Bean, M.D. A reprint is in Olmsted County Historical Society archives, "William Worrall Mayo" folder.

Page 81

W.W.'s letters from New York are on microfilm at Rochester Public Library. I quote from *Rochester Post*, December 25, 1869, page 1.

McDowell's surgery, Wangensteen and Wangensteen, *The Rise of Surgery*, pages 228-230; McDowell's medical education, page 227; Dr. Clay's work, page 230.

Page 82

"Belly-rippers," Clapesattle, page 128.

Page 83

Microscope story is from Dr. William J. Mayo, "Discussion," following a report by T.E. Keys on "The Medical Books of William Worrall Mayo, Pioneer Surgeon of the American Northwest," printed in *Proceedings of the Staff Meetings of the Mayo Clinic*, Volume 16, August 6, 1941, page 502. Dr. Will's remarks were made on July 6, 1938. This document is in the Mayo Clinic Library.

The book by Rindfleisch is listed in the Keys article.

Page 84

Byford consultation and rectocele surgery, Clapesattle, pages 129 and 130.

Cauterization, Wangensteen and Wangensteen, pages 21-23.

Mayo's "People's Party" attempt, Clapesattle, pages 96-98.

Mayo organizing M.S.M.S. (really reorganizing—the society was begun when Minnesota was a territory, but it had ceased to meet) is from Clapesattle, page 121.

Page 86

W.W.'s speeches before M.S.M.S. are from the Hartzell papers.

W.W. saving a man's hand, Gertrude Berkman interview, Clapesattle notes, Box 1, Interviews by Dr. Beard (folder 1).

Dr. Hill and the move to St. Paul, Clapesattle, page 134.

CHAPTER *9*

Page 87

Walk from Kasson, *Rochester Post*, March 14, 1874, page 3; "plans to return," March 21, 1874, page 3.

Page 84

Edgar story, Clapesattle, page 91; *Rochester Post*, May 30, 1874, page 2, and June 6, 1874, page 1.

Page 89

Henry Wellcome is from "Adventures of Two Prairie

Pioneers" by Alvin B. Hayles, M.D., and Jack D. Key, M.A., M.S., from the file "William Worrall Mayo" in Mayo Clinic archives. It first appeared as an address and is copyrighted 1979 by the Mayo Foundation. I also used a biography of Wellcome from the Internet, "Henry Solomon Wellcome and the Sudan" by Ahmed Awad Abdel-Hameed Adeel, September, 2000. Wellcome's speech to the American College of Surgeons, *Surgery, Gynecology and Obstetrics,* December, 1927, page 857. His obituary, *Rochester Post Bulletin,* July 25, 1936, page 1.

Charlie's conversation in the buggy, Clapesattle, pages 171, 172.

Page 90

Dr. Will on W.W., "Discussion," after Keys article, pages 497-505.

Page 91

Dr. Charlie as anesthetist, "Early Days," pages 8 and 9.

Frank B. Kellogg is from the Internet, "Frank B. Kellogg – Biography" at www.nobel.se/peace/laureates/1929/kellogg-bio.html

Page 92

Stories of Will and Charlie, Clapesattle, pages 166, 180, and 113.

Phoebe's accident, *Rochester Post*, February 27, 1875, page 3.

W.W.'s trip to England, *Rochester Post*, August 26, 1876, page 3.

Page 93

Information on Lister, Sherwin B. Nuland: *Doctors, The Biography of Medicine.* New York: Vintage Books, second edition 1995, pages 372 and 365; and Fisher, *Joseph Lister,* page 223.

Dr. Hodgen's speech in *Transactions of the International Medical Congress of Philadelphia, 1876,* edited by Dr. John Ashhurst, Jr., from the Mayo Clinic Library.

Page 94

Marriage of Gertude Mayo and Dr. David Berkman, *Rochester Post*, June 29, 1877, page 3.

Moving to the farm, Clapesattle, pages 104, 105. *Rochester Post*, August 10, 1877, page 3.

Page 96

Dr. Will on his education, Wilson interview, page 4.

Albert Younglove's comment, Clapesattle, page 751.

Dr. Will's description of his brother, *The Daily Post and Record*, June 23, 1916, page 5.

Dr. Charles W. Mayo's comment, *Mayo: The Story...*, page 27.

Page 97

Charlie's new coat, Clapesattle, page 169.

Sister Carlan Kraman spoke of similarities between W.W. Mayo and Mother Alfred in an interview, Rochester, Minnesota, August 2, 2003. Mother Alfred's description is from Sister Carlan Kraman, O.S.F., *Odyssey in Faith, the Story of Mother Alfred Moes.* Rochester, Minnesota: published by the Sisters of St. Francis, 1990, page 24. Father Thomas O'Gorman's part in bringing Mother Alfred to Rochester, page 121. This story is also told by Whelan in *The Sisters' Story,* pages 35, 36.

Page 98

Phoebe's accident with Nevil, *Rochester Post*, September 7, 1877, page 3. Her accident in 1878 is described by her sister, Gertrude Mayo Berkman, the Beard interview, Clapesattle notes.

Information about the children the Mayos took into their home from an interview with Barbara Withers, granddaughter of Gertrude Mayo Berkman.

Page 99

The first telephone in Rochester, Clark W. Nelson, *Mayo Roots, Profiling the Origins of Mayo Clinic.* Rochester: Mayo Foundation for Medical Education and Research, 1990, page 162.

Page 100

The Waggoner surgery, Clark W. Nelson, "Historical Profiles of Mayo, Dr. William Worrall Mayo's Gynecologic Surgical Practice," *Mayo Clinic Proceedings*, 1977, and also Clapesattle, page 142.

Smash-up of Mayo's carriage, *Rochester Post*, March 25, 1881, page 3.

Dr. Charles W. Mayo's comment is from his book, page 15.

CHAPTER *10*

Page 101

The quote from W.J. Mayo, Nelson, *Mayo Roots*, page 32.

Page 102

W.W.'s birthday party, *Rochester Post*, June 3, 1881, page 3.

Mayoral election results, *Rochester Post*, April 7, 1882, page 3.

Mayo's speech about farmers, Clapesattle, pages 94, 95.

Sir George Clark, *English History, A Survey*. London, England: Oxford University Press, 1971, pages 417, 423.

Page 103

Mayo Park, Dr. Will's interview with Wilson, page 24.

The rock quarry, Dr. Charlie's interview with Beard, page 4.

W.W. and the Fox book, Clapesattle, page 750.

Dr. Will and Listerism at the U. of M., Clapesattle, pages 197, 198.

Page 104

"A good many do not learn easy...," Nelson, *Mayo Roots*, page 32.

The Record and Union on the Mayo offices, Nelson, *Mayo Roots*, page 164. W.W.'s earlier partners, Nelson, page 18.

Dr. Will and the three cataract operations, Wilson interview, page 5.

Page 105

Dr. Will on the tornado experience, Wilson interview, page 5. Clapesattle (page 760) was familiar with this interview but chose to follow Dr. Charlie's tornado story from "Early Days," page 5. One brother (Will) said they were working at the slaughterhouse when they responded to the storm, and the other (Charlie) claimed they were still on their way to the slaughterhouse when they turned back to town. I followed Dr. Will's story. It was longer, more detailed, and, to me, more convincing.

Rochester Post description of the tornado, August 24, 1883, page 2.

Page 106

Mother Alfred's conversation, *A Century of Caring, 1889-1989*. Rochester, Minnesota: Saint Marys Hospital, 1988, page 12, in St. Marys Hospital library. I have spliced into it the "But you have sons" conversation, from a newspaper report mentioned in Kraman, *Odyssey in Faith*, page 171.

Page 107

"They came to us like soldiers...," W.W.'s address at the dedication of St. Marys Hospital's first addition, April 4, 1894, *Saint Marys Hospital Annals*, page 41.

Tornado damage, the Hon. Joseph A. Leonard, *History of Olmsted County, Minnesota*. Chicago: Goodspeed Historical Association Publishers, 1910, pages 149, 150.

Mother Alfred's vision, "Inside Mayo Clinic," a 1992 PBS video now at Mayo Clinic, Scottsdale, Arizona, an interview with Sister Carlan Kraman, O.S.F. Sister Carlan also told me in our interview of Mother Alfred's vision.

Page 108

Mother Alfred's handling of money and the sisters' sacrifices, Kraman, *Odyssey in Faith*, pages 172-174, and page 143. (Sister Joseph Dempsey's "all for God" comment was made before the late 1880s but was still appropriate in 1889.) See also *A Century of Caring, 1889-1989*, page 15.

Sister Joseph Dempsey's comment is from Whelan, page 38.

Dr. Will's speech to the medical students, Clark W. Nelson, "Historical Profiles of Mayo, Dr. William J. Mayo's Advice to Medical Graduates," *Mayo Clinic Proceedings*, 1998; 73:4 in Mayo Clinic Library.

Page 109

"That big needle trick...," Wilson interview, pages 10, 11.

Page 110

Will and Hattie's wedding, Clapesattle, page 238.

Phoebe's death, *Rochester Post*, May 22, 1885, page 3.

Page 111

Dr. Will on Gerster, Wilson interview, page 11.

Edwin Jacobs' and the baby's surgeries, *Rochester Post*, December 4, 1885, page 3.

Page 112

The Record and Union tells of the waterworks, October 31, 1890, page 3.

Charlie's medical school, Clapesattle, pages 203-205 and page 239.

Page 113

The common pocket book of Drs. Will and Charlie is well documented. In his interview with Wilson, page 26, Dr. Will said it began as a three-way purse.

Beautiful site for St. Marys, Whelan, pages 45, 46.

Page 114

Dr. Will and the ovariotomy, Wilson interview, page 3; Clapesattle, page 231.

CHAPTER 11

Page 115

Sister Joseph's quote, interview with Dr. Richard Beard in Clapesattle notes, Box 1, Folder 6, "Interviews with Sisters and Staff."

Sarah Mayo Thorp is in the Berkman genealogy of the Mayo family.

Dr. Charlie on Europe, "Early Days" speech, page 1.

Dr. Charlie's visit to Pasteur, Clapesattle, page 241.

Pasteur's work against rabies, Bettmann, page 287.

Page 116

Dr. Charlie and physical exams, Beard interview, page 11.

Dr. Will and Dr. Joseph Price, Wilson interview, page 13.

Dr. Charlie's surgeries and "Everything was slushing," "Early Days," page 7.

Of 52 votes by the sisters in all, 31 were cast at the meeting in Rochester, and 21 more sometime later in Ironton, Ohio, Kraman, *Odyssey in Faith*, page 165.

Page 117

Mother Alfred and Billingsley, Whelan, *The Sisters' Story*, pages 46, 47.

Page 118

Newspaper description of Saint Marys Hospital, Clapesattle, page 251.

Dr. Charlie's surgical table, "Early Days," page 7, and Clapesattle, page 257.

Page 120

Edith Graham's journal is untitled and unpublished. Written in 1889, it is in the Olmsted County Historical Society.

Gertrude Mayo Berkman's remark, Beard interview.

Hospital description, Whelan, *The Sisters' Story*, pages 48, 49, 63, 69, 70, 71.

Page 121

Dr. Will's comment about hospital sisters, Wilson interview, p. 16.

Page 122

Sister Ellen Whelan's quote, Whelan, page 78.

John Willis Baer on his short term as superintendent, *Souvenir of Saint Mary's Hospital*. Rochester: Saint Mary's Hospital, 1922, page 16.

Mother Alfred's work as superintendent, Whelan, page 51.

Page 123

The cesspool problem, *Souvenir of Saint Mary's Hospital*, page 15.

Page 125

Dr. W.W.'s hospital work, *Souvenir of Saint Mary's Hospital*, page 7.

Dr. Will and Dr. Charlie's work, Nora H. Guthrey, *Medicine and Its Practitioners in Olmsted County Prior to 1900*, page 48; and *Sketch of the History of the Mayo Clinic and the Mayo Foundation* by the Division of Publications, Mayo Clinic. Philadelphia and London: W.B. Saunders Company, 1926, page 15.

Page 126

Dr. Will, "By the greatest effort,..." Wilson interview, page 17; Bishop Cotter remarks, page 18.

Statistics on mortality in the first years of the hospital are from *Souvenir of Saint Mary's Hospital*, page 16; and Whelan, page 69.

CHAPTER 12

Page 127

Whelan, *The Sisters' Story*, page 73.

Dr. Charlie's elevator story, "Early Days," page 7. The elevator was completed in 1891.

The elevator's deficiency, *Souvenir of Saint Mary's Hospital*, page 15.

Dinah Graham's career is from an interview her grandson, Chris Batchelder, conducted with his mother, Edith Olin Batchelder, in 1991, a typescript manuscript in Mayo Clinic archives. An error appeared in a 1926 Mayo Clinic publication saying Dinah was the first anesthetist at Saint Marys Hospital. She was still in nursing school when Dr. W.W. Mayo trained Edith Graham for this position in 1889.

Dr. Charlie on Dr. Stinchfield's hiring, Beard interview, page 12. Dr. Will on Stinchfield, Wilson interview, page 20.

Page 129

W.W.'s letter to Edith Graham, January 18, 1892, Olmsted County Historical Society archives, in a folder, "William Worrall Mayo."

Page 130

W.W. on Chicago World's Fair, January 22, 1893, from the Hartzell letters.

Page 131

Donnelly's career, Richard B. Morris, *Encyclopedia of American History*, page 248.

J. J. Hill's career, Minnesota Historical Society's site

on the Internet, "http://w.w.w.mnhs.org/places/sites/jjhh/aboutjames.html"

Quotes of Mayo and Hill, Dr. Charlie, Beard interview, page 5.

Dr. Charlie to Edith Graham, November 22 and 26, 1892, Hartzell letters.

Page 132

Mayo-Graham wedding, *Rochester Post*, April 7, 1893, page 3.

Riverside Hospital has been called…", Clapesattle, page 265.

Rochester Post, November 11, 1892, page 3.

Senator Mayo's trip, *Olmsted County Democrat*, May 4, 1893, page 3.

Page 133

W.W. and Chicago fair, *Rochester Post and Record*, August 23, 1901, page 6.

Christopher Graham information, Nelson, *Mayo Roots*, page 126. Dr. Will's comment about Graham, Wilson interview page 20.

W.W. and hospital addition, *Souvenir of Saint Mary's Hospital*, 1922, page 7. The dollar amount of the sisters' contract, Whelan, page 71.

"Never hold a knife," *Souvenir of Saint Mary's Hospital*, page 8.

Page 133

W.W.'s speech, *Saint Marys Hospital Annals,* "Address of Doctor W.W. Mayo at the opening of the First Addition to Saint Marys Hospital," page 41.

Dr. Allen's career, Guthrey, *Medicine and Its Practitioners*, pages 50, 51.

Sister Joseph Dempsey's interview by Dr. Richard Beard, "Interviews with Sisters and Staff," is in Clapesattle notes, Box 1, Folder 6.

CHAPTER 13

Page 135

The first trip using the new ambulance, taking a patient to St. Marys Hospital, in *Rochester Post*, July 30, 1897.

Page 136

W.W.'s letter to Carrie Mayo, written from Hotel Alcazar in St. Augustine, Florida in 1896, is in Mayo Clinic archives.

The ladder accident, *Rochester Post*, August 19, 1898, page 1.

Page 137

The brothers' decisions about money, Wilson interview, page 23.

Trip to St. Louis, *Rochester Post*, January 13, 1899, page 3, and January 20, 1899, page 2.

Dr. Charlie's letters to Edith, March 15 and 24, 1899, Hartzell letters.

Page 138

W.W.'s retirement, *A Souvenir of Saint Mary's Hospital*, page 8.

Dr. Charlie's comments, Beard interview, page 5.

Dr. Will's "proudest day of my life," Wilson interview, page 14.

Dr. Chuck Mayo, from his interview with Helen Clapesattle in boxes of Clapesattle notes, Box 1, Folder 4.

The new office, Guthrey: *Medicine and Its Practitioners*, pages 51, 52.

Page 139

50th wedding anniversary is in both *Post and Record*, February 8, 1901, page 9, and *Olmsted County Democrat*, February 8, 1901, page 3.

Page 141

Dr. Will's story of Dr. Plummer, Wilson interview, pages 21, 22.

W.W. in Europe, *Post and Record*, September 6, 1901, pages 6, 7, and 9.

Page 142

W.W. and Willson in Pacific Northwest, *Olmsted County Democrat*, September 12, 1902, page 1. Trip to Mexico, same newspaper, April 29, 1904, page 2.

Page 143

The 85th birthday party is covered in a long article in the *Post and Record*, June 3, 1904, page 7. Unfortunately, W.W. placed his statement of religious faith directly after his quote about Bismarck's faith, and many writers, beginning with Clapesattle, have confused the two.

CHAPTER 14

Page 145

The election, Clapesattle, page 375.

Statistics on surgical cases, Clapesattle, pages 437 and 481.

Will's remarks on Dr. Wilson, Wilson interview, page 28.

Dr. Wilson and quick-freezing, Clapesattle, pages 444-446.

Page 146

"Charlie and I consulted God too...," Whelan, page 89.

Dr. Will's remarks to the A.M.A., Clapesattle, page 440.

Page 147

Louise's letters, from "Letters From My Grandmother" by Martha M. Blethen, a typewritten document in the W.W. Mayo House archives.

Dr. Chuck Mayo's comments, from his book *Mayo: The Story...*, page 5.

Page 148

W.W.'s trip to Japan, *Olmsted County Democrat*, June 14, 1907, page 5; Clapesattle, page 471, and Dr. Charlie's Beard interview, page 5. Returning from this trip, W.W. said he was willing to take a trip around the world, but I can find no credible evidence that he ever took one.

First Baptist Church speech, Meloney, *The Delineator*, page 46.

Page 149

Dr. Will on Dr. Judd, Wilson interview, page 26.

W.W.'s accident, Beard interview with Gertrude Berkman.

Page 151

Phoebe Mayo Walters, from "Reminiscences of William James Mayo, M.D.," a talk she gave at Mayo Clinic, July 12, 1977, in private papers of her son Waltman Walters, page 5.

The funeral, *Rochester Daily Bulletin*, March 7, 1911, page 2, and the *Post and Record*, March 10, 1911, page 2.

Sister Joseph Dempsey's remarks, Clapesattle, page 473.

CHAPTER 15

Page 153

Size of Saint Marys Hospital, Whelan, page 77; patient numbers, *Souvenir of Saint Marys Hospital*, page 18.

Dr. Will's remarks, Wilson interview, page 30.
Dr. Charlie's remarks, "Early Days" speech, pages 10 and 11.

Page 154

Harry Harwick's comment, from William Holmes, *Dedicated to Excellence, the Rochester Methodist Hospital Story*. Rochester: Johnson Printing Company, 1984, page 30.

Louise's letter, "Letters from my Grandmother" by Blethen, page 4.

Phoebe Mayo Walters about Louise, "Reminiscences of William James Mayo, M.D.," pages 4 and 5.

Page 155

Dr. Chuck's comment, from his book, page 15.

Louise to Meloney, *The Delineator*, pages 9 and 46.

The Mayo Building, from edited version of Helen Clapesattle: *The Doctors Mayo*, copyright 1969. Rochester, Minnesota: Mayo Foundation for Medical Education & Research, 1990, Fourth Printing, pages 324 and 325.

Page 156

Incorporation and beginning of the Mayo Foundation, from the same 1969 version of Clapesattle, pages 331-339.

Page 157

Statue ceremony, *Olmsted County Democrat*, June 4, 1915, pages 2 and 3.

Page 158

Rochester Daily Bulletin, July 15, 1915, page 5.

Page 159

"I am a good soldier...," from Guy Stanton Ford, transcript of a tape recording he made on April 23, 1962, at Clark Nelson's request, for Mayo Clinic archives.

The "lost oration," edited version of Clapesattle, pages 338, 339; and "Historical Profiles of Mayo: 75th Anniversary of the Mayo Foundation" by Clark W. Nelson, in *Mayo Clinic Proceedings*, 1994, 69, page 308.

Page 160

"I started all this," from a eulogy by Dr. Frank Doran about W.W. Mayo, printed in *Rochester Post Bulletin*, June 12, 1929. This document is in the William Worrall Mayo folder, Olmsted County Historical Society archives.

Index

A

	Page
Allen, Dr. J.S.	70
Allen, Dr. W.A.	132, 134
Ayer, Dr. Otis	48, 50-51, 55, 59

B

Balfour, Dr. Donald C.	71, 153
Beecher, Rev. Henry Ward	81
Bellevue Hospital	23, 28, 80, 135
Bell, Dr. John	83
Berkman, Daisy Louise	98, 132, 136
Berkman, Dr. David	94, 106, 154
Berkman, David Mayo	112, 158
Berkman, Helen Phoebe	109, 135, 148
Berkman, John Mayo	16, 136, 147
Berkman, Martha May	98, 146
Booker, Dr. Gertrude	138-139
Burroughs and Wellcome & Company	88
Byford, Dr. William H.	84

C

Calvary Episcopal Church	75, 118, 131, 151, 158, 161
Chief Little Crow	56-57, 60
Clapesattle, Helen	21, 103
Clay, Dr. Charles	81
Cronan's Precinct	42
Cross, Dr. Edwin C.	64, 67, 79, 86
Cross, Dr. Elisha W.	79, 86, 104
Cushing, Dr. Harvey	137
Cut Nose (A Dakota brave)	45, 60, 62, 73, 61

D

Dakota Sioux Indians	44, 53
Dalton, John	15-20, 23, 25, 28, 73, 75, 87, 143
Daniels, Dr. Asa of St. Peter	55, 90
Deming, Dr. Elizur H.	25-35, 104
Dempsey, Sister Joseph	115, 123, 133-134, 151
DeWolf, Dr. Oscar	113
Dickinson, Anna E.	68
Doctors Mayo, The	21
Donnelly, Senator Ignatius	131
Douglass, Frederick	68
Duluth, Minnesota	40

E

Eaton, Burt	92, 137, 153, 156

F

Fenger, Dr. Christian	112, 137
Flandrau, Judge Charles E.	55, 57

G

Galbraith, Agent Thomas	56
Galloway, Dr. Hector	64, 79
Gerster, Dr. Arpad	111
Gorman, Governor Willis A.	40
Graham, Dr. Christopher	133
Graham, Edith (see also Mayo, Edith Graham)	118, 121, 123, 127, 129, 131, 133
Grand Centennial celebration of the Louisiana Purchase, 1903 St. Louis Fair	137
Grand Excursion of 1854	37
Greeley, Horace	68

H

Halsted, Dr. William S.	137
Hart, Daniel L.	30, 51
Harwick, Harry	153
Hewitt, Dr. Charles	109
Hill, James J.	50, 130, 148
Hodgen, Dr. John T.	34, 93-94
Hunter, Dr. John	90
Hyde, Dr. W.A.	64

I

Indiana Medical College, La Porte	25-27, 78
International Medical Congress, Philadelphia	93

J

Judd, Dr. Edward Starr	148

K

Kellogg, Frank B.	91
Kraman, Sister Carlan, O.S.F.	97, 108

L

Le Sueur, Minnesota	43, 45, 53, 57
Le Sueur Tigers	58
Lincoln, President Abraham	49, 51, 60, 159
Lister, Dr. Joseph	27, 87, 93-94, 103, 109

M

Manchester School of Medicine 20
Mayo, Anne Bonsall 15
Mayo, Dr. Charles William 33, 42, 100, 138
Mayo Clinic Building 155
Mayo, Edith Graham 118, 121, 123, 127,
  (see also Graham, Edith) 129, 131, 133
Mayo Foundation for
  Medical Education and Research 156, 158, 160
Mayo, Gertrude Emily (Trude) 19, 33, 38-53,
  63-112, 120, 136-160
Mayo, Hattie May Damon 110, 112, 117,
  132, 135-136, 151
Mayo, James 15-17, 46-48
Mayo, Phoebe Louise 43-46, 58-60, 64, 68-69,
  72, 73, 91-94, 98-101, 104,
  109-110, 134, 136, 148, 151, 154, 155
McDowell, Dr. Ephraim 81, 83
Millet, Dr. Melvin 139
Minnesota State Board of Health 109
Minnesota State Medical Society 10-11, 80,
  85, 90, 99, 109, 111, 146
Minnesota Territory 36
Missouri Medical Department in St. Louis 34
Moes, Mother Alfred, O.S.F. 97-98, 106-108,
  113, 116-117, 120-122, 134, 143

N

New Ulm, Minnesota 49-50, 53, 55, 57-60, 90
New York Postgraduate School 109
Nichols, Eda 98
Nicollet County Agricultural Society 43
Niles, Sanford 72, 96

O

Ochsner, Dr. Alfred 137
O'Gorman, Father Thomas 75-76, 97, 122, 157
Olmsted County Medical Society 13, 79, 86, 151
Ostrander, Sarah Totten Wright 75
ovariotomy 13, 81, 83-84, 99, 113-114, 127
Oxford, the 21-23

P

Paget, Sir James 90
Parkes, Dr. Charles 112
Pasteur, Louis 115
Peterloo Massacre 102
Pine Street School 21
Plummer, Dr. Henry 139, 141, 145, 147,
  151, 153, 155-156
Preston, Dr. Harriet 10

Q

Quaker 18-19, 75-76, 143

R

Ramsey, Governor Alexander 53
Rerum book 20, 24-26, 32-33,
  38, 43, 49, 64, 68, 72, 94
Riordan, Father William 121
Riverside Hospital 132-134

S

Saint Mary's Church 15
Saint Marys Hospital 116, 123, 125-126,
  129-136, 138, 143, 145-146, 151, 153, 160
St. Louis County, Minnesota 40
Sands, Dr. Henry B. 109
Semmelweis, Dr. Ignaz Philipp 78
Senn, Dr. Nicholas 112, 131
Simpson, Dr. James Young 63
Sisters of Saint Francis 97, 106,
  117, 122, 133, 143, 147
Society of Friends 18-19, 76
Stinchfield, Dr. Augustus W. 114, 127,
  135, 138, 151, 153
Stone, Dr. A.J. 114

T

Tefft, Dr. N. S. of Plainview, Minnesota 90

W

Wellcome, Henry	88-89, 91, 97
Weschcke, Dr. Carl	55
Whelan, Sister Ellen, O.S.F.	122, 127
Wilson, Dr. Louis B.	145
Women's Medical College of Philadelphia	11, 80
Wood, Dr. James R. of New York	63
World's Fair in Chicago (Columbian Exposition)	132

Praise for *I Started All This*:

"At last W.W. Mayo, this feisty, fascinating, pioneering, remarkable little giant in nineteenth century medical practice — and his equally fascinating, practical, energetic, resourceful, admirable wife, Louise — are getting deserved recognition, for the Mayo brothers, their sons, grew up in the soil and soul of these parents. Thank you, Judith Hartzell, for your illuminating first chapter, really, of the Mayo Clinic story." Charles Mayo Rankin, grandson of Dr. Charlie

"I am indebted to Judith Hartzell for doing the research required to tell the story of my great-grandfather Dr. W.W. Mayo's life. He was gone before I was born, so my only knowledge of him came from either stories my mother told me, photos, articles in various books, or the tour my wife and I took thru his house in LeSueur, Minnesota. Judith's book brought all these random pieces of information together for me into a wonderful story of a fascinating and famous pioneer man. Thank you, Judith!"
Waltman Mayo Walters, grandson of Dr. Will

"W.W. Mayo, my great-grandfather, was a man who had a tenacious will to learn, to do, and to teach. Judith Hartzell has captured these qualities, as well as the personalities that meant so much to him. Great job!"
Dr. Charles Horace Mayo II, grandson of Dr. Charlie

Praise for *Mrs. Charlie*:

"Balfour, Damon, Plummer, Harwick, Berkman and so on. Your book has given me a context in which to place these names. Though I know something about history, I have much to learn about my own town. Your work has helped me appreciate the place I live in…. Of course, the real gem of the book is Edith Mayo herself. A human being, a woman, a wife, a mother, a grandmother, a nurse, a friend, a worker, and a pioneer — but in the end, a person like you and me. I was especially interested in her relationship with Doctor Charlie, to learn about their love."
Benjamin Pennington, Rochester native

Judith Hartzell with her husband Tom

Photo by John Berk

Judith Hartzell is a freelance writer who especially enjoys writing and reading biography. She was educated at Cornell University and earned her master's degree in English language and literature from the University of Michigan. She is married to Tom Hartzell, William Worrall Mayo's great-grandson. Her previous biography was *Mrs. Charlie: the Other Mayo*, published in 2000 by Arvi Books, Inc.